DAMAGE CONTROL

How to **TIPTOE AWAY** from the **SMOKING WRECKAGE** of Your *Latest* **SCREW-UP** with a MINIMUM of **HARM** to Your **REPUTATION**

DAMAGE CONTROL

DAVID EDDIE
WITH **PAT LYNCH**

McClelland & Stewart

Library and Archives Canada Cataloguing in Publication

Eddie, David
   Damage control : how to tiptoe away from the wreckage of your latest screw-up with a minimum of harm to your reputation / David Eddie with Pat Lynch.

ISBN 978-0-7710-3041-3

1. Faux pas – Humor. 2. Embarrassment – Humor. 3. Excuses – Humor. 4. Interpersonal relations—Humor. I. Lynch, Pat, 1972- II. Title.

PN6231.E8E34 2010   395.3   C2009-905145-1

We acknowledge the financial support of the Government of Canada through the Book Publishing Industry Development Program and that of the Government of Ontario through the Ontario Media Development Corporation's Ontario Book Initiative. We further acknowledge the support of the Canada Council for the Arts and the Ontario Arts Council for our publishing program.

Published simultaneously in the United States of America by McClelland & Stewart Ltd., P.O. Box 1030, Plattsburgh, New York 12901

Library of Congress Control Number: 2009942490

Typeset in Electra by M&S, Toronto
Printed and bound in Canada

This book is printed on acid-free paper that is 100% recycled, ancient-forest friendly (100% post-consumer waste).

McClelland & Stewart Ltd.
75 Sherbourne Street
Toronto, Ontario
M5A 2P9
www.mcclelland.com

1 2 3 4 5   14 13 12 11 10

For Pam

TABLE OF CONTENTS

THE BIRTH OF DAMAGE CONTROL

Most of the advice-seeking souls who regularly read David
Eddie's Damage Control column in *The Globe and Mail*
probably don't know that one of their favourite newspaper
destinations had a previous life in the magazine universe.
The birth of Damage Control, in fact, is intertwined with
that of *Toro*, the men's magazine that conceived it and put
a roof over the column's head between 2002 and 2007, when
Toro met its untimely demise.

Almost six years ago now, I was hired to edit *Toro*, which,
at that time, was something completely new on Canada's
media landscape – a general-interest magazine for men. If
that wasn't a daunting enough challenge, the affluent gentleman who was paying for *Toro*'s creation gave me about
eight weeks in which to do it. I don't mean eight weeks to

edit the stories and design the magazine. I mean eight weeks to hire a staff, find an office, buy computers, woo advertisers, and dream up what the magazine was to be about before commissioning, editing, designing, and fact-checking all the stories it would contain. This was an insane proposition, and I was experienced enough at the time to fully understand the glorious horror of what I was taking on.

My fear was often tempered in the early days by, well, alcohol. *Toro* didn't yet have an office, so, for about a month, the editorial team met in various bars and restaurants in Toronto's Little Italy district, trying to hammer out what kind of magazine Canadian men might want to read. We decided then that we wanted *Toro* to have an advice column, but one with a twist.

I remember trying to explain our concept to the Toronto novelist and journalist Russell Smith (who also has a column with *The Globe and Mail*), that we didn't want it to be your typical advice column. We wanted the column to have some tension, which we planned to achieve by making it a forum for guys who found themselves in situations of extraordinary or extreme discomfort (likely involving embarrassment) and needed help. As I tried to articulate all of this to Russell, he interjected at one point and said, "So it's kind of like damage control for men."

"That's it!" I yelped.

"What's it?"

"Damage control. That's what we're going to call the column: 'Damage Control: Advice for Guys in Sticky Situations.'"

It didn't take me long to decide who I wanted to write it. David Eddie had written an excellent book two years earlier called *Housebroken: Confessions of a Stay-at-Home Dad*.

Housebroken was essentially a book-length advice column on the stickiest situation any man will ever find himself in: marriage. In fact, when I read *Housebroken* I'd been married for about a year. Like David, I'd landed a wife whose beauty and career success were several notches above what I'd expected or deserved. And while my wife and I didn't have children at that time, I'd begun to realize that my quasi-pathetic freelance writing life had sent me swerving rather dangerously into househusband territory. Which is why I remember clinging to the words on each one of the book's pages, hoping David could help me find a way to avoid the sort of emasculation neither my wife nor I could have lived with for long.

I don't want to give David all the credit for the fact that I remain married to the same woman, but *Housebroken* had a profound effect on me. And when, as an editor, I imagined the kind of man I'd want to consult when I found myself in a sticky situation, David's voice was the first one that came to mind. It was the perfect mix of humility, insight, *cojones*, honesty, and, best of all, humour.

In the early days of the column, there were the obligatory girlfriend/wife questions – "What do I do if she finds my hidden stash of pornography?" – but there were also more than a few queries that came across the transom we probably never could have invented. Here's one that jumps to mind: "On a ski trip in Northern Italy last winter, after my first day on the slopes, I went down to the hotel's spa for a sauna. I walked in with a towel around my waist, only to discover a crew of naked young Germans, half of whom were women. I sat down and kept my towel on, but I'm sure they were talking about me the entire time. What's an uptight North American guy to do?"

(In case you're wondering, David told him to leave the towel on again next time.)

I also recall David's advice to the guy whose squash playing partner never offered to buy the post-match pints: "Obviously your friend's welshing is eating away at your innards, but let's face it: it's not the male way to confront friends, to bring up issues, to 'want to talk.' It's too similar to whining. If you must say something, better to make a joke with teeth – like, 'Yeah, that's okay, there's a Raquel Welch* movie I want to see on Showcase, anyway.' Or 'Maybe I'll just sit here and have a Welch's grape juice.' If he has any sense, he'll get it eventually."

There was also the occasional question that forced David to put on his reporter's cap. I remember helping him hunt down a lawyer who specialized in drunk-driving cases because a reader's inebriated friend had been charged after being found at the side of the road, asleep in the rear seat of his parked car.

The end of *Toro* magazine in early 2007 happened to coincide with the launch of a new Life section in *The Globe and Mail*, which adopted both Damage Control (in a non-male-specific form) and our sex columnist, Claudia Dey. The Life section was also fortunate to inherit a number of other *Toro* alumni, including Pat Lynch, who has been editing both versions of Damage Control since 2004.

I can fondly envision David walking into the *Toro* office on many an evening to meet Pat so that the two of them

---

* In case this reference is a little obscure, I, David Eddie, would like to add a slight footnote: it refers to "welching" on a bet; which actually, though I didn't think about it at the time, probably derives from a derogatory reference to Welsh people, unfortunately.

could decamp to a local watering hole to discuss the questions that had come in for the next column. Occasionally, one of them, in a futile effort to gain my sympathy, would make a crack about how much of their precious time this column was taking up.

"Don't worry, boys," I would say. "One day that column is going to turn into a magnificent book."

I can't tell you how happy (and proud) I am that it finally has.

Derek Finkle

ORIGINS, AND A FEW GENERAL PRINCIPLES, OF DAMAGE CONTROL

"People don't seem to understand it's a damn war out there." — JIMMY CONNORS

"All warfare is based on deception." — SUN TZU

THE DRIPPING FACE OF DOOM

Okay, so you screwed up.

Again. You're as surprised as anyone. You can't believe what a mutt, what a mook, what a plum duff you are.

"Oh, my God," you might find yourself thinking. "I'm a freak! A fool! I'm screwed!"

You may begin to hyperventilate, to start to *schvitz* from fear, your hyperactive hypothalamus douching your entire bodybag in a fine, sour-scented mist of flop-sweats.

Your heart might start fibrillating wildly, like a broken metronome.

To try to keep cool, you may go into the washroom to splash some cold water on your frazzled face. But when you look up from the basin at the mug in the mirror, it's not your face you see.

It's . . . the Dripping Face of Doom!

But take it easy. Relax, son. Sister, ease your foot off the panic pedal.

Team Damage Control, aka the cavalry, is here.

And we think we can help you. We're going to talk you through this, show you how to shake it off, and come out stronger, faster, smarter, and swinging harder than ever.

Take a deep breath. Inhale and exhale. Where's that famous smile?

There it is! Why, look at you: you're beautiful!

You may lose the odd battle here and there. But we want to show you how to win the war. We're going to absorb the details of your latest debacle, then talk you through the aftermath and beyond; show you how you can come out of a variety of fiascos smiling and snapping your fingers and humming a little tune and smelling – well, if not like a rose, then at least not like someone who was making a shit-shake and forgot to put the top on the blender.

The sun will shine again, sunshine.

Everything's going to be fine. Everything's going to work out for the best in this, the best of all possible worlds.

But before we go any further, we realize you may have a couple of questions.

Like, first: who are these guys, Pat Lynch and David Eddie?

And second: who do they *think* they are, calling themselves "the cavalry" and talking trash like "We're here, we think we can help you" and la la la and promising – what? To turn back time and undo our mistakes?

But no: we never said undo.

In fact, that is **Damage Control Rule No. 1: You can't undo.** There is no undoing. Trying to undo could be your undoing.

As Omar Khayyam (Persian poet, AD 1048–1122) put it: "The moving finger writes; and, having writ, moves on: nor all your piety nor wit shall lure it back to cancel half a line, nor all your tears wash out a word of it."

Or, to put it another way – and this is in fact one of Damage Control's corporate mottos, which we sometimes shout out on the dance floor at company parties:

"What's done is done and can't be undone/The bell that's rung, it can't be un-rung/The sands of time, they can't un-run/You did the deed, now it's gotta be spun!"

Then we all blow our little whistles and wave our glow-sticks in the air.

Or, perhaps, to put it in even simpler, almost cowpoke-type language (and if it helps, you may imagine us removing our ten-gallon hats, scratching our sweaty melons, squinting across a dusty prairie-patch, and spitting a brown stream of tobacco-laced saliva into a nearby spittoon as we say): "Son, you doggone gone and done what you doggone gone and done. And sister: ain't nothin' under the blazing sun gonna change that. The $64,000,000* question is: what're yew gonna do *now?*"

And that's where – *con permiso, certamente: gracias!* – Pat

---

* All figures adjusted for inflation. Also, Damage Control International was recently the beneficiary of a targeted governmental bailout, so we've got quite a bit of cheddar to throw around.

and I and the rest of the Damage Control team come in: on the what-you-should-do-*now* part.

But what *we* should probably do now, and without further ado, is introduce ourselves.

I, David Eddie, am CEO (Chief Error-rectification Ombudsperson), and Pat Lynch is COE (Chief Operating Editor), of Damage Control International, a vast, intercontinental aggregation of ameliorization artisans, smooth-over specialists, and turnaround technicians headquartered in a fortified underground bunker located somewhere deep in the Ozark Mountains.

Travelling by company helicopter (black, with Damage Control's logo tastefully emblazoned in gold letters on the door), and landing on a secret helipad, I, David Eddie, divide my time between the bunker and my fabulous mansion in downtown Toronto, where I am most likely to be found either (1) in conversational intercourse and spiritual communion with my wife, Pam; (2) tousling the hair of, or playing catch, or Frisbee, with, one of my three male off- spring, saying stuff like "Attaboy!" or "Nice throw, kiddo!" or "You're really improving!"; (3) engaged in the never- ending, disgusting, Sisyphean task of walking my dog, Murphy, around and around the park across the street; watching him squat, knees trembling, a faraway look on his shaggy mug; then picking up his stinking, still-steaming "offerings" with a plastic bag from my pocket. . . .

And, sometimes, all of the above, all in the same afternoon.

Pat, meanwhile, is still single, still "out there," which, if memory serves, means saying "Dude!" a lot while "high- fiving" his "bros"; drinking shots of Jägermeister in loud, crowded, crepuscular bars; grabbing some "dinner" on the fly by sticking a quarter* in a peanut-dispensing machine at the pool hall and twirling the knobs; holding up lighters at concerts;† jumping off the speakers and onto the heads of the terrified-looking crowd;** all the while keeping an eye peeled for the twitching, elusive miniskirt of Ms. Right as it disappears around the corner of the various lofts, watering holes, and brunch spots of the city. . . .

And, sometimes, all of the above, all in a single evening.

Lynch and I have been working together for some time now, just a couple of cogs in the advice-dispensing machine known as Damage Control.

As The Dogfather™ aka "Dapper" Derek Finkle mentioned in his excellent Preface (thanks, Dog!), we honed our chops and made our bones cranking out advice for the late, lamented men's magazine *Toro*, which, unfortunately, floated belly-up to the top of the tank after four years (it was an *intelligent men's magazine*: perhaps in that single, almost

---

* I may be dating myself here. It's probably more than a quarter, at this point.

† Oh, wait, I read somewhere recently they don't do that any more: it's illegal because it's a fire hazard – so they hold up their *cellphones* now, which is so sick and wrong, for so many reasons, I don't even want to talk about it.

** Well, they always looked terrified when I did it in my long-ago twenties: of course, it could be because I'm 6-foot-5 and weigh 240 pounds.

oxymoronic phrase one can begin to detect the seeds of its eventual demise); then, more latterly, we've been disgorging our advice-nuts for Canada's blue-chip national daily newspaper, *The Globe and Mail*.

We work well together, I think.

My tendency, as you are perhaps slowly becoming aware, is to weave elaborate word-tapestries to enchant the eyeballs and dazzle the cerebellum.

Whereas Lynch's inclination is to say, "Get to the point, you pomo Soho boho mofo."

Lynch is at the centre of a stern, gruff, often silent, but always deadly, cadre of manly men and guy's guys – guys who would have no time for word-tapestries, and if someone were to attempt to weave a word-tapestry in their presence they'd tell that person to shut up: "We're listening to Sabbath on vinyl!"

The yin-yang action inherent in our interpersonal and inter-professional dynamic results in a good look for both of us, I think. In fact, it is no less than my belief that over the years Lynch and I have achieved some sort of Vulcan mind-meld, and our two individual melons have fused into a single Supermelon™, capable of generating advice that is enchanting, bedazzling, and to the point, all at once; and all at record speeds.

At the same time, a crack crew of crisis-management consultants and extrication experts has accrued around us, coral-reef-style, over the years. As The Dogfather mentioned in the Preface, whenever a particular question falls outside the comfort zone of our skill set, we reach for the phone and contact various experts, each outstanding in his/her field.

And if a particular expert whom we have contacted appears to us to be imbued with not only genuine expertise but also what used to be known as "good old-fashioned horse sense," we invite him or her to join our team (on a strictly pro bono basis, natch) to consult on all future questions falling within his/her purview/bailiwick and enter his/her name into our electronic Rolodex.*

Currently, Team Damage Control – or, as we call it in warmer moments,† "the Damage Control family" – includes not one but three different types of lawyer (civil, criminal, family); several marital and financial counsellors; a number of authors; journalists and columnists; a CEO; several VPs; a small-business man; two brand-management specialists; a publicist. . . . Name a knowledge-worker type of profession, basically, and chances are we have one on our (pro bono) payroll.

We have one woman who seriously makes a living as an "ethical counsellor."** We even have a nudist – oops, we

---

* Well, I say "electronic Rolodex," but that's a bit of a canard, a nerve-agent powder I blow in your eyes to make myself seem more techno-savvy. In fact, I use an old-fashioned Rolodex, into which I painstakingly enter all names, addresses, e-mail addresses, phone numbers, cellphone numbers, pager numbers, and so forth, with an antiquated artifact known as a "pencil."

† E.g. in the hours right after I send out a company-wide memo saying corporate profits are up and everyone's getting an extra-special Christmas bonus this year.

** We first met her because her office is in the same building as a friend of ours, a graphic designer. She charges people $60 an hour to tell them mean "naturist" – on the team: Stéphane Deschênes of the Federation of Canadian Naturists.

He's outstanding *nude* in his field.*

Along with Team Damage Control,† I, David Eddie, have assembled, over the years, an inner circle of wise, village-elder-type friends and associates whom I refer to simply as The Panel.

I consult The Panel on most things, both personal and professional. I'm a big believer in the power of advice** to help clarify matters for us poor, confused humans down here on earth, to help steer us on the right course.

And I need it as much as anyone. Thus it is that, though I dish it out by the wheelbarrow-load, I am a net consumer of advice.

---

what she thinks is the right thing to do in any given situation. We should probably mention here, right from the jump, that *we* will not always necessarily advise you to do the "right" – aka the high-road, Angelina Jolie-esque, "noble" – thing. We want you to be good/moral/etc. But we also don't want you to be a sucker, or a chump, or a doormat, either.

* We originally contacted him when we got a question from a couple who were worried that a friend-couple of theirs was avoiding them because they'd secretly become nudists – a question included in the "social whirl" chapter.

† Team Damage Control is not to be confused with Team Dave Eddie, though there is some overlap: Pam, for example, is a leading consultant on the former, and Chairperson of the latter.

** I'd be in the wrong business if I wasn't, wouldn't I?

But I do not always abide by the rulings of The Panel. In these cases you, gentle reader ("and still gentler purchaser," as Byron would say), get two points of view for the low, low price of one.

I believe in advice. But I also believe in the truth of the old Yiddish saying "Seek advice from many but in the end follow your own counsel."

Same goes for you, dear reader. Listen to our advice. Take it seriously. But follow it only if it accords with what the "little man" or "little woman" inside you has to say.

Your inner voice* knows all.

GENESIS

Damage Control was not always the vast, intercontinental empire it is today.

It – we – had humble beginnings. As he was quick to point out in his Preface, Damage Control was the brain-child of Derek Finkle, aka The Dogfather, whose oversized, idealized portrait hangs in every room in the bunker.

(Not to mention the towering, Michaelangelo Buonarroti-esque fig-leafed marble nude in the foyer, depicting The Dogfather in the act of running his fingers through his long, flowing hair – a statue that is usually the first thing to greet

---

* You know the one we mean. We mean the one that says, when you're not quite sure about something: "You should probably double back and deal with that." *Not*, repeat *not*, the one that says, "Nah, don't worry about it, it'll probably be fine."

the eyes of visitors to the bunker when their blindfolds are whipped off.*)

The Dogfather, perhaps in a frenzy of overcompensation,† was contemplating launching a men's magazine with the hyper-masculinist moniker *Toro*.

And he needed an advice columnist.

But The Dogfather was tired of the typical type of advice promulgated in newspapers and magazines and everywhere else.

It was all too effete, dainty, and sanctimonious. There's too much tut-tutting, pooh-poohing, and finger-wagging in most advice that's out there, he felt; too many verbal doilies, fingerbowls, and antimacassars.

Too often the advice boils down to "Well, you shouldn't have done *that*. But now that you have, uh, seek counselling."

Oh, thanks a pantload, Mr. or Ms. Advice Columnist!

For one thing, the poor zhlub who wrote in *knows* he/she screwed up.

And he/she *did* seek counselling: you, Your Highness the Advice Columnist. And you failed him/her utterly.

---

* Some scream and recoil in shock and awe; others fall into a sort of erotic reverie or trance and cease to respond to external stimuli, such as shouts or snapping fingers: these will often have to be sedated and transported to the infirmary in one of the bunker's golf-cart-like Personnel Conveyance Units (PCUs) for rest and observation.

† For what, we may never know: shortly after completing the massive marble nude, the statue's sculptor, who had been heard to mutter darkly about the "reality" of what lay behind the fig leaf, met with a mysterious "accident," falling down one of the bunker's air shafts, and was never able to tell the world his story.

And so often the advice is delivered with such *fauxracular* certainty, it makes you want to peel back the curtains of the advice columnist's life and see how wonderfully he/she has everything arranged.*

The Dogfather had a vision of a new type of advice: advice that was realistic, straightforward, and blunt-yet-compassionate.

No verbal antimacassars, doilies, or tea cozies.

Since it was aimed at men, it had to be pretty straightforward, hovering on the edge of brutal, almost brutish truth.

But at the same time, it had to be imbued with compassion and understanding and empathy – less from-on-high and more eye-to-eye.

Kind of like the advice you might get from a good, old friend, over, say, a drink.

A friend who might say, "I feel your pain. I went through something similar a while back. Let me first tell you a bit about what I learned from that messed-up situation; then, based on my experience and such wisdom as I've managed to acquire, give you my best guess on where to take it from here."

——

* Not well, you can bet – and it strikes us that most advice columnists, like most shrinks, are probably more, rather than less, cracked, kooky, and hanging on by a very thin thread than the rest of us regular/double-double Joes. Take Abigail "Dear Abby" Van Buren and her sister, Ann Landers. The heads of two competing advice juggernauts, global syndicates, they fought like a pair of spitting cobras their entire lives and went through long stretches when they weren't speaking to one another: but of course that didn't prevent them from dishing out how-to-get-along-with-your-family advice by the steaming boatload.

But when it came to finding the right man for the job, The Dogfather hit an impasse.

Sitting in a high-backed leather chair in the back room of a restaurant, his face half-obscured by shadow, a coat draped over his shoulders but his arms not in the sleeves, sipping espresso from a tiny cup in a tiny saucer, The Dogfather pondered the question:

"Who will do this thing for me? I need someone who is well-liked, reasonably well-respected, but who has a lot of direct, first-person knowledge of screw-ups. Someone, basically, who screws up all the time! But whom do we know fitting this description? Whom, dammit, whom?" The Dogfather demanded, pounding his desk, causing his tiny espresso cup to rattle in its little saucer. "Would someone please tell me?"

That's when The Dogfather's *consiglieri*, "Gentleman" Russell Smith, standing in the shadows behind him, wearing an elegantly cut bespoke suit, his handkerchief peeking out of the pocket *just so*, leaned forward and whispered something in The Dogfather's ear.

After considering for a moment, The Dogfather silently nodded and reached for the telephone.

BRAVISSIMO! ENCORE, ENCORE, FAUX PAS-VAROTTI!

It was inevitable the name David Eddie should come across The Dogfather's transom.

My work in the area of the faux pas alone is globally renowned, without serious peer or challenger.

I am the King of the Faux Pas. Wherever I go, my sub-
jects – basically anyone who has ever blurted out something
dumb at a party – bow down low before me, saying "Hail,
sire," and kiss my pinkie ring and/or the golden knob of my
royal sceptre.

For example, at a crowded magazine-industry awards ceremony party recently,* I was like some kind of crazy faux-
pas generating *machine*.

I was . . . Faux Pas-Varotti: I opened my mouth and they
just came out in one seemingly never-ending faux-pas-ria.

My wife, Pam, in a dress special-bought for the occasion
(a slinky, silky low-backed crimson number, if memory
serves), was at my side: wincing, cringing, and shaking her
head in disbelief as Faux Pas-Varotti sang into the night.
Once she even ground her heel down, hard, on my toe, in
an attempt to ward off a fresh one.

But nothing can stop Faux Pas-Varotti once he's in full
flight.

One by one, miffed, offended, insulted, my interlocutors
mingled off, leaving me staring into Pam's aghast face.
Then she too turned on her three-inch heels to hit the bar
and refill her glass.

Leaving me in what is probably man's most natural state:
alone. Kicking myself and asking, "Why? Why? Why do I
ever leave the house?"

The title of my faux-pas-ria, incidentally, could have
been "Dave Doesn't Remember Anyone; and Even If He
Does, He's Got You Mixed Up With Someone Else; and If
By Some Miracle He Does Figure Out Who You Are and
How He Knows You, He Doesn't Know Any of the

---

* I lost, but hey: it's an honour just to be nominated, right?

Background Details About You That He Really *Ought* to Know, And/Or He's Got Them Wrong: A Reprise."

People kept coming up to me, and above the maddening din of the chattering mob, they'd be like "Hey, Dave, what's happening? Long time no see! Hey, by the way, did that rash Adam had behind his left knee the year before last ever clear up? Did you try that zinc ointment I told you about? And did Dr. Zuckerman give you any other tips? Oh, and how did J.J. enjoy the reptile specialist you hired for his eighth birthday? And how are *you*, you old bugger, you, we haven't seen you around much lately!"

And I'd be staring at the person thinking: "Have we met?" Because as far as my misfiring sieve-like cerebellum was concerned, I had never seen this person before in my life.

("Nice to meet you," I said to one person, who countered: "Dave, I *drove* you to that parenting panel, don't you re*mem*ber?")*

So it was with some relief, when, hearing a voice behind me saying, "Hey, Dave," I turned and came face-to-face with a face that was blessedly familiar: the subtle, cynical, mahogany-hued mug of a certain Arjun, Montreal magazine editor and man-about-town.

Now, with Arjun I was on somewhat more solid footing. I'd written a number of pieces for him; we'd chatted on the phone; e-mailed; were Facebook friends; and whenever he

---

* I do sometimes think it's other people's duty to be a bit more memorable. Everyone's the same these days, you ever notice? Same hairstyles – practical bob on the ladies, short-shorn for the men; same cottony, practical clothes; similar opinions and politics (vaguely liberal). It's like trying to tell one Big Mac from another!

came to town he would invite me to parties and/or we might go out for drinks together.

About him I knew, at least, several indisputable facts: (1) he was married; (2) he'd recently been promoted, from editor of one magazine to some kind of overseer of several magazines; (3) he had at least one, quite possibly two, but certainly not three or more, children, somewhere between the ages of two and twelve (fourteen at the outside); (4) he lived in Montreal.

Therefore I was able to pepper him with several semi-intelligent questions re: his career and personal life. We were even having a reasonably decent conversation, when Pam rolled up on us with a fresh-filled glass of wine.

"Arjun," I said, attempting to be smooth, soigné, urbane, and Rico Suave. "I don't know if you've met my wife, Pam?"

The face he turned to me was sarcastic, scornful, and suffused with an admixture of contempt and irony.

Me thinking: *what*? How could *that* possibly be a faux pas?

"Yes, Dave, I've 'met' her," he said, voice dripping with condescension and venom. "Hel-*lo*? I've been to your *house*? I've played with your children – *remember*? Pam has served me drinks, and we've sat around the fire and chatted, with your kids running around, so, yes, in that sense, we've 'met.'"

Ah, I thought. Interesting. Damage Control's Faux Pas Management Department (FPMD) should find this one fascinating.

Out loud I said, "Oh, yeah, Arjun, ha-ha, of course, yeah, right, I forgot about that night, yeah, sure, it's all coming back to me now: we were all sitting around the fire, and . . . "

But he'd already turned away from me, and toward Pam, and, with a courtly little bow, said pointedly, "Nice to see *you* again, Pam."

And, turning on his heel, Arjun flounced off in a huff (*cough-cough* like a poopy-pants prima donna ballerina who didn't get to do her solo *cough-cough*), leaving me thinking, "Everyone's so touchy these days. Sheesh! And they expect you to remember *everything*."

He'd been to our house, once, for like an hour: years ago. So I forgot! Sue me! Yeesh!

Still, I thought, watching him melt into the crowd (me trying not to catch Pam's eye; her, I could see in my peripheral vision, trying very hard to catch mine), that's probably one magazine – or group of magazines, I supposed, now that he's been promoted – I won't be pitching any pieces to, anytime soon.

TOE-CURLERS, FACE-GRABBERS, AND . . .
THE BOVINIZER

But that wasn't my worst one. Oh, no. Not by a long chalk. Not by a country mile.

After a series of exhaustive studies conducted on students and indigents and anyone else willing to be blindfolded, brought to a secret location, and experimented upon in the bunker's windowless underground laboratory for ten dollars an hour, Team Damage Control's Faux Pas Management Department (FPMD) devised a sliding-scale Faux Pas Rating System, or FPRS.

At the low end of the FPRS scale are **Toe-Pinchers**, or **Toe-Curlers**, so-called because perpetration of this garden-variety form of faux pas may cause the subject's toes to curl up inside his or her shoes, and/or pinch each other, a bit.

Next rung up the ladder is the **Face-Grabber** (self-explanatory) and its many variants, e.g., the **Rocking Face-Grabber**, which derives its name from the way a subject will actually rock back and forth, as if in an invisible rocking chair, while grabbing his or her face, when the incident is recalled.

Above that is **The Tosser**, so-called because that's what you call yourself as you toss and turn, unable to sleep: "Argh, why did I do that? Oh, man, I'm such a *tosser!*"

And then, at the farthest end of the FPRS scale, with the needle buried deep in the red zone, we come to . . .

The Bovinizer.

The Bovinizer refers to a faux pas so spine-tingling that the mere recollection of the incident causes the subject to emit a low, cow-like bellow or moan of mortification – to *moo* with shame, as it were.

I'm pleased and proud to say my last **Bovinizer** was quite a while ago now.

But the memory is still as fresh as a hot bagel from mama's oven.

The setting for my rube-like display of uncouthness was appropriately bucolic: the annual corn roast at my new book editor's farm.

Call her Madame X. She'd "inherited" me from my old editor, Doug, who'd flown the coop, heading south for the mighty skyscrapers and numbered avenues of New York City.

———

Now, let me pause for a moment to inform you, dear reader, that in publishing, this business of "inheriting" authors is a ticklish phenomenon.

A new editor is a new broom: he/she wants to clean out the Augean stables and assemble a stable of authors that reflect his/her taste, style, beliefs, and so on.

The last thing he/she wants is some nag from the last regime filling up the place with the aroma of his old-school verbal droppings.

But Madame X had done me the honour of saying she would be "psyched" to keep publishing my stuff.

Also, in a certain sense, being invited to this corn roast meant you'd "arrived" and had become part of the "*crème de la crème*" of literary society (though more like the upper-crusty, extra-tangy layer of a bowl of curdled sour cream, if you knew what pickle-faced sourpusses most authors are), here in the hyperborean hinterlands of Canada.

In any case, suffice to say I was anxious, at this corn roast, to impress upon Madame X that in hitching her wagon to my star she had not gone far wrong; that I was a man, and therefore an author, of rare intelligence and perspicacity; a man/author who saw into the heart of things, who perceived instantaneously, with razor-sharp insight, that which might elude, or need to be patiently explained to, others.

Which is probably why, when Pam and I were approached by a woman who looked exactly like Madame X, but with a halo of snow-white hair surrounding her head, I opened my big, dumb mouth and jammed my size-13 retro-styled Adidas track shoe right in it.

"Ah," I said. "You must be Madame X's mother."

She froze. Her face fell. The moment that followed was both awful and immortal: it hangs forever suspended in time, like a giant, rubbery matzoh ball in a bubbling vat of greasy chicken broth.

"Oh, no," I had time to think. *"The horror . . . "*

"I'm her *sister*," she finally managed to say, her throat constricted with wounded vanity and stung pride. "We're nine years apart. I knew I should have kept dyeing my hair. People tell you that you should let it go naturally grey, but . . . "

Her voice trailed off.

If, ladies and gentlemen, at that moment a flaming pit of molten lava had suddenly opened up at my feet, I would have turned to Pam and said, "Pam, tell the boys I loved them more than they could ever know – you, too, by the way: I don't know what I ever did to deserve you, but our time together was as close as it is possible to come, I believe, to heaven on earth."

And then, with a little salute and an odd look on my face, I would happily have jumped in.

No such pit opened up to save/incinerate my bacon, though. I was left stammering: "I . . . I . . . "

But Madame X's sister and I had already wordlessly begun to back away from one another.

Pam and I headed toward an antique swing near the edge of a cornfield to recoup and regroup.

"Dave. What were you thinking?" she asked as we walked.

"I don't know," I said, miserably. "I guess I was trying to impress her with how perceptive I am."

"I knew it!" Pam said, triumphantly. "I know you so well! I know you better than you know yourself!"*

My answer was a bovinized moan of pained self-loathing.

---

* A frequent boast of hers. I kind of like it.

"Dave," Pam said. "Will you promise me that in future, before you say anything, you'll ask yourself: 'What is the upside, what is the downside, of what I am about to say?'"

"Yes, darling, I know, I know. You're right, as usual," I said.

Depressed, defeated, I sat down heavily on the antique swing – and there was a horrible splintering, sundering sound, as this valuable antique, obviously some kind of sentiment-saturated family heirloom, became a piece of crap.

And that's kind of the sound it made, too, as it gave up the ghost: *krrrraaaaaap!*

"Oh, man," I said, looking up at Pam from my newfound seat on the ground. "If one more thing happens, we may have to leave."

"We may have to leave as it is," she said.

LEARN, BABY, LEARN

But I recovered from the above heinous, hair-raising faux pas, boys and girls.

Damage control was done with due diligence. Madame X accepted my profuse apologies with great grace ("Oh, it was just an old swing, and listen: your thing with my sister makes me think I seem younger than I am"), and I lived to type another day.

I learned from this episode, people. "Poverty is a great teacher," they say (and I agree: it taught me, for example, as a struggling young author, how to cook). So is pain. So is shame. I absorbed the pain from this incident, and it remained in my system like a piece of shrapnel until it had worked its way out and I had learned its lesson.

Thus it was a couple of months later I *almost* committed an even more hair-raising faux pas – but I didn't! Happy ending! High five!

It was at a goth-run Hallowe'en party in which guests were encouraged to come dressed as "the undead."

I wasn't even invited: I came with a friend of mine who knew the host.

The host's outfit was brilliant, downright Dickensian: stovepipe hat; drainpipe pants; "winkle picker" shoes; long Victorian frock coat; all covered in a fine, whitish "grave dust." His face was powdered, and festooned with very realistic-looking scars and suppurating sores; and his teeth were all snaggly and grey and cobwebbed with cracks.

We were all sitting around sipping drinks and everyone was complimenting him on his outfit.

"I love your hat!" one person said.

"And that's a cool coat!" someone else said.

"The 'grave dust' is a great touch," another one said.

"And your scars are so realistic!" another person exclaimed.

And, ladies and gentlemen, I *almost* said: "And your teeth are really gruesome, too!"

But I didn't. I stopped myself. I opened my mouth to speak – but then Pam's words started ping-ponging around in my cranium: "What's the upside, what's the downside?" And instead of saying something, I kept my mouth shut.

And hoo doggy am I ever glad I did.

"Oh, no, those are his real teeth," the mutual friend who brought me to the party told me a couple of days later. "That's the way they naturally are. And he's *really* sensitive about them."

"So, suffice to say," I said, "if I yelled out at his party that his teeth were really gruesome, that would have been a truly *awful* situation?"

"Dave," the mutual friend said, placing a hand on my shoulder, staring into my eyes, and shaking his head, all at once. "No one in that room would ever have been the same."

That night, lying in bed, I sent up a little prayer: "Thank you, God, for sparing me that spine-tingling comeuppance, at least."

"No problem, Dave," I imagined God answering, evenly, sitting at His or Her desk, polishing a fresh thunderbolt with FOR DAVE: NEAR FUTURE embossed on the side. "On this occasion it amused Me to spare you humiliation. Just watch your step and also, FYI, watch your mouth when you talk to Me, pal."

"What are You talking about?"

"What's all this 'at least' shit, hm? After all I've done for you? Laid Pam and three beautiful boys on you, for starters? You, who, were he to get what he deserves, would be in a Turkish prison right now, screaming and begging for mercy! Listen to Me, smart-ass: I've got some love-taps up My sleeve that would make a Turkish prison look like a seaside holiday, so keep a civil tongue in your head when you talk to Me. Got that, Danny me lad?"

"Uh, it's Dave, actually. And I didn't mean to be disrespectful, it's just that . . . "

But He, or She, had already hung up.

Anyway, let's go ahead and make that **Damage Control Rule No. 2: Learn, baby, learn.**

If you don't learn, if you fail to interpret, to read, in tea-leaf-like fashion, the particular meaning inherent in each of your screw-ups, you are doomed to repeat the same mistake over and over again.

And that doesn't sound like much fun at all. Especially when there are so many fresh, dynamic, exciting *new* screw-ups out there waiting for you to commit.

It's probably a cliché and overexposed notion, but we think it bears repeating: from each mistake, you must learn, baby, learn. Life is a learning experience. What we call "problems," failures, disasters, screw-ups, are often signposts pointing the way to a brighter, more festive and rewarding future.

E.g. you break up with someone who wasn't quite right for you. "Oh, no, this is terrible, what a disaster," you lament. But next thing you know you meet Mr. or Ms. Right, and that never would have happened if you hadn't broken up with the other one.

It's like that with a lot of things. It may just be that God has a greater design for us than that which we design for ourselves. Maybe our plans don't work out; but maybe our failures and screw-ups are part of a larger plan.

As my favourite philosopher, Epictetus, puts it: "I am content with that which happens, for I believe that what God chooses is better than what I choose."

Remember, also, that other wise and incredibly pithy old Yiddish saying: "Man plans, God laughs."*

Which doesn't mean we feel you should lie around passively and let yourself be buffeted hither and thither like a leaf in the wind. No, you have to keep throwing yourself at

---

* Variant: "I thought I was going to do X, but life had other plans." Take me: I thought I was going to be another Charles Bukowski. "But life had other plans." Instead I turned into a bearded, bespectacled, 6-foot-5, 240-pound, tattoo-covered Ann Landers.

your problems, like a policeman at a door in a TV movie, until something gives.

And you may fail, again and again. But you have to keep trying. Maybe everything is a failure. Maybe all winds up in failure in the end.

Doesn't matter. Keep fighting. Keep trying. Things will improve. Or, as Samuel Beckett, who, it sometimes seems to me, summed up all of human existence in the following six words, put it: "Try. Fail. Try again. Fail better."

CURB YOUR HUBRIS

Yes . . . **learn, baby, learn**: It's rule No. 2 in terms of importance (after "you can't undo").

But it's the last thing you do, chronologically speaking.

Chronologically speaking, the first step in becoming a seventh-dan Shaolin priest of damage control is **Damage Control Rule No. 3: Curb your hubris** – or, as we say around here, for short, CYH.

CYH: that acronym is embossed on all the hydraulic doors and stickered on the back of all the company-issued clipboards here in the bunker; it's also monogrammed on the pockets of all the lab coats.

Long before a screw-up happens, or, as we put it here at Damage Control HQ, "between screw-ups," * you must train yourself to kick your hubris to the curb.

---

* A phrase that's central to our philosophy and approach. There's a Preston Sturges biography called *Between Flops*, because Mr. Sturges made so many movies that were box-office duds. But Mr. Sturges didn't

The first step, Grasshopper, is to believe, to *know*, it will happen to you. You are not exempt. You will screw up – or, at the very least, *become embroiled in a screwed-up situation* (another way you can find yourself marinating in hot water).

Now maybe it hasn't happened to you in a while. Perhaps you are enjoying a long hiatus "between screw-ups." If that's the case, if that's *your* case, then we say unto you: kudos and congratulations. Here at Damage Control Central we all salute you and put our clipboards under our arms and applaud you, "slow clap" style.

But we urge you not to be guilty of the sin of hubris and think that just because it hasn't happened for a while, you are somehow exempt.

That's hubris. And hubris will bring you down every time. "Pride goeth before a fall." Remember that one? Hubris will turn you into an Icarus, and you will find yourself frantically flapping your melted wings in vain, as you plummet to the cornfields at the rate of sixteen feet per second per second, before you can say, "Outplacement counsellor? Why would *I* of all people need an outplacement counsellor?"

Here at Damage Control Central, whenever we hear, on the monitors or over the audio feeds in our Surveillance Room, someone uttering a sentiment along the lines of "Ah, I haven't screwed up in a long time, maybe I'm the type of hotshot who doesn't screw up at all, anymore," we exchange worried glances.

"Uh-oh," a junior staffer might say.

let any of his flops faze him; he shook them off and pressed on. One of the most successful filmmakers of his time. That sums up our maybe-you-lost-the-battle-but-you-can-still-win-the-war approach.

"Here comes another client," the office wag, a man nicknamed Doomsday Dan for his pessimistic, cynical *Weltanschauung,* can be counted on to say, sometimes spraying some powdered sugar and crumbs from his doughnut as he does so.

(And we all say "Dan!" and throw pencil erasers and pieces of balled-up paper at him, because really: we wish only the best for everyone. We don't *want* you to become our client – but we'll help you if you do.)

Because we believe that these types of statements cause the gods to frown, furrow their brows, and head for their celestial bullpens to limber up their thunderbolt-throwing arms.

LOVE YOUR PROBLEMS

Most people don't love their own problems, let alone yours. That's the reason most advice you get, both personally and professionally, sucks.

You'll say something like "I did X, Y, and Z. Now what should I do: A or B?"

And, barely looking up from her newspaper, or tearing his eyes from the television screen, or typing away on a Crackberry, the person you're talking to will say, "Uh, do B."

"But what about the Y factor? Doesn't that militate against me doing B?"

"Oh, okay, then do A," they'll shrug, then pick up the clicker, or turn the page, or return to their thumb-typing.

In *Civilization and Its Discontents,* Freud said: "Men are not spontaneously fond of work." Likewise, you could say most people are not spontaneously fond of their own problems, let alone yours.

We are, though. We love problems! We subscribe to the Zen saying that "without problems, life would lose all interest, all colour, and all meaning."

Same could be said of screw-ups. You *should* be fond of your problems and screw-ups. In fact, you should *love* your problems and screw-ups. **Damage Control Rule No. 4 is: Learn to love thy problems and screw-ups as thyself.**

Because your problems and screw-ups *are* you, in a sense. And how you deal with them says more about who you are than how you handle ordinary, un-screwed-up situations.

Your screw-ups, and the screwed-up situations you became embroiled in, are your stories, for one thing.

For example, say you go to Jamaica, and everything's fine: smooth flight, comfortable hotel, everything goes well and you get a beautiful, tawny tan.

When people ask you about your trip, what happened, you've got nothing: "I had fun and everything went smoothly and I got a good tan."

Boring! "Huh, well, that's, uh – *yawn*! sorry! – fantastic, Dave. Nice to hear everything went so well. Say, will you look at the time? We gotta go."

But if the airline loses your luggage; if your plane's engine explodes, and drops, flaming, into the ocean; if a nude woman in a tub full of bath bubbles falls through the ceiling of your hotel room; if you pass out drunk and high on the beach, wind up getting stabbed and rolled, and you have to beg your father-in-law to send some cash via Western Union so you can get home at all. . .

Then you've got a story! Everyone's riveted! On that, you can dine out for weeks! Suddenly, you're the life of the party!

Another reason you should learn to love thy problems and crises as you love thyself is because, as we hinted before, events that present themselves to us as "disasters" are often just the culmination of some way in which we have been, as the rappers say, "living foul."

And the "disaster" or crisis that has befallen us is just the goose we need to cattle-prod us back onto The Path of Righteousness.

We know it's corny, but technically this is a self-help book so we figure we're allowed the odd corny-ism – so here goes:

You know how (and if you don't, well, bully for you) when you get fired and everyone crowds around you and says, "Hey, don't worry about it, it's all for the best, this will turn out to be the best thing that ever happened to you, you'll see"?

And you're sitting there thinking, "Thanks for the *Schadenfreude*-wrapped gift basket of empty clichés: I'll try to bear your thoughts in mind when I'm picking up my groceries at the food bank"?

But it's weird, though, how often that clichéd sentiment turns out to be true. It's tautological but no less logical that if you get fired from your job you probably weren't, to use a current corporate neologism that we actually kind of like, a "good fit" in the first place.

Either that, or you weren't giving it your best shot; or maybe a bit of both? Hmmm? Hmmmmmmmmm?

In any case, it doesn't matter. Getting fired, getting dumped, getting your comeuppance, or "coming a cropper," as they used to say, can zap you out of your rut, cause you to pull up your socks, and be a valuable signpost to the future: it can point you in the direction of doing the type of work, being in the type of relationship, and becoming the type of person you were *really* put on the earth to do and be.

If that makes sense.

GENERALLY SPEAKING, ACTION IS BETTER THAN INACTION

When you've screwed up, or become embroiled in a screwed-up situation, doing nothing and just hoping it will all go away is natural – but will tend to be a big mistake.

That's why **Damage Control Rule No. 5 is: Generally speaking, action is better than inaction.**

In the words of Lao Tzu: "The sage, because he confronts all his problems, never has any." You have to go toe to toe with your problems, gaze right at them in their bloodshot eyeballs and stare them down, lest they grow bigger, nastier, and beastlier than ever. They'll wrap their hairy arms around you and, laughing and jouncing up and down, and sticking a hot, wet tongue in your ear, ride you into the ground.

There are exceptions to this rule (see the question at the end of this chapter). But most of the time, it behooves you to act, and usually quite quickly, to repair the short-term damage. Next, you step back and take a look at the longer-term picture.

The term "damage control" comes from the British navy, and it referred to the sequence of events sailors had to follow when their ship was hit by this terrifying new weapon, wielded suddenly and without warning by German U-boats slinking through the inky blackness deep below the waves: The torpedo.

First, sirens wailing and lights flashing, they had to rush to the site of the breach in the hull and attempt to repair that, so that in the short term, their vessel did not tilt up on one end and with a mighty BLOOP! sink below the surface, leaving them to tread water and be plucked under the waves one by one, screaming, by circling sharks.

They acted fast, because they *had* to.

Second, assuming they'd successfully repaired the breach, they needed to look at the long-term damage to the ship.

And that's a pretty good metaphor for how Team Damage Control goes to work on your problems.

First, with sirens wailing and lights flashing, Pat and I roll out of our cots and, grabbing our (metaphorical) welding masks and (metaphorical) oxyacetylene torches, with grim faces and a high awareness that every second counts, we go to work on the immediate damage. If there's something we can't handle, we quickly get on the blower to someone whose area of expertise speaks to that particular issue.

Later we step back and make sure your vessel is ship-shape, fit for a long voyage and chugging off in the right direction.

GOD, OR IT MIGHT BE THE DEVIL, IS IN THE DETAILS

But enough of the general rules of Damage Control.

We could go on and on, but it's better if we start to look at some individual cases.

Because each screw-up is unique, like a snowflake, like the individual that perpetrates it. That's why we have chosen in this book to unveil our mystical truths, mind-bending revelations, and kabbalistic profundities in question-answer format: to attempt to arrive at the general through the specific. If there were a bunch of rules you could apply to every situation, we would just print up those rules, make seven billion copies, and hire seven million students at ten dollars an hour to hand them out on every street corner of the world.

No, the solution to many problems is often in the details. We've heard two variants of this saying. One is "God is in the details."* The other is "The devil is in the details."† We're not sure which is right. Probably both. Perhaps neither.

In any case, whatever lurks in the details, it's important to pay attention to them. Often, the solution to a particular problem lies in them – as in the case of the following curious dilemma.

---

* This saying is popularly attributed to the architect Ludwig Mies van der Rohe (1886–1969).

† The exact provenance of this saying is unclear.

THE PANTIES, PAM, THE PANTIES

THE QUESTION

My wife and I share a cleaning lady with another couple who are friends of ours. Recently the cleaning lady told us she saw the husband of our friend-couple coming out of the bedroom in the middle of the day, obviously having had sex with a woman who was not his wife!

Then, later, the cleaning lady found a pair of panties in the laundry that obviously did not belong to the lady of the house, and that were of a type (thong) the lady of the house would never wear.

Now the cleaning lady's asking us what she should do. Should she tell the wife (who signs her cheques) or keep her mouth shut? I think she should keep her mouth shut, but my wife doesn't agree! She says she would want to know if it were her and is accusing me of "condoning adultery"! Now it's caused friction in our own marriage, believe it or not, and I've spent the last two nights on the couch because of this. How can I smooth it over?

THE ANSWER

Okay, this one's ticklish. A regular Gordian knot, with several strands of problems all intertwined. The cleaning lady had a problem. The husband of the friend-couple had a problem. The wife of the friend-couple had a problem. The guy who wrote in, aka our "client," had a problem.

My first loyalty, as always, is to the "client," he who wrote in for help. But I couldn't see how to tackle this fellow's problem, at first. I thought of feeding it into Damage

Control's bank of problem-solving supercomputers* for some preliminary analysis, but Karl, the bunker's head tech guy, said the computers were down.

And I sensed my questioner needed a quick answer! So I had to go "manual" and figure this one out with that exhausted old grey nag, my brain.

I paced around. I scratched my melon. I took long walks in the snow. I sat on park benches, staring into the middle distance with thousand-mile, parking-lot-attendant stares, puzzling and puzzling until my Puzzler was sore.

Then one night I was sitting with Pam in front of the fireplace, as is our wont of a chilly winter evening, after we've put the kids to bed: me sipping a quintuple bourbon, brooding and gazing moodily into the fire; her reading some fat, fashionable new novel – when it hit me like a bolt from the blue.

"The panties!" I said aloud.

Pam looked up from her book.

"I beg your pardon?"

My eyes burned into hers like two red-hot embers into a piece of paper towel.

"The panties, Pam! Of course! How could I have been so blind? The panties are the key to everything!"

"What are you talking about? And will you please stop saying 'panties'?"

"But Pam," I said, "it's all in the panties! The panties are the solution! *What did the cleaning lady do with the panties?*"

Pam just rolled her eyes, shook her head, and went back to her book. By now, after seventeen years, she is used to her

---

* Purchased from the Pentagon, second-hand, on the q.t., when they upgraded their system.

husband's "eccentric" (*cough, cough* madman-like *cough, cough*) ways.

The next morning I typed my answer to my reader with fingers of fire: "Do nothing!" I told him. "The panties will take care of everything for you. You don't have to do anything!"

Ask yourself this, I told him: what did the cleaning lady do with the panties? Sure, she might have stuffed them in her pocket and taken them home. But that seems unnecessarily collaborative, conspiratorial and collusive vis-à-vis the husband, and an egregiously overt act of betrayal vis-à-vis milady, who after all, as the cleaning lady took great pains to point out, signs her cheques.

No, what she probably did [I typed] was put them into the system, i.e., the laundry, along with milady's own unmentionables and delicates; in which case they will inevitably make their way into milady's own unmentionables drawer, and in fact at this very moment, as I type [I typed], she is probably holding them with a puzzled frown on her face, the wheels inside her noodle turning and churning.

"The panties will tell her everything she needs to know," I told him. "They will in effect become the *deus ex machina* of the piece, and relieve you and your wife of all moral agency.

"Therefore you should compliment your wife on her good judgment, assure her if push came to shove you would do it her way, but explain to her as I have to you that all action is unnecessary,* that you can let the panties do all

---

* This is actually a rare case that contradicts Rule No. 5 ("Generally speaking, action is better than inaction"), but so be it. Let's say it's "the exception that proves the rule."

the work in this case. As soon as your wife sees 'the logic of the panties,' you'll be back in your marital king-sized in no time," I predicted.

A couple of weeks later, I took the unusual step of checking in with the chap who wrote in, and sure enough, all had come to pass as I predicted. My questioner and his wife did nothing, the panties revealed their hidden secrets, the cheating husband confessed and was now installed in a budget hotel in a seedy part of town, and both he and milady were flipping through the Yellow Pages in search of divorce lawyers.

Which you can guess was probably not much fun for them. But, hey, they weren't the Damage Control "clients" in this case. If the husband of that couple wrote in I could probably help them (though I'm not a huge fan of adultery – more in our "marriage" chapter).

At least my "client," aka the guy who wrote in, was out of the doghouse and back in his wife's good graces, all snuggled up and cozy under the marital duvet.

He thanked me profusely. He stopped short of saying I saved his marriage, but I could tell he felt indebted to Damage Control and would gladly contribute to any charity we endorsed.

(Not that we endorse any: we have enough on our plates with our own problems and those of others – though we applaud all those Angelina-Jolie-esque types who devote so much of their time and energy to help out the less fortunate.)

And that's when I realized I'm some kind of Sherlock Holmes of advice, chasing down clues, solving mysteries, in my deerstalker, smoking a custom mixture in my briar pipe.

"How the deuce did you solve this one, Holmes?"

"The panties, Watson. Follow the logic of the panties and all will be revealed." Puffing on my pipe. "Now leave me, old friend. I want to smoke a couple of bowls and twiddle with my fiddle a little."

And that's when I knew The Dogfather had done right, unleashing Pat and me and the rest of the Damage Control team on an unsuspecting world. That we had a gift, and it was our duty to share that gift with as many people as we could reach.

DAMAGE CONTROL IN LOVE AND COURTSHIP

"Oh tyrant Love, to what do you not drive the hearts of men?"
                                              – VIRGIL

SILENT, UPON A PEAK IN DARIEN

As I mentioned in the Introduction, Pat's still "out there," high-fiving his "bros," downing shots of Jägermeister, chasing the elusive, twitching miniskirt of Ms. Right as it disappears around the corner of the various bars and lofts and brunch spots of the city.

I feel for the boy. It's like trying to find a needle in a haystack – a needle made out of hay! A needle that looks exactly like all the other pieces of hay in the haystack!

Me, I found my Ms. Right seventeen years ago, the semi-divine superheroine Pam.

And everyone's been congratulating me on my so-called luck ever since: "Oooh, Dave, you're so lucky, how'd you get to be so lucky, you're such a lucky bastard, I mean, you're a

42

great guy and everything, but how'd you pull a babe like Pam, you must have rabbit's feet out the yin-yang, you must have horseshoes up the hoo-ha," and la la la.

It can almost get a little . . . insulting. In the roll-up to our wedding, the cacophonous chorus of you-lucky-bastards grew so deafening I made it the theme of my speech: chance, and its various permutations; fortune, and the role it plays in our lives; the slow-dropping other shoe of Providence.

If I hadn't made luck the theme of my speech, I think my wedding guests might have arisen as one and smitten (smote?) me on the spot.

(Sorry to brag, but my wedding speech *killed*, by the way, boys and girls. I don't remember much about the body of the speech, but I ended it by saying: " . . . and so, in conclusion, I would like to say to everyone who's been reminding me in the past few weeks what a lucky bastard I am: thank you. I feel lucky. My only sadness is I only get forty years or so with her. Forty years isn't going to be enough. Forty years with Pam is going to go by like *that*."* I snapped my fingers. "Thank you." End of speech. The crowd, especially the ladies, went bananas. You can use that line if you like in your own speeches, boys. I give it my personal Dave Eddie Guaranfriggintee to be pure gold, a crowd-slayer.)

———

* A statement that's looking truer every day. Seventeen years have already passed in a flash. Where'd they go? Every year seems to go by faster. "Enjoy childhood, kids," I tell my boys. "Savour the moments, and especially how long a day, a summer, a year seems to last – because when you get to be my age a year goes by like a week, it's awful!" They listen with serious faces.

Of course, I know what people are referring to when they drone on and on about my "luck."

Pam's a babe, no doubt. As hot as a vat of bubbling grease, in which a basket of fries are quickly turning golden brown. If she were TV news station, she'd be Fox News. Way "out of my league" – *seemingly*. Apparently. To a lay person.

Yes, to the untrained eye, it might appear I "punched above my weight," that my shagging, tagging, and bagging a babe like Pam was a stone fluke, sheer dumb luck.

When we met, Pam was one of the most sought-after bachelorettes in town. Not only tall, shapely, elegant-yet-sensual, and a little bit famous from her job as a breakfast-television news reporter, she was also Smart, Sexy, Sensible, Sane, Soulful, Strong, and Single.

All seven of The Seven Esses™ every bachelor seeks, in other words.

Which is extremely rare. Ask any bachelor. Ask Pat. An on-the-prowl single man might hope, in his wildest dreams, to encounter "in the field" a woman who embodies two, possibly three, maybe even four of The Seven Esses.

But all seven, in one easy-on-the-eyes package? I felt like I'd said "Open Sesame" and come across the lost treasure of Ali Baba.

She could have had any man she wanted. Lawyers, bankers, doctors, musicians, TV hotshots, advertising slick-sters – yea, even (cue celestial music) architects – threw themselves at her feet, sobbing, begging for a shot, offering to whisk her away to private islands and shower her with champagne and caviar and, I don't know . . . Fabergé eggs or whatever.

(Asking me, a poor ink-stained wretch of a writer, to try to imagine what rich folk shower each other with on private islands is like asking an Indian Brahmin which type of steak he prefers.)

And yet she chose me.*

And who was I, in this era? A thirty-one-year-old man with a part-time job and literary ambitions, living above a store in a part of town (Toronto's Kensington Market) some considered sketchy, others downright dangerous. Trying to look stylish in thrift-store clothes. Arguing about art and literature with my similarly impoverished, bespectacled, vintage-clad pomo boho po-folk friends.

Throw a stick in a crappy neighbourhood in just about any major North American city, in other words, and you'll hit six like me.

So why me? Why me and not the investment bankers, ad slicksters, movie moguls, TV hotshots, and (celestial music) architects?

Well, as with most questions, there's a long and a short answer, boys and girls. But I feel obliged to inform you that despite whatever euphonious horse-feathers I may have fed the credulous, half-crocked rabble at my wedding (who

---

* And make no mistake, that's how it works, boys. Scientists used to think the strongest, fastest alpha-sperm would outswim all 500,000,000 other contenders and head-butt his way through the egg's wall when he got there. But we now know quite a few sperm arrive at the egg's ramparts at about the same time and blindly bump their heads against her wall. After considering her options for a bit, the egg then *reaches out and pulls one in*. And of a more apt/succinct analogy for the dating scene I cannot think, gentlemen.

ate it up with a spoon: of course the unholy miscegenation of a goddess like Pam with a regular Joe* like me could only be the purest form of fool's fortune and blind happenstance), luck had very little to do with it.

Which is not to say luck didn't play any kind of role at all. Of course it did! Mostly in the fact of my meeting her in the first place.

Whenever anyone asked Calvin Trillin, the author of *About Alice*, a classic of what might be called the "literature of uxoriousness,"† and a memoir so moving that hardened New Yorkers would press it into the hands of total strangers on the subway, saying "You must read this," what his secret was – in other words, what is the secret of a long and happy marriage – he would merely smile quietly to himself and say, "Have the good luck to wander into the right party in the first place."

(In his case an early-sixties, proto-pomo boho Greenwich Village "mixer," one that probably featured men in turtlenecks, smoking pipes; women in berets and capri pants; and Charlie Mingus or Miles Davis on the Wurlitzer or whatever.)

Meaning: it really helps if you meet the right person in the first place. Which is a little coy, in our view, and more than a little simplistic. There is so much more to launching and maintaining a happy marriage (we'll get into what, exactly, a bit more in the next chapter).

We will concede, though, it will probably save you a lot

---

* Or, on my best days, perhaps a double-double Joe.

† Admittedly, it's a pretty thin field.

of pain and tears and bad blood and probably a king's ransom in lawyer's fees if the person you hook up with in the first place is right for you.

So in that sense, yes, I was "lucky." I "wandered into the right party" – in my case, the launch of my friend Doug's* difficult, experimentalist, labyrinthine first novel, *Amnesia*.

Pam was standing shyly by the canapés, wearing a silky, summery, floral number that caressed but did not cling to the turbo-curves of what was clearly some kind of Wonder-Womanly, Amazonian über-body.

Even from across the room, her beauty was like a rabbit-punch to the solar plexus.

At that moment, I think I felt something akin to the way the poet John Keats imagines the explorer Cortez† must have felt when he saw the Pacific Ocean, and "all his men/ Look'd at each other with a wild surmise – silent, upon a peak in Darien."

I was "silent, upon a peak in Darien," as I gazed for the first time upon the woman who would one day become my wife and bear me three handsome male heirs.

I'm no Keats, though. Here is a transcript of my thoughts at that moment: "Muh . . . muh . . . me. Me want. For me."

Then, when the mists of lust had dissipated a bit: "Target acquired. I'm going in."

———

* Not *all* my friends are named Doug, though it's true quite a few are.

† He had his parties muddled, though: it was Vasco Núñez de Balboa who first saw the Pacific, not Hernán Cortés.

Poor Pam! Poor sweet, soulful Pam. To this day she believes we're "soulmates"; that it was "fate," aka "destiny," that brought us together, a fate or destiny foreordained and pre-approved by no less an authority than God Him/Herself.

About the "soulmate" part, I agree. But as to the rest of it? She never suspected her seduction and conquest was in reality the *chef d'oeuvre* of a Machiavellian master-bachelor! That behind all the "fortuitous circumstances" and "happy coincidences" of that first fortnight, now so long ago, it was I (cue ominous organ music and bwa-ha-ha-type villainous laughter), The Puppetmaster, all along, behind the scenes, pulling strings.

Little does she realize that for a brief period I became Fate itself, Destiny incarnate!

MY MASTER PLAN

To tell you the truth, I don't like to reveal too many details of the intricate Web of Doom I wove around Pam.

I'm worried that if certain aspects of my Bachelor Campaign were to fall into the wrong hands, they could be converted into a Weapon of Mass Seduction, and all over the city, all over the country, perhaps all over the world, impecunious zhlubs like me would make off with all the top babes.

And lawyers, doctors, investment bankers, yea even (cue celestial music) architects would stand there stunned, open-mouthed, their Porsche keys dangling uselessly from their fingers.

Society itself would teeter on the brink of collapse.

———

All I'll reveal for now is: for a while there, it must have seemed to Pam like everywhere she went, doors flew open; and behind those doors, people were talking about *me*, what a great guy, how talented, etc.

I had half the city working for me, undercover. I turned my crappy little vermin-infested bachelor pad into an HQ, from whence I masterminded the whole operation. I gave "field promotions" to my lieutenants and *consiglieri* who demonstrated outstanding initiative and enterprise in action; I unceremoniously stripped underperformers of their rank and status.

A crucial watershed, or Waterloo (for Pam), came to pass when I "turned" one of Pam's top operatives, her best friend, Julia.

I captured this Julia behind enemy lines and dragged her back to my HQ, where I interrogated her mercilessly. After three or four Chardonnays she sang like a canary about Pam's likes and dislikes in men, where men had failed in the past, etc.

(It was terrifying, to be honest: "She likes you, Dave, she thinks you're funny, but she also likes men with a bit of gravitas, so be funny but not too funny – you know what I mean?")

She also agreed to act as a double agent and feed me information on Pam's moods and movements from inside her camp. And with intel like that, how could I, a student of Sun Tzu (one of the world's first advocates of espionage in warfare, a man who believed "an army without spies is exactly like a man without eyes and ears"), lose?

———

But enough! I've said too much already!

Though I do want to say one other thing for the benefit of the current crop of bachelors out there, who strike me as hopelessly weak-willed, namby-pamby, and vacillating:

Gentlemen: there was nothing ambiguous or half-hearted in my seduction of Pam.

In *The Art of War* (which actually makes for a handy seduction guide: all you have to do is replace words like "battlefield" and "attack" with "the city" and "woo"), Sun Tzu says, "While we have seen a blundering swiftness in war, we have yet to see a clever campaign that was prolonged."

His sidekick, Tu Yu, adds, "An attack may lack ingenuity, but it must be delivered with supernatural speed."

My attack did not lack ingenuity. And it was delivered with supernatural speed.

It was all over in ten days – ten days that changed the world, for me. The book-launch party at which we met was held on a Wednesday night. By a week from that Friday, the deal was signed, sealed, and delivered; the target, neutralized.

Or, to put it in more romantic terms: we were in love.

Which is not to say I view that ten-day period through the hubris-goggles of hindsight and think my Bachelor Campaign was without flaw.

On the contrary, I committed at least two ultra-rookie errors, either of which could have turned out to be a deal-breaker.

Potentially Fatal Courtship Error No. 1 was **Poor Choice of First-Date Venue**: a memorial service.

Well, it wasn't an official date. But a couple of days after the first night we met, I held a private party in my HQ – I mean, apartment – and sparks had flown. She'd even stuck her neck out and done me the honour of being my last guest. Then, when I showed her out, and led her toward her car, just before she got in, we'd kissed – a kiss that lasted several hours, gentlemen, and during the course of which I was running my hands all over her body.

A kiss that lasted until the birds chirped in the trees and rosy-fingered dawn started to creep over the tenement roofs of my poverty-stricken, crime-ridden, artist-, student-, and-rodent-infested neighbourhood.

Finally, after refusing numerous entreaties to come back up to my apartment,* she tootled off in her car, a cute little white Suzuki Swift.

Two days later, she was picking me up in that self-same Suzuki Swift to go to the funeral of a woman who had gone to my high school but whom Pam had also known.

In the car, Pam played it pretty cool – made no mention of the sub-erotic activities of two nights before.

Finally I couldn't take it any more.

"So," I said, heart pounding, "any thoughts about the other night?"

"What about it?"

Still all cool, and coy.

---

* "We don't have to do anything!" I kept saying. "We could just cuddle!" Displaying the admirable common sense I would later come to cherish so much in her, Pam mocked my stratagem: "Do I look like I just fell off a turnip truck, Dave? Does that line still even work for you?" Ruefully, I had to admit it worked better in college.

"Well, you know, it was pretty . . . amorous."

"Well," she said, laughing a savage, raw, dismissive laugh – a type of laugh I hadn't heard her emit before, "I was pretty drunk."

Thus plunging me into a funky pit of despair. I opened my window, as I remember, lit a cigarette, and started to sulk.

At the memorial service I started to get it in my head Pam was "dissing" me, ignoring me, snubbing me, acting cold toward me, etc.

And so, to "show" her, in a hissy-fit-a-licious display of pique, like a little ballerina who couldn't find her tutu or toe shoes, I hopped in a cab, without a word, long before the memorial service was over, and pissed off to my apartment.

Luckily, I didn't say anything before departing. And perhaps that should be **Rule No. 1 of Damage Control in Matters of Love and Courtship: Sometimes, silence is golden, because it is almost impossible to interpret, and you haven't gone on the record one way or another.**

It's when you open your mouth and actually say something – like, I might've gone up to Pam and laid a piece of my melon on her, chewed her out, explained to her *why* I was leaving the memorial service in a huff. . . .

But that might've cremated my chances of a relationship with her, right there. R.I.P. Dave's chances with Pam.

As it was, she might've suspected. But I still had deniability: sometimes a crucial weapon in courtship's early going.

(Later, they can read your mind; and you lose this competitive advantage.)

———

I don't remember what damage control I did on that one, to be honest, ladies and gentlemen. There's an outside possibility I lied: told Pam I'd been "too overcome by grief" to stick around.

If I did go that route – and for the record, I admit nothing – she must have forgiven me, at least enough to acquiesce to a proper first date.

I borrowed a bunch of money from my mother and took Pam out to a medium-nice restaurant.

I'm a naturally chatty fellow in the first place. On that date, trying to impress this shapely goddess, my tongue grew wings and soared to new heights of loquacity and oratorio. Basically, I dropped all my best material on her, pure gold, stuff I'd spent years workshopping in the company of friends and in front of the word processor.

She laughed at the jokes; then when I laid some of my more "moving" material on her, her big, hazel eyes welled up with tears and she reached across the table to take my hand.

Success! That night she did not demur, and accompanied me back up to my apartment afterwards.

As a gentleman, naturally I must draw a veil of tact and discretion over the events that followed. Also, for some time now, I have been instructed by Pam to refrain from writing* about our sex life.

Then I made **Potentially Fatal Courtship Error No. 2: Not festively throwing caution to the wind in the early going.**

---

* Any more than I already have.

The next day, surfing a wave of seratonin and endorphins, I thought I'd be a clever fellow and employ a classic romantic gesture of sending her some flowers at work.

But at the florists I, a man struggling to make ends meet with only a part-time job, balked at the price of a dozen roses – something like $36 – and instead bought a bunch of carnations: $2.99.

Telling myself: "Roses are cheesy anyway!" And: "It's the thought that counts!"

Another terrible misstep, as the fullness of time revealed. In the newsroom where she worked, Pam's high-performing, high-expectation, high-maintenance, superbly coiffed and shod cadre of female colleagues gathered around, wrinkled their foreheads (*cough, cough* to the extent they could, what with all the Botox *cough, cough*) and turned up their curiously *retroussé*, perfectly sculpted (*cough, cough* by a surgeon's scalpel *cough, cough*) noses at my offering; and declared it wanting.

Vis-à-vis the obviously impecunious young man proffering the offering, they advised her to give this new cheapskate suitor the old heave-ho without delay.

"Dave, everyone *knows* carnations are the cheapest flower," Pam explained to me many years later. "You weren't fooling anyone."

If Pam had been a lesser woman, I might have lost her right there. But she didn't listen to her colleagues, bless her, and I lived to kiss my way down her neck, and nibble on her clavicle, another day.

In this case, it was impossible to do "damage control" because I never found out about the actual error until years later. But Pam viewed it as anomalous to my overall aura of generosity. So let's make that **Damage Control Rule No. 2**

in Matters of Love and Courtship: It is indescribably helpful if your offence is perceived as anomalous to your overall character, i.e., "unlike you."

It's good to bear in mind. You can make any number of mistakes in the early going, so long as the object of your affection, attention, and lust is enjoying the overall cut of your jib (we'll explore more about this later in the chapter).

And so I navigated potential problems, beat out other suitors, and was able to secure a pole position, so to speak, with the woman of my dreams.

And we've been together ever since. Those ten days led to seventeen years and counting; three children, all boys; cohabitation in, first, a loft, then a house, then another one; an indescribable feeling of tranquility, rootedness, and being loved for my true self.

And what if I'd blown it in the early going?

Once in a while, walking Murphy on, say, a blustery fall or blizzardy winter's day, I like to mess with my own head, a bit, by trying to imagine what might have become of me had I not met Pam; or, having met her, had blown it in the early going, and we'd decided to part ways.

Sometimes, I think everything would've worked out fine for me.

Other times, though, it seems to me things might not have gone so swimmingly. That I might've wound up sleeping on a cot in a room with a hundred other guys, the air fetid with flatulence and foot odour; the darkness pierced by whinnying screams, and ripped by ragged, chainsaw-like snores; me tossing and turning, clutching my wallet – or maybe a knife! – under my pillow.

"Brrr!" I'll say aloud, pulling the drawstrings of my parka hood tighter, trying to shake off this dystopian vision.

And Murphy, startled, will prick up his ears, cock his head sideways, and look up at me as if to say, "Master?"

"Oh, it's nothing, Murphy. Come on, boy, let's head home."

And I'll point my size 13s toward the house, and start to walk a little faster, Murphy scruffily scurrying ahead of me.

But why dwell on such downbeat scenarios? Better to avoid blowing it in the early going, wouldn't you say? Or, having blown it, perform a little quick damage control, yes?

Okay, let's look at a few of the ways one might blow it in the courtship phase, and how to handle it if you do.

THE FORTNIGHT TEST: DON'T BE TOO INTENSE . . .

THE QUESTION

Recently I started dating a woman I think is my soulmate. For nearly a month, everything was aces. Then I took her to a local community centre to play table tennis. Unfortunately, I got kind of competitive, smashing the ball and doing some "joke" trash-talking. She was not impressed. Also I made a remark about an Asian woman playing at a nearby table. It was a positive comment (something to the effect of what good ping-pong players Asians are). I swear to God I'm not racist, nor overly competitive, but I guess I was a little "off" that afternoon. Now the love of my life has been "busy" the last week. What do I do to salvage this situation? I feel like George Costanza, here!

THE ANSWER

Oh, you're a Seinfeld fan. What up? Me, too.

But you sound a bit more like Kramer, what with the racist component, and all.*

Sorry if this sounds too politically correct, but after giving the matter some deep, heavy thought, we've arrived at the conclusion it is no longer cool to make racial generalizations, even positive ones.

There is a *Seinfeld* that addresses this topic. In the episode entitled "The Chinese Woman," George's phone line gets crossed with a woman named Chang (who turns out not to be Chinese but Jewish: her family changed their name from Changstein).

"I should've talked to her," Jerry says to Elaine when he tries to call George but gets Donna Chang instead. "I like Chinese women."

---

* Fans and non-fans alike may recall that, post-Seinfeld, Michael Richards aka "Kramer" had an onstage meltdown during his stand-up comedy routine and started hurling racial epithets at an African-American heckler, including the "n-word" and the bizarre comment "Fifty years ago we'd have had you upside-down with a fork up your ass!" (A statement over which we're still scratching our melons a little bit, to be honest.) In the midst of the fiasco that followed, he tried to do some damage control, going on TV to apologize and so forth, but it was no use. Another case of someone beyond the reach of conventional damage control. Career-wise, Michael Richards may well have to say, as Kramer says in "The Butter Shave" episode: "Stick a fork in me, Jerry: I'm done."

"Isn't that a little racist?"

"If I *like* their race, how can it be racist?"

But sorry: it is. I mean, I'm of Norwegian extraction. But I don't want people coming up to me and saying: "Oooh, you Scandinavians are such great tennis players. And I love your furniture, it's so practical and easy to assemble!"

Even if they're trying to be complimentary, it's insulting:* it robs people of their individuality, their uniqueness; it tars everyone from a particular group with the same brush, which is not a good look for anyone.

In order to enhance your dateability and maximize your chances of getting lucky, if I were you, friendo, I would cease and desist all "racial profiling" *immediatemente*, posthaste, and *prontissimo*.

Your other grievous sin, IMHO,† was to display unwarranted aggression and poor impulse control in the early phases of your relationship.

That can be a real deal-breaker, a supreme luck-limiting move in the early going, in my experience. In fact, I would go so far as to say that unwarranted aggression and poor impulse control are the two biggest red flags for women in the first fortnight of a relationship.

(Apart, perhaps, from taking her to a porno theatre, à la Travis Bickle in *Taxi Driver*.)

* It's an "insultiment," about which you'll read more in our "social whirl" chapter.

† Oh, you don't speak "text"? It means "in my humble opinion."

It's my firm belief that in the early going every man must pass what I call "The Fortnight Test."

For readers born after about 1868, it may be necessary to explain that "fortnight" = two weeks. And during this two-week period you best believe, boys, your actions are under intense scrutiny. She is deciding whether you are a "keeper"; or, to continue the fishing analogy, whether she will practise a "catch and release" policy upon you.

And if, during this two-week period, you are unwilling or unable to contain your aggressive/wrathful/lustful/obnoxious/overly argumentative impulses, she will know, deep in her DNA, that you are not a gentleman; that you have been insufficiently civilized; and that you could well wind up beating her, cheating on her – or at the very least becoming the type of bullying bore who ticks off points on his fingers during arguments, and just keeps talking louder and louder over whatever it is she is trying to say.

The type, in short, she will probably wind up having to divorce, out of sheer attrition, enervation, irritation, and boredom.

Moreover: excessive intensity vis-à-vis recreational/peripheral matters is the hallmark of the powerless, low-status man. A busy man, a man of gravitas and substance, a man concerned with great affairs or achievement, does not care if he loses the odd ping-pong point. You think Bill Clinton (to choose a somewhat random example of a man who seems to have a fair amount of personal power) trash-talks, smashes, pumps his fist, and performs a little "victory dance" when he wins at ping-pong?

No, he probably just says mildly, in his southern-fried accent, something to the effect of "Nice point, better luck next time."

(Whereas Saddam Hussein, say? Definite ball-smasher, fist-pumper, and victory-dancer.)

I know that women love men who are passionate, ambitious, and competitive. Men who are forceful and intense. Men who are driven.*

But they need to know all this intensity and passion is directed outwardly, toward the world, and on their behalf; not the other way around.

In terms of what steps you should take to get back in her good graces:

I would say, first, apologize. Not too humbly: no need to grovel – what you did wasn't *that* bad, in the grand scheme of things. But do whatever you need to do to get a second chance.

And if a second chance is granted, use it wisely, sir. Show her, through words and actions, that you are indeed a gentleman; you are indeed sufficiently civilized; and that your boorish rec-room comportment was in fact an anomaly.

You have to convince the object of your affections that your table-tennis tantrum rec-room racial-profiling antics are "not like you." (See **Rule No. 2 of Damage Control in Matters of Love and Courtship: It is indescribably helpful if your offence is perceived as anomalous to your overall character, i.e., "unlike you."**) From here on in, until such time as I tell you to stop, which will be never, you need to treat her with exorbitant, elaborate, ostentatious, almost Old-World civility and even courtliness.

Now, don't get me wrong. You need not become a perfect gentleman overnight. Women know the process of

---

* Especially those who are "driven" by chauffeurs – ah, ladies, take it easy, I'm just kidding. Teasing! I love you all, mwah!

civilizing the rough beast known as the male of the species is a lifelong project.

Ask Pam, who's still putting many finishing touches on her husband of seventeen years, i.e., me – e.g. whenever I pour myself a drink, I must always and without fail offer her one, too.

That one's fairly obvious (though sometimes I still forget, and upon these occasions there's hell to pay, I get the full silent treatment, complete with crabby face, followed by begging her to let me know what's wrong – all before I'm even *allowed* to apologize). But it can get quite subtle, too.

For example, when we're at a restaurant, she likes me to order for her. (Pam likes to be "the girl," sometimes.) But I'm not allowed to say to the waitress, referring to Pam, "She'll have such and such." I have to say, for some obscure, unfathomable, inscrutable reason, "My wife will have such and such." Or "Pam will have such and such." (Even though the waitress doesn't know Pam's name.)

Or else it's "rude." Why? Go ask it on the mountain. But I don't fight it. I figure she somehow has access to subtleties of punctilio completely lost on the male of the species.

In any case, ours, gentlemen, is not to reason why, ours is to do as Her Nibs says or in Tarnation we shall fry. Tabernac!

The main thing is to demonstrate (a) you're willing to improve, (b) you recognize there's room for it.

She'll take it from there!

Which brings us to **Rule No. 3 of Damage Control in Matters of Love and Courtship: You must demonstrate to potential girlfriends, boyfriends, spouses, or whatever, that you are on that person's side, or "team," at all times.**

Make it exquisitely clear, through words and actions, that it is the two of you vs. the world, not you vs. her. That you are if not the CEO then at least Head Cheerleader of Team [Object of Your Affection's Name Here].

Otherwise you risk doing to your chances with her what Michael Richards did to his career.

. . . BUT DO GO STRONG TO THE HOOP

THE QUESTION

There was this guy in my social circle, I was into him and I know he was into me, too. But he would never make a serious move. I knew he wanted to. I waited and waited. And we did make out quite a few times, and even slept together a couple of times, but whenever it seemed to be getting serious he would always pull back and act all unsure and tortured and say he wasn't sure he was ready for a "commitment" or a "serious" relationship.

This went on for years. So finally I said, fine, and now I'm dating another guy completely. But now the first guy is coming on strong, saying he realizes I'm "the one," the only one he's really cared about and so on. But it's too late, I've moved on. I'm in love with my new boyfriend, who at least is sure I'm what he wants. I really care about my ex "boyfriend," since I secretly think that's what he really was, but I've lost interest in him, romantically. What should I say to him?

THE ANSWER

"Cancel my subscription, I don't need your issues."

You know, I've always considered myself to be a hip, cool, "happening" dude, *au courant* and *au fait* with the youth of today, and an all-around relaxed and easygoing guy.

Lately, though, mostly for the fun of it,* I've been trying to cultivate my "inner curmudgeon." So I would like to ask you to imagine me standing on my porch in a ratty old bathrobe and crusty slippers, my gamy, bandy, hairy, fish-white legs gleaming in the sunshine, as I shake my bony old fist at you and yell out:

"You kids these days! I just don't get you at all!"

In my day, when a man was interested in a woman, he grabbed a bottle of wine or beer or (best) tequila, gnawed off the cork, spat it on the ground, poured as much of the contents down his throat as he could handle, and cha-a-a-arged, with steam coming out of his ears.

And the object of his affection squealed, giggled, and started running around his coffee table, as fast as her skin-tight miniskirt and high heels would allow.

(Then if she liked you, she sort of slowed down at one point and let you catch her.)

But these days it's all "hooking up" and "hanging out," "booty calls" and "fuck buddies," pardon my French. Toss in "Facebook friends" and "online dating" (a total oxy-moron if you ask me), and it's no wonder men and women are confused, lost in a hazy mist of romantic grey areas and half-assed sort-of relationships.

---

* Also, perhaps, in preparation for the inevitable onslaught of old-codger-dom.

Mainly, twenty-first century men strike me as the worst collection of namby-pamby ambivalence junkies and too-little-too-late artists to come along in a long time. You could be dating one of these wishy-washy characters for six months and not even be aware of it!

"Oh, I thought we were just hanging out."

"Nah, baby, we been hooking up, definitely."

"Oh."

"So, you wanna hang out . . . ?"

"Uh . . ."

So we already discussed how women don't tend to go for men who are too intense. They also don't like men who seem too horny, needy, or desperate.

At the same time, though, they like a man who, when he sees an opening, goes strong for the hoop.

But why take only my word for it? Let's ask a real, live, va-va-va-voom, boom-chika-boom-chika-wow-wow babe (Pam).

Now, I mentioned above that I went strong to the hoop when it came to Pam. But let's hear her side of the story.

. . . but, uh, first, let me ask: we're getting to be friends, now, a bit, right, dear reader? We can tell each other stuff, now, don't you think?

Because earlier, I told you people are always coming up to me and telling me what a lucky bastard I am, and so on.

What I didn't want to reveal, at least until we got to know each other a bit better, is that people will often come up to Pam, with me *standing right there*, and ask her, in tones of ultra-insulting incredulity: "Pam, when you first started going out with Dave, like, no offence* Dave, but tell us, Pam, just what exactly did you *see* in him?"

Now, as with most questions, there's a long answer and a short answer.

Interestingly, though, Pam in effect chooses neither.

Instead she uses the opportunity to ascend her bully pulpit/ soap box and send a message out to bachelors everywhere:

"Well, there were a lot of things I liked about Dave when we first started seeing each other," she'll say. "But I'll tell you one thing. I was never in doubt about how he felt about me. He made it abundantly clear, right from the start, that he was *very* interested in me. And I liked that."

He who has ears, let him hear.

In other words, gentlemen: if you see something you want, cha-a-arge! Ladies: wear your ovaries on your sleeves. Don't self-censor! Don't say "out of my league." Anything under the sun is possible, if only you aim yourself at it, and, like one of those out-of-a-cannon circus daredevils, shoot yourself toward the object of your desire with your guts churning and senses tingling.

Life is short. Sexy members of whichever sex you happen to prefer don't just fall in your lap and start to undulate. (Well, maybe once in a while, at a party, when you're in your twenties: but you can't count on it happening with any kind of consistency.) When you're single, you know one thing: Mr. or Ms. (or Dr., or best, ladies, Frank Lloyd) Right isn't in your apartment.

---

* I love how people say something insulting preceded by "no offence." As I'm constantly telling my kids, though, saying "no offence" before an insult (e.g., "No offence, that's a really dumb joke, Dad,") does not in fact change anything.

You've got to get out there.

It's like anything else: if you want something, *fight* for it! Become an opportunistic organism. Seize the day, and the night.

Otherwise, you'll never know what you missed; you'll always wonder what might have been; and that doesn't sound like any kind of fun at all.

Even if the object of your affection isn't interested, at the moment, or is otherwise entangled, it never hurts to plant that seed, the seed of "I like you."

You never know what time will bring. Say she's seeing some dude – an architect, for instance. And he wins the Prix D'Or at the annual architectural conference in Barcelona, or whatever.

And it goes to his head; and he becomes an insufferable, egotistical prick; and winds up having an affair.

And the long-ago object of your affection breaks up with him, and becomes single again.

Late one night, watching *Sex and the City* reruns, sipping Chardonnay, she might wind up scratching her pretty little coconut and thinking, "I wonder what ever happened to [Your Name Here]? [Your Name Here] seemed like a pretty nice guy. And he certainly was keen on me! Wonder if he's single, these days?"

And she'll track you down via Facebook or whatever; maybe you'll start e-mailing one another, then chat on the phone, and agree to have a drink.

And then, perhaps, at long last, you, patient pilgrim, will reach The Promised Land after all.

MISOGYNY AND MISANDRY: LUCK-LIMITING MOVES

So far we have concentrated mostly on some common ways men can blow it in the early going.

But let's take a look, now, at what I think is one of the most common mistakes modern women make, before the early going even ever gets going.

THE QUESTION

I have a female friend who's a bit of a "man-basher." She's great, she's really attractive, but she's had quite a few disappointments in love and she seems quite angry with men. She's always saying men are stupid, pigs, and dishonest – stuff like that. Meanwhile, she's begging me to set her up. Truthfully, I know a couple of great single guys, but I'm reluctant to set them up with her because she has such low expectations going in. I keep putting her off, but she's starting to get mad at me. Am I obliged to set her up?

THE ANSWER

It never ceases to amaze me: women who say all men are pigs, and bastards, and the scum of the earth, in one breath; then wonder why they're single in the next.

Like the horrible women of the aforementioned, now-defunct (thank God) TV show *Sex and the City*. They sit around their coffee shop or whatever, complaining about, rolling their eyes at, and making derogatory generalizations about men – and then wonder where all the single men are.

What the shallow, materialistic, footwear-obsessed characters of that show don't see, as they stride confidently down the streets of Manhattan, off-screen wind machines ruffling their hair, brave looks on their faces, is all the men flattening against walls, ducking into doorways, and crossing the street.

Man-bashing has become so widespread lately, sometimes I think people don't even know when they're doing it.

In every sitcom, the man is a useless, ignoble, overweight, hapless, helpless, duplicitous, shallow, self-serving slob – and those are the good guys.

In the ads interlarded* between the shows, men fare even worse. They're foolish beyond belief; cretinous in a way that defies credulity.

As I write there's a commercial on TV of a fat, foolish-looking guy tattooing the name of a casino onto his chest, in front of a full-length mirror (as if). His wife or girlfriend or whatever comes in and says to him: "You know . . . it's backwards."

He turns around to face her. It is backwards. "No it isn't!" he says.

She just rolls her eyes and exits. He turns back toward the mirror, and is relieved: phew, it's not backwards (because, duh, the image in a mirror is reversed).

I mean, Jesus, advertising industry: how moronic are we men supposed to be?

Meanwhile, "man jokes" proliferate on the Internet.

Some, I confess, I find kind of funny:

* At last, I get to use my favourite word.

Q. How do you get a man to do sit-ups?
A. Put the remote between his toes.

Q. What do you call that insensitive fleshy thingie at the base of the penis?
A. A man.

Others, though, are kind of disturbing:

Q. How many men does it take to wallpaper a bathroom?
A. Three, but only if you slice them very thinly.

Now, I get that a lot of this is backlash for millennia of male misrule.

But what a lot of women don't realize, I think, is the person they're hurting the most with their male-bashing ways is themselves.

My aphorism here (sorry it's a little convoluted) is "Just as women love men who love women, so men love women who love men."

Get it? We like women who like us, basically. Duh! And our eyes start to dart around, looking for escape routes, when we encounter those who obviously don't.

Just like you, ladies! Let me put it to you this way: say you were at a party, and some bitter, angry-seeming guy was standing over by the fish tank, muttering about how all women are bitches, and making other angry and pejorative generalizations about your gender, e.g., "Women are all the same, they all want the same thing!"

You'd avoid him, wouldn't you? And if you couldn't, if he cornered you by the canapés and asked for your phone number, you wouldn't give it to him, would you? Or else give him a false one?

Well, we're the same way! At the first sign of a man-basher in the vicinity, we melt into the crowd/moonwalk for the exits/hide behind a ficus.

Well, some of us, that is: the smart, discerning ones, the ones who actually care about women and relationships and stuff other than sex.

The horny cheeseballs, the ones who don't care about anything, as long as they get some, stick around, not caring; or maybe even thinking, "Cool, that chick sounds really mad at men. So whatever I do will not surprise or disappoint her! I can be a total douche and it will only confirm what she already believes about men!"

That's why male-bashing is such a self-fulfilling prophecy. All the good men are "in the wind," but the horny cheese-balls remain. These dudes abide, their eyebrows bobbing up and down – because they don't care! They're too horny to care if you like them, or they you. They like *it*, that's all that matters to them.

And so your friend winds up surrounded by this type of man, thus reinforcing her *weltanschlong*:* "All men are horny cheeseballs who don't even care about feelings, all they care about is sex." Uh, no, honey, just the ones who were still left in the room when you finished your anti-male tirade.

If you really want to help your friend, get her out of her vicious cycle of male-bashing and douche-dating; you

---

* A German word meaning, I believe, one's view of men in general.

should attempt to convince her of some or all of the above.

Explain to her that, given our druthers, all other things being equal, we men have to admit we'd prefer it not be someone who is going to be bitterly angry at us and/or hate our guts and/or bad-mouth us to anyone who'll listen, for the rest of our lives.

We want someone who loves us, not only for our individual personalities, but for all the occasionally counterintuitive, often annoying, and occasionally downright dumb, flat-out fucked-up stuff (e.g., puddles of water outside the shower, stepping over something on the stairs you *obviously* left for us to pick up) that makes us what we are: men.

Or at least someone who has a sense of humour about it all.

Tell your friend to try to make an effort to ease up on men, a little. If she digs in the heels of her Jimmy Choos and says, "But men *are* such pigs," maybe say, "That may be true, but you won't meet one of the few who aren't if you keep this up."

Of course, you can still go ahead and set her up with whomever. As long as they're consenting adults, whatever happens is up to them.

(Though be prepared, as with all set-up situations, to be interrogated for information by both sides.)

It's a give-her-a-fish-and-she'll-eat-for-a-day-teach-her-to-fish-and-she'll-eat-for-a-lifetime kind of deal. Help her look for what is good, decent, positive, brave, noble, and loveable in men; that'll be a much better look for her.

You can't find love until you open your heart. Can anyone disagree with that? Help her with that. Even if it's just an act, at first; I guarantee as soon as she does she will immediately begin to meet a better class of men.

And then maybe she will begin genuinely to fall in love with us, warts (and towels on the floor and remotes between the toes and stepping over stuff on the stairs) and all.

TWO THINGS YOU NEED: (1) MOMENTUM, (2) EXCLUSIVITY

THE QUESTION

My boyfriend and I dated for almost two years, but he just broke up with me. He was aware that I talked to a guy friend I've known for over seven years, but the messages that my "friend" and I were sending back and forth became rather inappropriate about a month ago.

Despite my best efforts to deal with this uncomfortable situation privately, my boyfriend (while we were still going out) read messages in my Facebook inbox, and my responses, where I told my "friend" of seven years I cared about him emotionally and how I found it hard not knowing how he felt. Now my (now ex-) boyfriend feels as though I am completely untrustworthy (because I have cheated in the past) and that there is no hope for a future between us, other than as friends.

Is there any way to assure my estranged love that I am indeed capable of being trusted?

THE ANSWER

Well, for starters, I'd like to know how your boyfriend got into your Facebook inbox. Did you give him your password and/or neglect to log out? You didn't write about your "feelings" for your "guy friend" on his/your Facebook Wall, did you?

You say your ex-boyfriend "feels" like you're untrustworthy. Could that be because you *are* untrustworthy, hmmm? I'll tell you, if I had a girlfriend who "cheated in the past" who was Facebooking some random dude to tell him she had "feelings" for him, that would be not only a red flag for me.

It would be a checkered flag telling me our relationship had just zoomed past the finish line.

But, hey, you're my "client" here, and like a lawyer zealously representing an obviously guilty offender, sure, I can tell you how to re-seduce your ex.

Re-seduction is the same as seduction, except with more familiarity and fraught, haunted undertones thrown in for spice. This may be the techno-savvy twenty-first century, but the way you seduce/re-seduce a man is as old as Time itself (or at least as old as my ratty bathrobe and crusty slippers and gamy, bandy, knock-kneed legs).

And it's as simple as frying an egg. Like with the egg (crack, fry, done), it's basically two simple steps: (1) Wave something eye-catching, something that might pique his interest, under his nose; then (2) snatch it away.

Got that? Wave; then snatch. Wave; then snatch. Like a matador, with the red cape. Could be cleavage. Could be a little leg. "To get what you want you got to shake what you got," as I heard a woman on a bus put it once.

Soon enough, if he's going to be interested, he will be; his testosterone will begin to simmer, his corpuscles commence to bubble. And he will *chaa-a-a-arge,* with nostrils flaring and steam emanating from his collar.

———

But is that what you really want? As your (advice) counsellor, I must urge you, my client, to ask yourself if this is the best course of action.

I'm not a big fan of reuniting with exes in the first place. It's returning to a poisoned well.

In your case, he's full of doubt and regret and, frankly, doesn't sound all that interested. Meanwhile, you're interested. But, pardon me for (re)iterating this observation, frankly, madam, you still seem to have fuzzy, underdeveloped notions about monogamy and exclusivity.

Sounds like a recipe for slow-roasted Szechuan disaster, with spicy, saucy, hot-and-sour encounters, served on a sizzling platter, followed by a fortune cookie that says, "No matter how hard you flog it, a dead horse can no longer pull the cart."

If I were you, I'd find someone with whom to start fresh, wipe the slate clean, and reboot your whole approach to relationships.

Earlier in the chapter, I said chemistry was one of the "necessary but not sufficient" conditions for taking your relationship to the next level, dropping the booster rockets, and blasting off into orbit together.

The other two crucial conditions, if you're interested in pursuing this type of romantic trajectory, are **Momentum** and **Exclusivity.**

Without **momentum**, a relationship is like a rocket shot into the air with insufficient fuel: bound to come crashing to earth, scattering debris and shrapnel everywhere.

And **exclusivity**, if I may use a different but equally elaborate metaphor, is the water you put on the little tiny plant-shoot of your relationship: with it, the plant will grow strong and robust; without it the plant will turn brown, wither, and die.

Momentum and exclusivity are mutually reinforcing. As I mentioned earlier, when Pam and I met, we came together* like a thunderclap: ka-boom! With enough momentum to propel us through time, to send us hurtling through the next seventeen years like a bullet.

And a big reason we were able to come together with such decisiveness is we were both emphatically, unadulteratedly, unadulterously single.

I could look her in the eye and say, "So. You one hundred percent single, Pam? No shadowy dudes in the wings, or guys in New Orleans you still have sort of a thing for, or regular late-night booty calls, or recidivist trysts with still-infatuated exes I should know about?"

And she could look me in the eye and say, "Absolutely not. I am one hundred percent single. What about you? Any of your bimbos still lurking around?"

"Not a chance, Pam. I am so single it hurts."

"I suggest we initiate countdown to full-fledged makeout sequence."

"I concur."†

And we could do whatever we felt like: take off all our clothes and run around nude, if we felt like it, in the eternal sunshine of a spotless conscience.

---

* Not sexually, madam – romantically! Get your mind out of the gutter.

† I'm paraphrasing, of course. We don't *actually* talk like this to one another.

Whereas shadowy entanglements – having to get rid of some long-distance dude who lives in New Orleans or whatever, before you can properly commit to the object of your affections – just bollocks things up in the early going.

Then, once you've got the momentum rolling, and left the liftoff phase, entered the part of the atmosphere where the air's a bit thinner, Part 2 of your two-pronged approach kicks in: the "exclusivity" bit.

I feel very strongly about exclusivity. Who knows? Maybe I'm a bit of a freak, a bit OCD, about it.

But here's how I feel: there's an old Canadian saying, born of the intense cold we experience during the winter, up here in the hyperborean hinterlands: "If you don't have heat, you don't have an apartment."*

By the same token, I think it could be said that if you don't have exclusivity, you don't have a relationship.

But hey, that's just me. Sorry to all the Mormons and assorted orgy guys and gals and "swingers" and spouse-swappers and other "polyamorists" out there. I know you feel you have a point. But in my view, as George Michael sang in the eighties, sex is best when it's (turn Auto-Tune™ to freaky basso profundo) "one . . . on . . . one."

Same holds for love, IMHO.

---

* Like, one person will say to a friend, in mid-February: "The heat's gone out in my apartment again." And the other guy will say: "Dude, if you don't have heat, you don't have an apartment."

IF YOU'RE GOING TO LEAVE, SOONER = BETTER

THE QUESTION

I was recently treated for cancer in a downtown facility where there are about a dozen volunteers. One of them took a liking to me and asked me out for a drink a couple of times. It was nice to get some positive attention and to forget for a while I had cancer. At any rate, after a couple of dates, we had sex. I wasn't that into him, but the idea that I was desirable to someone, while bald and pale, was overwhelming.

And having sex in the shadow of death was life-affirming.

But he's since resigned from his volunteer position and now wants to be my boyfriend. I told him I'm not interested, that I'm too vulnerable for a relationship, and we should stop socializing. My treatment, which is going very well, is almost over. I feel some obligation to this guy, but I do not want to continue seeing him. What should I do? I'm feeling like a user.

THE ANSWER

Well, you wouldn't be the first person in the history of humanity who's used someone else for sex.

Nor would you be the first to discover that sex is an excellent antidote to anxieties about one's own extinction.

There's a lovely scene in *Clea*, the fourth book in Lawrence Durrell's sweeping English-expats-in-Egypt quadrilogy.

. . . well, I thought the scene was so moving in college, anyway. I just re-read it and I have to admit, even I found it tough to swallow Durrell's baroque, one might even say *rococo*, word-tapestries.

Anyway, the narrator and his girlfriend, the titular Clea, are walking around Alexandria. Suddenly offshore warships start shelling the city, air-raid sirens go off, and everyone starts scrambling for bomb shelters.

The narrator says, "Clea, we should shelter."

She takes him by the lapels and says (don't say I didn't warn you), "I am too fastidious to die with a lot of people in a shelter like an old rats' nest. Let us go to bed together and ignore the loutish reality of the world."

The narrator's up for it: she's gorgeous, he's bookish, and while the two of them have been spending quite a bit of time together, lately, walking around Alexandria and chatting and having coffee, this would be the first time they would be conjoined in the, uh, throes of consummation.

Let the bombs fall where they may, the narrator thinks (I'm paraphrasing). *Thank you, warships!* They go back to her place and "so it was that lovemaking itself became a kind of challenge to the ... thunderstorm of guns and sirens. . . . And kisses . . . became charged with the deliberate affirmation which can only come from the ... presence of death."

Look past the flowery language, it's a profound sentiment, I feel. Now I'm no Durrell, but basically he's saying this: there's nothing like a little nookie to thumb your nose at the Reaper.

A sentiment that certainly applies to your case, and I would say makes it hugely sympathetic and relatable. Anyone, I would think, especially anyone who's had any first-hand experience with cancer, could probably understand why you might want to get away from the "loutish reality" of it for a few stolen moments.

But, anyway, it sounds like you've beaten it and may outlive us all. Therefore, let me give you the same advice

I would give anyone who wants to get out of a relationship he or she may have backed into for the wrong reasons but feels too guilty to extricate him or herself from. And in a way it's an adjunct to the advice to the wannabe re-seduction girl, above.

Damage Control Rule No. 4 in Matters of Courtship and Romance: If it's not going to last, don't forget you're wasting the other person's time, too. Therefore, the sooner you release the other person from your clutches, the bigger a favour you're doing that person. Your volunteer friend needs to get on with his life. He needs to find someone who will love him and appreciate him not just for sex but for every little facet of his character that makes him unique and special.

You are obviously not into him in this way. Therefore you will never be anything but a painful episode in his life. Better you should make it a brief painful episode rather than a protracted one.

He'll hate you less, later, when he looks back on it all.

And you need to get on with your life, too. What a lot of people don't realize is: when you allow these shadowy half-boyfriends or half-girlfriends to hang around, you're hurting your chances of meeting Mr./Ms./Dr./Right.

Think about it this way. Right now, somewhere across town, Mr. Right – a handsome young architect, say, who's also inherited a fortune and a stately home and is a crack cook who loves kids and considers cleaning the house a form of Zen relaxation – may be talking to a female friend of his who knows someone who knows you, and saying (about you): "Gosh, I think [Your Name Here] is very attractive and soulful and special. I really like her. Do you happen to know if she's single?"

And the friend of a friend of a friend might answer: "Nah, I think she's seeing someone. Some volunteer guy, or something . . ."

And the handsome young architect will shrug and pick up the phone and punch in some other woman's digits – some woman who's genuinely single and unencumbered and unattached.

And they will end up happily ever-so-together forever-more.

And the saddest part is you'll never know what you missed: "Honey, did you see my T-square? I need it for that soccer stadium I'm designing in Brazil."

"Oh, you silly Billy, it's right there on your tilty table, where it always is!"

"Thanks, honey!"

Kissy-kiss!

Basically, do yourself *and* this volunteer guy a favour and dump him with maximum bluntness and dispatch. Have the courage to be single, so when Mr. Right does cross your path, you can enjoy not only the transplendent pleasure of turning your backs on "the loutish reality of the world," but also all the other perks of being in a real relationship: love, companionship, and the sense of not being just you alone against the world, but the both of you together, as a team, taking on whatever life tosses at you.

No matter how much time you have left on the planet, you want to take your best shot at having that, don't you?

HURDLES:

(1) THE CONFESSION OF IMPERFECTIONS CONVERSATION

THE QUESTION

Two months ago, I was single and hopping from bed to bed. But I met this guy at a wedding and since then we've settled into a really sweet – but hot – relationship. Last weekend, during a little pillow-chat, we made the mistake of bringing up our histories. Actually, he started the conversation and didn't hesitate in telling me how many women he'd slept with and who his biggest hang-ups had been. I thought it was a tender moment of honesty, but when I told him (honestly) how many men I'd slept with, he freaked out and told me that if he'd known how much I slept around, he might not have thought himself so special. Things haven't been the same since. I don't feel like I have to take any of that back – he asked, I answered honestly – and now we're in the midst of our first big rift. Any way I can claw my way back to bliss?

THE ANSWER

There's two ways these types of scenarios can go: (1) well; (2) badly.

If it goes well, it can be one of the best parts of the early going.

It's that magic moment when you tell the other person something about yourself you don't normally tell other people, because you're too embarrassed/ashamed and/or don't want to horrify/disgust them:

"I have an STD."

"I've killed a man."*

"I have a vestigial tail, it wags when I'm happy."

(Okay, okay, I stole that one from a movie, *Shallow Hal.*)

It's a way of saying you trust the person. It's a way of saying, "I separate you from the herd, in a good way." The first step toward the two of you vs. the world, as opposed to you vs. him/her and the rest of the world.

The "confession of imperfections" conversation should happen, in my opinion, around the third or fourth date.

If the other person laughs at your confession, or recoils in horror, that obviously doesn't augur well for the future.

Best case: they express compassion, and then reveal some imperfection of their own.

"Vestigial tail? That's nothing. Check this out!"

Unzzzzzzzzzipppppppppp!

At which point, of course, your job is to arrange your own features into an expression of compassion, no matter what pops out next.

But that's maybe advice for the next guy. Maybe this guy isn't worth it. To be honest, he doesn't sound worthy, like a "keeper." He did fail the "confession of imperfections" test.

Maybe he's more the "catch and release" type. In any case, you shouldn't worry about how you should claw your way back into his judgmental embrace. He's the one who freaked out on you.

---

* Believe it or not, one of goody-two-shoes Pam's pre-Dave boyfriends – a dude named Moto Kross (she liked the bad boys, about which more later) or something like that – laid this line on her, in the early going. Cheque, please!

He's the one who should worry about clawing his way back into your good graces.

Bottom line: Tell him, point-blank: "This is me. This is the deal. Take it or leave it, and I'd rather know sooner than later because if you can't handle it I need to move along and find someone who can, someone who accepts all my history and my faults and loves me for them, because of them [i.e., because I'm the lusty, man-loving type and not a shy flower], rather than in spite of them."

If he decides he can handle it, that he can smile and enjoy the hair-raising tales of your sexual history, the ins and outs, then more power to him.

If not, buh-bye.

(2) MEETING THE CREW

THE QUESTION

I work in advertising and I've been going out with a lawyer for the past few months – I met her at a bar one night and things progressed really fast. She comes from a wealthy old family and I've been kind of putting on airs when she's around. We ran into a bunch of my old friends one night last week and to put it mildly, they're not the most sophisticated bunch. I felt like they were blowing my cover and was embarrassed by how they portrayed me in front of her, so I made up some lame excuse to bail out of there and gave one of my close buddies shit for acting like a jackass. Thing is, he wasn't – that's how we've always been. Now my friends think I'm a big jerk and my lady friend seems to be looking at me with different eyes. Do I have to come clean with her and level with my buddies or can I just keep up this scam?

THE ANSWER

Another great moment in the early going is when the object of your affection meets "the crew/the girls."

If it goes well, if your potential mate likes them, what a deal-sealer!

Pam met my boys after our third date. I was praying this motley crew of mostly ne'er-do-wells (but ultra-decent dudes) would rise to the occasion – and, in a way, they did, thank God.

They were mental! They were out there, practically doing handstands for Pam. One guy lifted up his shirt and showed her some kind of trick with his fab abs. Another guy (oh, wait, that might have been me) did a trick with a beer where he punched a hole in the bottom and it became a "beer shooter."

I was sweating the whole time wondering: "What must she be thinking of this funky bunch of FUBARs?"*

Here we have this pillar of virtue, this ultra-classy babe, this pillar of goodness and virtue à la Princess Fiona in *Shrek*. Would she see past the surface villainy of my crew to the rough-diamond sweetness underneath?

Praise be to God, she did. She laughed all night long. "I love your friends!" she said, later, back at my HQ.

Thank you, boys, I could kiss you all (on the cheek)! I said earlier the whole seduction of Pam took ten days. "Meeting

* Fucked Up Beyond All Recognition

the crew" happened on maybe day six or seven, and the fact she liked my homeboys was a crucial deal-sealant.

If you have nice friends, it means you're a good judge of character, you're loyal, a good communicator – all things women are looking for in a man.

And if not, well, hopefully the object of your affection will be so smitten he/she won't care. Of course, if you're too attached to your "crew," that could pose problems down the line, too. She doesn't want to marry someone who's going to go out with the boys every night.

Now, I don't know your boys. And I don't know you. But presuming your friends are, if rough, then still diamonds, stand by them, be loyal to them. It was well captured, I thought, in *Good Will Hunting*. Yes, Matt Damon is a janitor. But Minnie Driver, the Harvard student, sees his potential. And when she meets Ben and Casey Affleck, she sees they're loyal to him and they're his boys, and she likes him all the more.

The same should go, I think, for your new hoity-toity girlfriend. If she's the one for you, if she's a keeper, she should see beyond the rough-diamond qualities of your bros to the loyalty and solidity underneath.

If she looks at you "with different eyes," as you say, well, that could be good, it could be bad. If she sees you for who you really are, and likes it, then, good.

That is the goal of the early going: to find someone who knows you inside out, who sees you for exactly who you are, but loves you anyway.

YOUR TAKEAWAY DOGGIE BAG OF THOUGHTS AND OBSERVATIONS

Since this is (kind of) a self-help book, we want to do that self-help-y thing at the end of each chapter where we summarize everything we've said and leave you with a few "take-away" thoughts. So here goes:

- **Don't be too intense.** Over-intensity in the early going is a sign of poor impulse control and you could wind up getting served your Bachelor/Bachelorette Papers before you can even say, "Hey, wait, give me another chance."

- **Do go strong to the hoop.** This applies particularly to the gentlemen of the twenty-first century, but also to the ladies. Unless you're outrageously attractive, wealthy, and/or all of the above, sexy members of whichever sex you prefer will not necessarily just fall into your lap and begin to wiggle and nibble upon your earlobes. You see someone you want, even if that person is supposedly "out of your league," go get him/her!

- **Bitterly generalizing about the opposite sex is a luck-limiting move.**

- **Momentum and exclusivity are the twin engines of the early going.**

- **If the horse has died, stop flogging it.** If a relationship is clearly not working, the sooner you get out of it the better. If you feel guilty about leaving, counteract the guilt with the following thought: the less of the other person's time you waste, the bigger a favour you are doing him/her.

- **The goal, ultimately, is to love and be loved for who you are and who the other person is.** This process is initiated in the early going. Therefore, you don't have to be perfect. If the object of your affections can see your flaws, and flawed friends, as part of your "humanity," that's actually a good thing.

Basically, when you're single, you know one thing for sure: Mr./Ms. Right is not in your apartment. Therefore, you have to get "out there," soldier, mix it up, and sometimes take it on the chin, with all the rest of us flawed fools and semi-attractive bumpkins!

How Not to **Blow It** in the **Long Run,** and Wind up
Thumbing Your Way Through the *Yellow Pages*,
Looking for **Divorce Lawyers,** or If That **Really** Can't
Be *Avoided,* How to Minimize **Disaster** and **Distress**
for **All Parties Concerned**

DAMAGE CONTROL IN THE MIDST OF MARRIAGE AND OTHER LONG-TERM ROMANTIC ENTANGLEMENTS

KUDOS, FIRST OF ALL

Okay, so you managed to hang on through the early going.

You've passed "The Fortnight Test," dispersed the competition, and somehow managed to convince the object of your affections that you're The One for him or her; and vice versa.

And do you know how you know when you've passed The Fortnight Test and have entered the realm of potential keeper-dom? For guys, it's the moment the object of your affection, attention, and lust buys you, or forces you to buy, a new pair of shoes.

Yes. Women like to "make over" their potential mates, and they usually work from the feet up, starting by making sure he's well-shod, ending when he's suitably coiffed and everything in between is working, as well.

I would also like to add that I was speaking recently to one of our female Panel-ists, who informed me: "I knew I was serious about John [her husband, and the father of her recently born first child] when I stopped telling my girl-friends about sex with him."

So: gentlemen, there you have two reliable yardsticks by which to guesstimate a potential commitment is being made, or at least contemplated. Some grooming tips, and a switch of loyalties.

Ladies: it's the same for guys. Well, we tend to stay away from the grooming tips. But when we transfer loyalties, it's a big thing. If we tell you something we really shouldn't, for example, that might get us in trouble with one of our "bros"; or if we let you in on one of our insecurities (see "confes-sion of imperfections conversation," in previous chapter) – then it means we're starting to take you seriously.

Like – I don't mean to generalize too much, but let's say in many cases – if a guy finally comes out with a painful, tormented statement like "I wish I were more successful," ladies, then you know you're in, because that's not some-thing he's going to tell *anyone* but a potential mate-for-life.

But before we proceed, ladies and gentlemen, we should pause and say: if you've gotten there, if you have selected and been selected as The One, we here at Damage Control would like to take a moment out of our busy schedules, tuck our clipboards under the arms of our lab coats, and salute you: well done, son! Good going, girl!

Maybe you've even taken it to the next level, and there's been a ceremony, presided over by some sort of religious, legal, or nautical figure.

Or maybe there hasn't. Maybe, like Johnny Depp and Vanessa Paradis, you've decided simply to cohabit.

Cool, dude! You're a rebel! Hey, man: you don't need "The Man" to bless your union or "a piece of paper from the city hall," as Joni Mitchell said. You don't need a piece of paper to tell each other how committed you are! No one's going to put a label on you!

Or maybe you've even got a tattoo to commemorate your undying love. Even cooler! Totally gangster!

(Though you should be sure if you do that: ask Mr. Depp, who, when he and the actress Winona Ryder broke up, famously had to change his "Winona Forever" tattoo to "Wino Forever," which is kind of dumb, in our view.)

The main thing is: you have entered the Arena of Commitment. You've decided to set aside childish things, throw your lot in with another human being, for better or worse wake up next to that person every single day for the rest of your life and never have sex with anyone else, ever again!

Right?

I LOVE YOU SO MUCH MY HEART IS ON FIRE

Me, I took a belt-and-suspenders approach when it came to Pam: I married her *and* (more recently) got a tattoo celebrating my undimmed admiration for her.

Well, not just her. The kids, too. It's a huge, flaming heart, on my right bicep, with Pam's name and the names of our three children (Nick, J.J., and Adam) emblazoned around it, in the type of super-serific, quasi-calligraphic, ultra-florid font tattoo artists all seem to favour.

The flaming heart is a reference to the fiercely passion-ate birthday and Xmas cards my second-oldest, J.J., used to write, in which he'd tell us, his parents: "I love you so much my heart is on fire."

. . . actually, maybe I should dip ever-so-briefly into the back-story behind this particular work of "body art."

It'll be instructive, I think, for those of you who aren't married yet, or haven't been married long. It's emblematic of the types of adjustments and evolutions you have to make in order to keep a marriage fresh and vital, or at least alive and kicking.

And the rest of you can all chortle and chuckle along as you gorge yourself on the torment-tapas of *Schadenfreude*-filled snicker-snacks that is my life.

It began innocuously enough. One morning, over break-fast, Pam said, "I have an idea for a movie script *I*'d like to write."

(I'd been working on a spec script, a romantic comedy, for what seemed like several lifetimes, hoping some day to make oodles of boodle from the fruits of my noodle.)

I looked up from the paper. Oh, great, I thought, she'll probably write it in like three weeks and boom: instant worldwide boffo box-office *smash*!

But all I said was: "Really? Share."

It was about an intrepid reporter, she told me, covering a crime story of these two guys who were found shot dead in a Land Rover in a sketchy part of town.

Pam had covered a similar story for the news, about a year previous, so I said, "Oh, so your script is kind of autobiographical?"

"Yes."

"Okay, good. I like autobiographical stuff."

"The opening image is she comes upon these two guys, shot, in the front seat of their Land Rover, which is still running."

"Oooh, good opening image," I said. "I like it. So where does it go from there?"

Well, during the course of investigating her story (Pam explained), this intrepid reporter gets all caught up in this underworld of seedy characters, when she meets this ultra-buff, tattoo-covered, jiu-jitsu dude, a badass Hells Angel biker-type, "and she finds herself really attracted to him . . ."

"Wait a second! Hold up!" I said, interrupting her. "Is this part autobiographical, too?"

Blush, blush, squirm, squirm, hem, haw: "Yes."

"*What?* Who is this dude? What'd he look like?"

"Well, in the movie he might be played by Viggo Mortensen."

"*Viggo Mortensen?*" I started to feel ill. We all know how you ladies feel about Viggo Mortensen.* "Well, did you want to sleep with this guy?"

Hem, haw, blush, blush: "Why are we even having this conversation?"

Which is *not* a good answer, btw. FYI, ladies, if your husband asks you "Did you want to sleep with the random,

---

* Though I can't help myself from observing, through the seven veils of my jealousy, that like so many of his thespian confreres, he's probably (a) tiny, (b) boring, (c) crazy, ladies.

tattoo-covered Viggo-Mortensen clone you've just told me you were attracted to?" the best response is a vigorous denial followed by much dismissive pooh-poohing.

You can even throw in a little surprised laughter, if you like, for spice. Don't worry about laying it on too thick!

Good answer: "Wha-ha-ha-hat? Sleep with him? Ha-ha-ha, of course not, you silly fellow! Don't be ridiculous! You know you're the only one for me! Here, let me prove it to you."

Unzzzzzzzip!

[Dress falls to ground. Wife, suddenly nude, begins to nibble on husband's ear, whilst fumbling urgently with his belt buckle.]

Bad answer: "Why are we even having this conversation?"

Later even though she said she really didn't want to sleep with him, I felt zinged, zapped, zugzwanged. How was I supposed to compete with some ripped, tattoo-covered, Viggo-Mortensen-looking motherfucker?

I mention all this in light-hearted fashion, but seriously: the thought of my beloved, my teen queen, my soulmate, getting hot pants for, and wanting to sleep with, some random jiu-jitsu biker dude was like a boot-knife in the very ventricles of my irregularly-fibrillating-lately (must be all the coffee), suddenly-sinking-feeling-filled ticker.

But from pain sometimes comes enlightenment (hey, that'd make another good tattoo: maybe on my forearm, in Chinese characters). And all of a sudden, in a eurekalicious, epiphanic rush, I realized the following:

When Pam and I met, seventeen years ago – okay, I wasn't exactly a Hells Angel. But I was kind of cool and tough, an outsider: thin and tanned, with long, slicked-back hair. Also, I smoked a lot and didn't really want to get a job.

Rather a naughty fellow, in other words. Some might even say . . . a bit of a "bad boy."

And that, probably more than any other single factor, was probably what drew Pam to me in the first place. Suburban-raised, goody-two-shoes banker's daughter that she is, she had a bit of a taste for the bad boys.

What I didn't count on, what never occurred to me until that moment, was: she never changed. She still likes the bad boys.

Of course. Why would that change?

"So what do you think you're doing?" I asked the benign, slightly oafish-looking, heavily bespectacled* man in the mirror. "What have you allowed yourself to become? Whatever became of Dave Eddie?"

I decided I needed some of the old "bad boy" mojo back, *prontissimo*. I booked an appointment with Chris, a tattoo artist at Imperial Tattoo, around the corner from my house.

"Ha-ha, that's awesome!" Chris said, when I told him the sorry story of why I wanted to break my "body art" cherry. "Look, man, don't take it personally. All women love the bad boys. They can't help it."

Of course, Chris has a vested financial interest in spreading this notion around. But ladies: is he wrong? And of course I know women don't necessarily marry the bad boys, that even if they're attracted to bad boys, they often wind up marrying nice guys they think will become good dads.

---

* Lately I'd been trying to cultivate a "cool nerd" look. What a fool!

But a tattoo with your kids' names on it is the perfect nexus of bad boy and good dad, I figured. You're telling the world you're a bit of a badass, but also a loving father. ("You talkin' to me? About my family? I don't see anyone else around, so you must be talkin' to me, about my family.") A good dad who is also a "bad boy." I didn't see how I could lose.

Ladies: am I wrong?

GO TO FAILURE

Unfortunately, the initial reactions were far from auspicious.

I had planned the tattoo as a surprise – and, well, I think we can say I was successful on that score.

When I peeled off the bandage and showed Pam my still-bleeding, still-throbbing heart-of-fire tattoo, she was stunned to the point of near-zombification.

"I – I can't believe you actually did that," she kept saying, as if I'd just confessed to a homicide-filled, cross-country crime spree.

Then Adam, my youngest (at the time he'd just turned seven), came flying in, wondering what all the hubbub was about. He took in the tat and Pam's flabbergasted face and said, "Don't worry, Mom: it'll wash off."

When she informed him it wouldn't, that it was a tattoo of the non-temporary variety, he burst into tears.

"What's the matter?" I asked him. "I thought you'd like it!"

"I liked your skin the way it was!" he wailed.

———

But the family's growing used to Dad's tat – and even getting to like it, a little, I think.

What's not to like? I am both literally and figuratively wearing my fiery heart on my sleeve – even (or especially) when I'm not wearing a sleeve.

Also, cattle-prodded forward by fear, inspired by Pam's "movie idea" starring Viggo Mortensen, I've been going to the gym, every day, working out fiendishly. "Go to failure, go to failure," the huge dudes at the gym keep exhorting me – meaning, push the fucking weights until you can't push them any more. I've adopted it as my new motto, i.e., in life, as at the gym, you have to push and push until you just can't any more. "Go to failure."

My goal is to wind up like Mickey Rourke – to have a prissy, almost girlish little face and the body of a Minotaur.

And it's working, boys. I'm not where I want to be, yet, but in the interim, Pam can't keep her hands off this semi-buff bod.

THE MARRIAGE BENEFIT

So I've actually managed to extract a lot of useful juice from the pain of hearing about my beloved soulmate's hot pants for Jiu-Jitsu Boy: I'm getting buff; I'm en route to getting my mojo back; I've acquired some minty-fresh "body art" about which I don't care what anyone says (my mother was predictable: "That was a stupid thing to do, and you're going to wind up regretting it"), I love it; I have a new motto, "Go to failure"; and Pam can't keep her hands off me.

But that's not the reason I tell you this story. The point, in the words of Woody Allen, is that "it's important to make a little effort once in a while."

I like the line (it's from *Manhattan*, I think) because Woody's not saying "all the time," just "once in a while."

It makes me sad, and tired, when people say marriage is "a lot of work."

With marriage, as with sex, or writing, it's just possible that if it's that much "work" you may be doing something wrong (or perhaps you just don't have the talent). But it does require a fair amount of vigilance, and adjustments – constant adjustments, tinkering and tweaking. Pam and I are always checking in with one another: You okay? Yeah. What's the matter? You in a good mood? And so forth.

And that's my main point. Too many people, it seems to me, emit an almost audible hiss of air, like a punctured tire, when they get married, as they say to themselves:

"Aaaaahhhhhhhhhh, married at last. Now I can finally relax, pull the ripcord, and *really* let myself go, begin the slow slide toward becoming the crabby, pear-shaped slob I've always dreamed of being. I can tick off the box marked Relationship, and concentrate on other things – like this family-sized bucket of extra-crispy fried chicken between my legs, and my box set of *Family Guy*. Let me just – *psssht!* – open this brewski, and – where's that damn remote? Honey? Honey! Have you seen the remote?"

Wrong approach, if matrimonial bliss is what you're after. My previously espoused opinion toward spousal relations is: once married, you have to have your shit wired even tighter than ever. To rephrase Tom Berenger as Lieutenant Barnes from the movie *Platoon*: "Out here in the DMZ of marriage you keep your shit wired tight at all

times, or I goddamn guarantee you a trip out of the bush –
in a bodybag!"

Cohabitation on its own is a damage-control minefield,
littered with shrapnel bombs, bouncing Betties, claymores,
and tripwires. Throw in exhaustion, kids, chaos, careers,
external pressure, stress, and temptation, and it's a wonder
any of us come out of it alive, let alone hale and healthy,
hearty and happy.

But that's exactly how it can work out. Marriage can be
fun! I was disheartened, recently, to read an interview with
a fellow named Mark O'Connell, author of *The Marriage
Benefit: The Surprising Rewards of Staying Together*.

Good, I thought, when I saw the book's title. Finally,
someone has stepped forward with a spirited defence of
marriage, an institution routinely rubbished, mocked, and
satirized in the mainstream media.

I flipped to the interview. One of the first things Mr.
O'Connell tells the interviewer is:

"Statistically, about half of all marriages end in divorce.
Of the half that remain, very few are actually happy, lively
and satisfying. Couples all too often achieve a state of safe
complacency where there's a great deal of distance and stag-
nation."

The interviewer, seeming a little taken aback, proceeds:
"Your book is called *The Marriage Benefit*. If we're all miserable, what is the benefit?"

His answer (and this is basically the thrust of the book):
"Some of us, as we go through life and endure hardships,
close off; we have short-term ways of managing that are
designed to make us feel better but not to grow. Other
people are willing to feel some of the discomfort from their

mistakes, and that's the bedrock of what it takes to grow." For those people "sustained intimacy can be an incredible crucible for growth. Ultimately, marriage can be a forum for learning through a kind of creative constraint. . . ."

In other words, marriage is a horrible crucible of suffering – but suffering can lead to spiritual development. Therefore, marriage, like, say, cod liver oil, is good for you. Like being stretched on a rack, it helps you grow.

That's "the marriage benefit."

With all due respect to Mr. O'Connell and his clinical research, I do not concur. Marriage can be an extremely congenial and agreeable state of affairs.

Now, of course, we know even the best marriages can hit rocky patches, sometimes. I have in my library a book called *Duel*, by James Landale. It's partly a history of duelling, partly the story of Mr. Landale's ancestor, who killed his bank manager in the last recorded fatal duel on British soil.

I have to say I smiled quietly to myself as I read the history-of-duelling part, thinking how much it reminded me of how it can feel, sometimes, to be married.

In Scandinavia, in one type of early duel the two combatants were strapped to one another and armed with knives; at the signal, they'd just start hacking at one another.

Being married can feel like that.

In another early duelling format, the two disputants were each given a large burlap sack; the object of the duel was to get your opponent into your sack while he tried to do the same to you.

Being married can feel like that.

In the early nineteenth century, two Frenchmen duelled in balloons above the rooftops of Paris. Each had a pistol and tried to pop the other's balloon so his opponent would plummet to his death.

Being married can feel like that . . .

Pam and I once had a terrible, marriage-threatening argument – over a tomato.

Well, it began with a tomato. But one thing led to another, and everything was called into question.

I wanted to throw the tomato out, she thought it could be used in a pasta sauce or something. We called each other terrible names. Our faces the colour of the vegetable – or, I guess, technically, it's a fruit, but I digress – under dispute, we said, or shouted, things to each other we knew we would regret the moment they came out of our mouths, or even before.

Our voices kept going up in pitch, timbre, and volume; and then, abruptly, fell silent (well, Pam fell silent first; I kept talking, but then after a while was able to infer, from her refusal to answer my comments and point-blank questions, that the "silent treatment," marital *omertà*, had commenced). We didn't speak to each other for twenty-four hours. In these cases, the grandeur and hauteur of Pam's froideur is something to behold. The temperature in the room will actually seem to go down. Her face, always beautiful, becomes even more austerely, forbiddingly beautiful in anger: it becomes like one of those faces on Easter Island, serenely, stonily impassive, indifferent to my fate and the fate of everyone like me.

Every time she encountered me during that twenty-four

hours, she looked at me as if I were a cockroach that had come scuttling out from under the stove, feelers twitching.

A cockroach covered in snot . . .

Where was I? Oh, yeah, what a delightful barrel of joy being married can be.

Well, it can be. The institution of marriage is so trashed in popular culture. For example, the married couple in *Knocked Up*: the wife is a horrible harridan, the husband a meek milquetoast.

But it doesn't have to be that way. And as time passes, marriage bestows upon the very lucky few of us the best gift life has to offer: a person who has absolutely no illusions or misconceptions about you, who knows you inside out – "I know you better than you know yourself, Dave!" – but somehow, miraculously, loves you anyway.

As Lao Tzu puts it: "To love someone deeply gives you strength. Being loved by someone deeply gives you courage."

And it can be a lot of fun. A lot of laughs. And I love nothing better* than snuggling with Pam in a warm bed on a chilly winter morning; then having the boys all come barreling in, vying for position (most coveted spot is between me and Pam "because then you get both parents": worst spot is on the outside of me, because that kid might only get a "wing" or a "drumstick" of Pam).

Vis-à-vis arguing, yes, you argue: but it is possible, and lo and behold I do believe it has come to pass with Pam and me, you can actually find yourself arguing less, over time.

* Well, almost nothing.

You simply work some things out, and become adjusted to one another's quirks and blind spots and bald spots and habits and snoring.*

The main thing, I think, is not to care about the outcome of an argument, i.e., who wins – but to know that getting along is more important.

Anyway, enough generalizing. Let's address some specific instances.

I want to work backwards, a bit, and start with a situation where negotiations have broken down completely:

STAY PUT, SOLDIER, OR RISK LOSING THE CUSTODY BATTLE

THE QUESTION
My wife and I are separating after a three-year marriage. We tried counselling – which was useless. We tried mediation, which has gone nowhere. Now, on the advice of my lawyer, I'm not going anywhere either, until we have a separation agreement. Without one, I'm told, I risk being viewed as the party who jumped ship and that would work against me when it comes to custody issues surrounding our two-year-old daughter. So we've been living under the same roof, in separate rooms, for three hellish months that just took a turn for the worse: Last weekend, my wife brought home her new boyfriend, who spent two days lounging on my couch,

---

* Though it can be tough if, as I do, you have a partner whose snoring is like a rusty buzzsaw cutting through a plate of sheet metal, which causes the windows to rattle in their frames.

watching my TV and sleeping with my wife in our marriage bed. It ended badly, with a shouting match between me and the new chump and we almost came to blows. I'm at my wits' end and might just leave to avoid a physical confrontation. Should I stay or should I go?

THE ANSWER

Okay, ten-hut, soldier.

This is domestic jungle warfare, hand-to-hand combat at its most savage and visceral, and you're behind enemy lines.

Your gun's jammed, full of mud, you've seen a lot of good men go down, and the soft pop-pop-pop of bullets hitting the ground is getting closer.

The temptation is to go scorched-earth, grab the radio, and scream for a napalm hosedown of the whole situation, leaving everything in the vicinity charred and smoking.

But don't do that. In fact, don't do anything. Stay ultra-cool.

Even if your wife praises her new boyfriend's sexual prowess in front of you, and mocks yours: do nothing. If screams of erotic transport shake the walls, and your daughter is screaming, bawling, saying, "Daddy, what's happening," comfort her, of course, but apart from that: do nothing.

Am I coming through loud and clear, soldier?

I'm basing my advice on the sage counsel of two members of Damage Control's crack legal team: criminal lawyer Irwin Isenstein and Eric Shapiro of the family law firm Skapinker and Shapiro. I've retained their services on a pro bono basis to help me with the legal aspects of your problem.

One thing upon which they concur: if you lay a finger on anyone in this situation, or utter anything resembling a threat, you are, jurisprudentially speaking and custody-wise, screwed.

Or, as Mr. Isenstein puts it: "All it takes is a phone call and you're gone."

If you're arrested for assault or uttering threats, and charged, the terms of your bail will probably be that you not return to your apartment. And you may even be prevented from seeing your kid.

And it'll end in tears for you in court. Even if you feel you're in the right, even if you're provoked – don't touch anyone. Don't even touch the phone.

In any situation involving couples, cruisers, and flashing lights, the possession of the Y chromosome puts you at a distinct disadvantage. Or, as Mr. Shapiro puts it: "In domestic disputes, everyone has their own version of events, there are usually no witnesses and, to be fair to the police, it can be hard to sort out what really happened."

You could get hauled off anyway.

I know it doesn't sound fair, soldier. But as Tom Berenger says in *Platoon*: "There's the way things ought to be. And there's the way things are." (Right after grabbing a joint some private is smoking and bringing his battle-scarred face up to the other guy's with a growl: "You smoke this shit . . . to escape reality? I *am* reality!")

But at the same time, crazy as it may seem, your lawyer is right: it would be a mistake to move out. If you do, Mr. Shapiro says, your soon-to-be-ex gains control of how often you can see your daughter.

"It could be every week, or it could be once a month," Mr. Shapiro says. "If you leave, it's up to her discretion. She gets control over the situation."

Leaving confers upon her a sort of instant custody. And that, too, will go badly for you in court.

So stay put, soldier, no matter how intolerable the situation becomes. If it gets to be too much, go for a walk, see a movie. But stay hunkered in your bunker until the issue is resolved. If you haven't begun litigation proceedings to get this case before a judge, do so immediately. From there, it can take six to eight weeks or possibly even longer, Mr. Shapiro says.

And that may be a time of hell, a time of pain for you. But what can you do? That's the reality of your situation. You can't escape reality. You can try, but if you do, well, I have one thing to say (and I want you to imagine the tip of my nose almost touching the tip of yours, my scarred, stubbled, and world-weary face filling your field of vision, and my spit spraying as I bark out the following):

"I *am* reality, you little worm! You want joint custody? Then take the pain, soldier! Stay still and don't utter a peep! Don't even flinch! Or I guaranfriggintee you will end up one of those sorry sad-sack sumbitches who hardly ever gets to see his kid! Do I make myself clear, maggot?"

Sorry to be such a hard-ass. But it's for your own good. I just want to see you make it back to civilian life in one piece, to see you and your daughter laughing and playing in the sunshine, waking up and making pancakes together.

Happy, in other words.

I felt so sorry for this guy that I followed up with him,* after the fact, to see how it all worked out.

* Like I did with the cleaning-lady-panty guy. I know it must sound like I do this all the time, but in fact I think these were the only two times I've ever done it.

He did as told, I'm happy to report, and after a period of extreme personal trial and duress, of walking through the fire, his custody and all other issues wound up working out reasonably well.

Well done, soldier! Way to keep it all bottled up inside! Of course, emotions and frustrations like these need to find some sort of outlet, and he's getting some "body art" of his own, I understand, to commemorate the situation: a large Japanese-style depiction of a samurai warrior thrusting his pike through a dragon's head.

I worried a bit, when I first heard about this. Any tattoo artist worth his or her needle will tell you it's not a good idea to get "ink" commemorating a negative incident, e.g., breaking up. I assumed the samurai warrior must be my advice-seeker, and the dragon his (now) ex-wife.

But I was assured this was not the case, that, yes, our advice-seeker was the samurai; but the dragon was his emotions – his rage: the mural (which covers most of his back, apparently) depicts his ability to conquer his emotions and is a reminder for the future also that he must over-come his rage.

Which all sounds quite positive. So: good on you, private. I'm happy to have been able to play a role, however small, in your evolution.

And now, soldier: onward. Hut-one, hut-two, time to march with confidence toward the future.

But for us, now, let's wind the clock back to take a look at a few of the intra- and extra-marital issues that could lead to the type of situation described above, and how we might head them off before things reach such a pass.

SHE'S KILLING ME

THE QUESTION

So we all know it's a long-running joke for men: get married, say goodbye to sex. Well, I married a woman whose sex drive always outpaced mine, and now, two years into our marriage she tells me she needs more than I can offer. That I "don't put out enough." That she expects me to be open to the idea of her sleeping with other men if I'm not interested or able to satisfy her (voracious) needs. I kept pace with her for the three years we dated and for the first year of our marriage, but I have to admit, for the last year, I'm just not that into it. And for that, she's threatening to cheat on me? I thought marriage was supposed to bring something more than just physical intimacy, and I'd lose my shit if I knew she was sleeping with other men, so what do I do? Suck it up and try to keep her satisfied or let her go off and do whatever it is she needs to do?

THE ANSWER

Well, that certainly is a twist on the old joke:

"Scientists have discovered a new substance that reduces a woman's sex drive by 90 percent."

"What is it?"

"Wedding cake."

But the little research I've done on the topic suggests a low sex drive in men is actually a bigger problem than is generally acknowledged. Michele Weiner-Davis, an American sex therapist, has even written a book called *The Sex-Starved Wife*, in which she "controversially" suggests this is a more widespread phenomenon than the media's portrayal of the "not-tonight-dear-I've-got-a-headache" type of spouse would have us believe.

I'd recommend this book to you, but it's kind of long, full of dumb jargon, annoyingly self-congratulatory, and shamelessly self-promotional: Ms. Weiner-Davis, or maybe it's Dr. Weiner-Davis,* hawks her "divorce-busting centres" and coaching services on page after page.

But, anyway, pick it up, if you care to and have the time. It might help. She does make some good points, the main one being: it happens. And also: the reason people don't know more about this phenomenon is men hate talking about it.

Men would rather admit to cheating than losing interest in sex, Ms. Weiner-Davis says. Which sounds about right to me. At least, when you cheat, you know the plumbing's still working. Also, she makes some good points along the lines of: it could be grief, depression, or an adverse reaction to medication, an Internet porn addiction, or perhaps some other physical/medical problem.

So if you think it could be something like that, see your doctor, of course.

But if you think it could be garden-variety long-term *monogamosis*, the side effect of over-familiarity over an overly long period of time, I do have a few stray thoughts that might help.

First, though, a couple of caveats. In this, as indeed in all

---

* And I'm sorry, I guess I'm not all that mature, but I can't help but observe that it's a good thing that young Michele Weiner married a guy named "Davis" and not a guy named, say, Phil Krinkler – because then she'd be Dr. Weiner-Krinkler, which obviously wouldn't be so good for business.

departments of life, beware false prophets, aka "experts." Sex is a (sometimes *un-*) holy mystery, and anyone who claims to be an authority in this department is probably full of it.

Damn! Recently I participated in what the advertising industry calls a "guru group" of so-called experts talking about sex and long-term "intimacy" (I was there as an advice columnist).

Prepare to snicker, shake your head in disbelief, roll your eyes, or all the above as I tell you: the whole thing was sponsored by a sexual lubricant company* and a bunch of lubricant executives were watching from behind a two-way mirror.

It was me, the lesbian owner of a sex shop, a woman who'd been married five times and thus considered herself an expert in marriage,† and a sex therapist.

And man, did we ever talk a load of crap on the topic of sex and long-term marital intimacy! The b.s.-mist in that room was so thick my eyes were watering.

And the fact the moderator kept trying to steer the conversation back around to sexual lubricant, for the benefit of the dead-serious lubricant executives behind the two-way mirror, lent the whole thing a risible, absurdist edge.

It was nuts; it was bananas; yes, our sexual-lubricant conversation had a nutty-banana flavour.

(Q. So, Dave, if you found it all so silly and such a waste of time, why did you do it? A. Some people will do anything for $350.)

---

* I won't tell you which lubricant company it was, but here's a hint: its initials are K.Y.

† To me, it's the opposite, but anyway.

Of the misleading, misguided, potentially damaging notions floated during that two-hour session: that couples who found their "intimacy" getting a little tepid should laugh and horse around and adopt other kindergarten-style tactics, to inject "fun" into their bedroom antics; that it might help to check out Tantric practices; and anyway it's probably hopeless (this from the five-times-married lady, with an enthusiastic second from the shrink), because it's been *scientifically proven* that lust for any one given person dissipates after four years.

Wrong, wrong, and wrong. I blame Hollywood, and Sting, and numerous other culprits, for the promulgation of all the wrong-headed notions about sex floating about these days.

If I may debunk for a moment:

1. If someone's laughing while you're having sex with them, then you're doing something wrong.

2. It shouldn't go on too long. Everyone was so impressed when Sting was overheard (by a journalist) boasting to "Sir" Bob Geldof about his six-hour "Tantric" sex sessions with his wife, Trudi.

But I think (a) it's cheesy to boast about sex, (b) six hours of sex sounds like a freaking nightmare to me. After an hour, I'd be begging Sting – or someone, anyone – to make it stop; after two, I'd start to panic; after three, I'd call the police.

A recent survey of sex therapists concurred that the "optimal" time for sex (not including foreplay) is three to ten minutes. In other words, vive le quickie.

Sex should be nasty, brutish, and short. . . .

3. And as for this "four year" business, Pam and I have been together seventeen years, and I don't think it violates

the terms of our non-erotic-disclosure agreement if I say: I'm more attracted to her than ever.*

So while I know there is a lot of truth to it, at least we can say that it is not an across-the-board truth. As anyone who's been in a long-term relationship knows: it goes in cycles. Some good, some bad. Some up, some down. When Pam and I had little kids in diapers, there was a period there, where, if we had sex once a month?

That was a *good* month.

But oops! Sorry, Pam, I forgot! I'm not supposed to speak about our sex life!

Starting . . . *now*.

Anyway, you absorbed the above complicated caveat, right? All of this is just one man's opinion, and you should take with a grain of salt anything anyone – even, or *especially*, soi-disant experts – says about your sex life. Because when it comes to sex, as William Goldman says about Hollywood: "Nobody knows anything."

Sexually, everyone's problems are unique, and only you can find the solution.

Having said that, I'll add a couple more thoughts:

Go to the gym. Sometimes not feeling like sex is less a matter of not feeling attracted to the other person than not feeling sexy oneself. The gym is the antidote to many evils, anyway; get in a good workout, then see if you still feel as

---

* Okay here I may be violating it when I say: "and she tolerates my advances more cheerfully than ever." She's sweet about it. Some of our encounters are so charitable in nature, on her part, I do believe a good accountant might be able to write some of them off her taxes.

erotically enervated and lacklustre as you did before. My guess is you won't.

Also, your wife needs to stop angrily, bossily demanding her shagging rights; and to cease and desist threatening to cuckold you. That's a wiener-krinkler non-pareil. She should try to seduce you rather than extract her "conjugal rights" from you. Never a good look; almost certain to blow up/backfire in the perpetrator's face.

I've known men who have gone down that road ("You married me; that means you have to have sex with me"), though I've never known a woman to try it. In any case, for either gender, it's a low-percentage ploy. Net result of demanding sex from your partner: you appear even less attractive to your partner than before; your partner wants to have sex with you even less frequently than ever.

Which is not the desired result, obviously.

Another potential ploy is for her to act like she doesn't want it. See how that works. Worked for me, in college, anyway, with my first girlfriend, Francesca di Mauro.

She was *really* sexy. And I . . . I was nineteen. I was all over her, all the time – and that's not attractive. She cooled to me, which of course made me even hotter for her than ever. . . .

It could have been a vicious, downward, never-ending spiral, but instead I learned, from a couple of books we were reading in a couple of my classes, *Anna Karenina* (whose unbalanced love of Vronsky leads to her suicide) and *Madame Bovary* (throughout a classic study of unequal love, in the end also leading to a suicide), that unequal love was (a) not uncommon; (b) no joke. It could kill you!

So I forced myself to pretend not to be all that interested.

It worked, boys and girls, and soon hot-blooded Franscesca di Mauro was all over me, all over again.

So: she should maybe try that, on you.

Meanwhile, you, sir, should look deep within. You wanted her once. Why don't you now? Are you angry with her about something? Are you seeking dominance or control over her? Only you can answer these questions, as I say, therefore only you can solve your problem.

What we can say with confidence about sex is it's partly about libido and partly about the status of your relationship; if both are functioning properly, your unit may follow suit.

But let's return to your wife's threats to cheat and leave and so forth. The most disturbing aspect of the scenario you describe, IMHO. I wouldn't put up with that for a second.

Put your foot down, sir. Say to her: "Listen, I know it's been tough for you, and I'm willing to work on our sexual issues, together. But in the meantime, touch one penis that isn't mine and I'll be serving you your Bachelorette Papers before you can say McBurnie, Whitticombe, and Taft, Attorneys at Law."

Don't let her push you around. Stand your ground. Grow a pair, and maybe it'll make you feel that much stronger, more muskily manly, and you'll suddenly find a certain . . . stirring for her you haven't felt before.

In any case, good luck. Sex or no sex, don't let her push you around and threaten you. That's offside.

———

OH NO. YOU DIDN'T USE THE F-WORD, DID YOU?

On a lighter, though no-less-potentially-deal-breaking note . . .

THE QUESTION

People never talk about the collateral damage of diets, but my wife's been on one and it's turning her into a monster. She bites my head off over nothing, she's always irritable, and we've been fighting like crazy. The other day I said I'd rather she was fat and happy than skinny and cranky – and she blew a gasket. "You think I'm fat?" she asked me. Then: "And cranky? I'm cranky because you never clean up around here!" And then she launched into a litany of complaints that were true but usually don't get to her so much. Is this the future? How can I ward it off?

THE ANSWER

Boy, do you ever have a lot to learn about how to speak to a woman. Never, ever even *hint* she's fat. Never even obliquely allude to weight or dieting or working out in her presence.

You can't win. I used to have a girlfriend who was so touchy on this topic that if I even asked if she was comfortable in a particular chair she would say, "Why? What are you saying? Why wouldn't I be? Are you saying I have a fat ass?"

"No, darling, I merely – oh, never mind."

In fact, before we go any further, since we're on the topic, allow me to clear up, once and for all, how to handle it when your wife or girlfriend asks you point-blank about her figure – particularly if she drops the dreaded: "Do you think my butt looks fat in this outfit?"

Good answer: "Darling [taking her hand in yours and gazing soulfully into her eyes], whenever I am in your presence I become so intoxicated it's difficult to focus on these peripheral matters. But since you ask, I have to say: unequivocally no, your derrière has never looked more shapely and alluring than it does on this day. In fact, it's amazing: as time passes your attractiveness only becomes more subtle and complex, you seem to glow with an inner fire – kind of like the diamonds in this Fabergé necklace I've taken the liberty of buying for you."

Bad answer: "Not as fat as it looks naked."

That could get you served your Bachelor Papers on the spot. Or maybe that's what you secretly want? To be single again? If so, keep up the unsolicited fat cracks. She'll serve you your Bachelor Papers and you'll be back "out there" with the rest of the dogs before you can say, "Two more shots of Jägermeister, please."

Otherwise, keep your flap zipped on the topic of fat and just concentrate on keeping your own physique cut and rippling with manly power.

Crabbiness is another matter. It is your right to live a crab-free existence – as long as you're pulling your weight in the relationship.

Often what men call crabbiness is a legitimate complaint expressed passive-aggressively. If she's asked you a million times to do something (clean up, for example) and you promised to do it and then failed to live up to your promise time and again, that's trouble, my friend.

You don't have to be perfect. But I predict you will be amazed at how much sweeter and more tractable her demeanour becomes when you show her you care enough to at least try.

But if you can honestly say you are doing all you can to be a good man and you keep up your end in the relationship and pitch in domestically, then I would say if she is unwarrantedly crabby, diet or no diet, push back.

Do not be afraid. Part of the reason, I think, wives and girlfriends these days are rolling their eyes at their menfolk so much is because the menfolk are not standing up for themselves.

Of course you should be compassionate and thoughtful about the fact she is in a calorie-deprived haze and is doing this at least partly for you. But her right to be crabby ends when it affects your well-being and enjoyment of life.

So if she's being unreasonable, let her have it right between the eyes. Say: "Darling, you know I'm your biggest supporter, but you crossed the line there and I can't have that. It's not acceptable."

I know it's a leap of faith, especially if this sort of thing isn't really your style. You just have to trust me on this one. As long as she knows you care about her and respect her, she will respect you back for not letting her walk all over you.

If I'm wrong – well, you can crash on my couch. At least until my wife crabbily demands that I tell you it's time you got on your feet and found your own apartment.

SECRETLY SNIPPED

THE QUESTION
My fiancée is baby-crazy. Ever since I proposed it's all she goes on about – the family we're going to raise, how many kids she wants to see sitting round the dinner table, how much her mom is looking forward to being a grandmother. I grin and bear it, because I love her and I hope she does have kids some day. Thing is, it won't be with me. I've never gotten into it with her because it always seemed like such a touchy issue, but I had a vasectomy after I finished university. I did it for all the predictable bourgeois reasons – guilt over bringing a child into a messed-up world, fears for the environment, angst over the arrogance of humanity's blind need to procreate – but since then I've regretted my decision. I'd have kids now if I could, mainly to make her happy. I know I've waited too long, but is there any way to break this news without having her call off the wedding?

THE ANSWER
Well, the good news is: it's reversible. The bad news is: it's a painful, expensive, and not-always-successful operation.

And the even worse news is: the mechanics of this horribly intrusive "procedure" may be the least of your problems.

Let's deal with the basic mechanics first, and assume you love your fiancée enough, and want to stay with her badly enough, and have changed your mind re: offspring to the point where you're willing to submit your throbbing onions to the surgeon's knife – again!

Then your path is relatively straightforward. Time to man up – which, in this case, means donning a little shorty gown that keeps flashing your derriere peek-a-boo fashion to the world, then wincing and chatting nervously with a nurse as she shaves your twitching, tingling testes; so a surgeon can slit your bag open like gutting a sturgeon and reattach the, uh, hitherto dormant sperm-delivery tubes in the nutsackular region of your groinus majoris.

(Sorry to be throwing around all this technical jargon; I've been reading a lot of medical journals lately.)

But it sounds to me like there are bigger issues at play here. A statement from your question is my clue: "I'd have kids now if I could, mainly to make her happy."

Now, I'm the last person in the world to pooh-pooh this sentiment. Lots of men have kids in a half-hearted fashion and wind up enormously happy about it.

I'm one of them, and I'll have more to say about that in our "family" chapter. Suffice to say, for now, that I never wanted kids (kids, I thought, would hurt my writing and lead to the driving of a mini-van; I was right on both scores), but after a series of negotiations with Pam, I wound up with three hanging off me, like ornaments on a Christmas tree.

I'm thrilled about it. Having kids made a man of me, I feel, and it's a source of never-ending, daily joy.

Furthermore, I now believe you should have them *before* you're ready. If I was ever going to have kids, I told myself, I was going to wait until I was forty-five, and had seen, done, and accomplished everything I wanted to see, do, and accomplish; but that would've been a mistake, I think.

For one thing, having kids trumps and renders derisory a lot of the things one might want to see and do and accomplish – like, say, going to see the Leaning Tower of Pisa.

I've been to see the Leaning Tower of Pisa. It wasn't that great. It's hot, crowded, expensive, and it looks just like it does in all the pictures. Exact same with Stonehenge. Meanwhile, my kids make me snicker and chuckle (and cry and scream and want to tear my head off with irritation, and throw it out the window) and fill me with joy 24-7.

I'd rather have that than see the Leaning Tower of Pisa.

But maybe seeing the Leaning Tower of Pisa is really, really important to you, and you want to have numerous other adventures besides, including squeezing your useless, blanks-shooting testicles* into a scuba suit, and looking at a bunch of fish underwater, blowing bubbles as you stare at them.

In any case, you have to decide, sir, where you stand on the issue. It's true, on the one hand, that you could wind up laughing at yourself and pooh-poohing yourself for ever having any doubts about having kids and becoming a parent, but it could go the other way, too.

And there's nothing worse than parents who go around town saying they wish they'd never had kids and if they had it all to do over again, "I'm not sure I'd do it, honestly."

That's not good for anyone, Sonny Jim. So make up your mind. What do you *really* want? If you can look the man in the mirror directly in the eye and honestly say you don't want kids, then I'm afraid you have to scream "Man overboard!" and jump ship.

Because if you're really not ready, you won't be doing your fiancée any favours by acquiescing on such a major matter. You'll just wind up resenting her, and them; and they you; and her you; and the whole thing is a recipe for a Stir-Fried Nightmare with Hot and Sour Sauce, served on a bed of flash-fried hopes and dreams.

---

* I, as a vasectomee myself, am allowed to make cracks of this nature, I believe.

And believe me, parenthood is fraught enough with resentment, second thoughts, haunted epiphanies, and dark nights of the soul, without having to entertain fundamental regrets as to whether you should have done it in the first place.

Take our next question, for example:

YOU'RE NOT THE ONLY ONE WHO NEEDS "ME TIME"

THE QUESTION

I love my kids, really I do, but sometimes they drive me nuts and I need a break. Last weekend, my wife wanted us all to head to her parents' cottage for a weekend escape.

I told her that I had to go in to work over the weekend and wouldn't be able to make it, but really I was planning a little escape of my own. An escape to my den. I just needed some time alone, without the kids, to relax, read the paper, and bum around the house without having to play daddy all weekend long.

When they came back on Sunday night, my wife asked me how the weekend went and I told her that I ended up doing some work from home, which was a good thing, since she'd already found my work security pass in the glove compartment.

She's not buying my story and, between accusations that I'm "no family man," has hinted that I may be cheating on her. I'm not!

I just needed a break from the family and couldn't bring myself to tell her. How can I break it to her without seeming like a deadbeat dad?

THE ANSWER

The biggest damage here is not being upfront with your wife. Never lie to your wife.

Remember, it's you and her against the world. You're a team, and for a team to work you need to communicate (remember, too, that she may be the one delivering your eulogy, and you don't want her doing the whole thing through clenched teeth).

So apologize for that and vow to yourself and to her to be more straightforward in the future.

Second, you need to address the question of "me time."

As I've mentioned, I would gladly take a bullet for Pam or the kids.

But at times, especially as the summer wears on, it can all get a bit much. The bickering, the squabbling, the endless demands, the tears, the emotional outbursts – and the kids can be quite difficult, too (badump-ching!).

At these moments, "parent porn" images unspool in your mind: you sitting in a wing chair, wearing some sort of velvety smoking jacket, sipping claret, reading Shakespeare.

And I'm a bit of a workaholic. I confess I too have done what you did – so many times, in fact, that my own children have started to twig to it: "You never want to go anywhere, Dad! You always say you have to 'work,'" they say, using their fingers to make air quotes, screwing their little faces into masks of irony and sarcasm. It's not true I "never" want to go anywhere. I go on some outings.

But I admit, while it's true I "have" to work, it's also true I want to. And it's also true I want to be alone, bathed in silence, able to hear myself, finally, think.

We all need time alone, to reconnect to our deeper selves. Thoreau said he could not feel healthy or happy unless he spent at least four hours alone every day, walking in the woods.

And I kind of feel the same way. Luckily, as a writer, I get a good chunk of solitude every day, to think and commune with my inner self and ponder the lint in my navel.

But many of us twentieth-century types are not afforded this luxury, especially those who have kids. We never get time alone, and if we do, it's jangled by cellphones and CrackBerrys and car alarms and honking horns and everything else.

Which may be part of the reason so many of us are slowly, inexorably going out of our minds. . . .

You, sir, should acknowledge you and your wife both need a bit of time to yourselves once in a while. When you need to be "home alone," be upfront about it, don't resort to these little deceptions. And try to be sensitive and figure out when she needs it, because she may not come right out and tell you.

Maybe part of the reason your wife's mad at you (especially in light of her accusation of cheating) is that she's a little envious and could use her own time alone, but doesn't want to say that. Also, I suspect she may secretly be hurt you didn't want to spend the time with her.

So, once you've apologized and vowed to be honest in the future, take your wife out on a date. (Remember: just because you got married, doesn't mean you should stop dating your spouse. We have to remember always to date our spouses, people.) Get a sitter, do it right. Take her somewhere nice – and try not to talk about the kids. Talk about your careers, the weather, anything but.

Then offer to take the kids once in a while so she can enjoy the inimitable pleasures of "me time" – maybe even make a schedule. Tit-for-tat. "You take the kids this chunk of time, I'll take the kids that chunk of time. Then we'll do such and such a thing all together; then you and I are going out for a romantic dinner."

That's part of the recipe for a happy marriage, I'm telling you. Let her go to the spa, shop, shoot pool, climb a rock, whatever she likes to do on her own.

When she comes back, she'll be refreshed, her batteries recharged, and (ideally) have missed you. Best of all, you'll have earned the brownie points you need to do whatever you need to do in the future.

Brownie points are the currency of marriage. But remember: they're a highly volatile currency, like the ruble or the zloty, subject to sudden adjustments and surprise deflations. One day a fistful will get you a lot, the next a wheelbarrowful will get you just about nothing. Cash in all brownie points quickly!

QUIT BEING AN AFFAIR ENABLER TO OTHER HOUNDS

THE QUESTION

Recently, as a favour to an unhappily married friend, I helped him woo another unhappily married person by delivering a romantic gift consisting of a CD, a single red rose, a compass, and a poem he'd written her. I didn't think too much about it, except that it seemed sort of touching and charming.

But when I told my wife, she was furious at me and asked if I were the type who thought cheating was fun and good.

Of course I felt a slight tremor of sleaze. But I figured it was mostly their business. Am I as morally reprehensible as she's trying to make me feel?

THE ANSWER

Musing long and hard upon this question, as I always do, scratching my coconut, stroking my beard, I found myself focusing more and more on one anomalous detail: the compass.

"Why a compass?" I wondered. When it finally hit me, I laughed out loud.

Obviously the compass came with a note that said something to the effect of "Carry this with you always, my darling, so that no matter where life's journey may take you, your heart will find its way back to mine."

Which is . . . I mean, it's just so, so . . . [Dave and Pat, overcome by emotion, simultaneously whip out handkerchiefs, dab tears from their eyes] so damn *touching*, is what it is. . . .

You know, it never ceases to amaze and amuse me how some people – men, particularly, it seems, though I could be wrong about that – undergo this magical personality transformation when they're trying to get some. Guys who normally sit in a stupor in front of their TV sets, scratching their nuts and quaffing a brew, suddenly become . . . poets, seekers, "troubadours of the soul."

They muse upon the loftiest questions of the human condition. They soar above the quotidian on wings of faux-philosophical b.s.

Perfectly captured, I thought, in the movie *Wedding Crashers*, when Owen Wilson says to a sexy bridesmaid, "People say we only use 10 per cent of our brains. I say we only use 10 per cent of our hearts."

Hilarious. Exactly the type of pseudo-romantic horse-puckey you'd feed a sexy bridesmaid on a moonlit beach, the hotel you're trying to steer her toward looming in the background.

And it is charming, in a way – if the guy's single. If he's married? Less so, in my view.

Yes, I hate to be the bearer of bad news, gentlemen, but if you're married and "wooing" a woman who's not your wife, you're not a poet or seeker or troubadour.

You're a schnauzer. You're a boxer. You're a Great Dane.

A dee-oh-double-gee, in other words, and even if you rise up on your hind legs with a rose in one paw and compass in the other to deliver a poignant speech about life's journey and the sweet fragrance of your desire, all I hear is "Woof, woof! Arf! Ruff! Ruff! Woof!"

Accompanied by the sound of a tail thumping on the floor.

I'm afraid being "unhappily married" is no excuse, either. You can't have your bone and eat it too. The rules here are simple: if you're tired of the person you're with and you want someone else, you first have to break up with the person you're with before you go after the other one.

I figured that out at age nineteen. True, it took another ten years to fully implement this policy, and to the girls I dated in my twenties I can only say, "I'm sorry, my dears, you were all so lovely, the spirit was willing but the flesh was – arf! Woof, woof! Arf!"

Anyway, lack of moral fibre in his kibble is your friend's problem, not yours. What possessed you to get involved, delivery boy? What made you go all UPS? You must cease and desist being an "affair enabler" immediately. It's all downside and no upside.

You have enraged your wife; if the woman's husband goes on a rampage he might kill you, too – and you don't even get any hot, naughty sex out of it.

And I think your wife's quite right: all this skullduggery makes it look like you endorse adultery. Perhaps it titillates you to play Lothario-by-proxy? Perhaps you enjoy the drama just a little, hmmm?

But it's a dangerous game and you could get your paws burned. Next thing you know you're giving your secretary a compass at the office Christmas party because you're her "Secret Santa," and shortly after that you find yourself circling "room for rent" ads in the local alternative weekly, wondering how it all went pear-shaped.

Nip that in the butt, bud – I mean the bud, dog. First convince yourself, then your wife, that it is in fact *fidelity* you find fun and charming and exciting, and that you're happy you're not out there with all the tomcats and pariah dogs. (And if you don't believe it, what are you doing in this relationship?)

Frequently and loudly pooh-pooh adultery and adulterers in her presence. (Newspaper: "LOVE TRIANGLE CULMINATES IN MURDER-SUICIDE." You: "These things always end in tears, don't they?") Court her. Woo her. Give *her* a compass, and a red rose. Show *her* that after however long you've been with her, *she* is still the one you're trying to impress.

Do this and I predict you'll be out of the doghouse and curled up in a basket in front of the fire in no time.

YOUR TAKEAWAY DOGGIE BAG OF THOUGHTS

- **To keep it healthy, keep your edge.** Too many people emit an almost audible hiss of air when they get married.

- **If things do fall apart and the two parties can't be reconciled, then you have suddenly to switch tack and start looking after your own interests, e.g., future custody.** The law is a Byzantine and sometimes counterintuitive creature: best consult a lawyer on all your moves when things start to get ugly.

  But let's hope it doesn't come to that! Marriage can be tough: perhaps the most important thing is that both parties *want* to solve disputes more than they want to be right. Both have to be flexible, and willing to back down, from time to time.

- **The best approach is, insofar as possible, to apply the same level of courtly manners to one another you adopted in the earliest phases of courtship.** Don't use the "F word" (fat) at all, but particularly not in reference to the object of your affection's derriere – at least, not if you want your relations to proceed in a peaceful fashion.

- **At the same time, no one should let their partner push them around too much.** Stand your ground if it's something serious, or your spouse will lose respect.

- **Everyone needs "me time."** Both parties should acknowledge that fact, not try to be deceptive about it, and negotiate a certain amount of it for one another.

- **And for God's sake, though it seems hardly worth mentioning, let alone repeating (but, human nature being what it is, we know it does): you must maintain exclusivity at all times.** Marriage without exclusivity is like a car without an engine: you might be able to push it along for a while, but really it can only go downhill. If you're married and "wooing" a woman who's not your wife, you're not a poet or seeker or troubadour. You're a schnauzer.

"**Outplacement Counsellor?** Why Would **I**, of **All People,**
Need to **Make an Appointment** with the **Outplacement
Counsellor?**" How to Avoid **Getting Canned,** While
Increasing Your Peace (of Mind) by **Expanding** Your **Brand**

DAMAGE CONTROL IN THE WORKPLACE, AND VIS-À-VIS YOUR CAREER IN GENERAL

SUBJECT: "DAVE, COULD YOU . . .

. . . come see me in my office, please?"

I was about a year into my job as a producer for a TV chat show, when I received the above e-mail from my boss.

Sitting at my paper-and-videotape-strewn "work station," I stared at this curiously bifurcated e-mail, on my computer monitor, with a species of detached fascination.

There was a fashion at the time – perhaps, in some quarters, there still is – of putting half of what you wanted to say in the "subject" line of an e-mail and the other half in the body of the e-mail.

People did it, I think, because it made them look busy, pressed for time, and in a race against the clock.

"Good Lord, man," this type of e-mail seems to imply, "do you really think I have time to compose both a subject heading *and* a whole separate e-mail besides? For Christ's sake, can't you see I'm far too busy for these types of frills and furbelows?"

My boss – let's call him "The Man," for fun – was definitely the type who enjoyed appearing stressed, harassed, behind the eight ball, and under the gun, at all times. With furrowed brow and put-upon mien, The Man walked swiftly and carried a big, stylish briefcase. He also spent a lot of time chatting on the phone, telling people how freakin' busy he was.

When he wasn't on the phone, he was either holding meetings with us, his minions, or sitting at his desk, furiously "rattling off" e-mails, with fingers of fire, to an untold number of recipients.

But it was all just dry ice, and flashing lasers. In reality, The Man accomplished very little. His big, stylish briefcase might just as well have contained soda crackers, or little airplane bottles of vodka (well, except for the clinking, of course, that might not have seemed too businesslike), for all the work he actually did.

His phone calls were just blowing smoke. No truly busy person has the time to tell everyone in that kind of detail how busy they are.*

And the people he e-mailed so furiously, when he wasn't on the phone, were mostly just fruitcakes, as I slowly came

---

* Take Pam: as a television news reporter, now she can get hella busy. The difference between a good day and a disastrous one, in her world, can literally boil down to a few seconds. So if I call at a "bad moment" – and her whole day is bad moments, basically – she'll just say, "Dave, I'm really up against it, can't talk right now." *Click.* Dial tone. Now that's

to learn; the types of balls-talking crackpots, loony lampreys, and hot-air-filled hangers-on a truly busy person would studiously stonewall.

Now, I don't want to be guilty of painting too one-sided a portrait. The Man was, and is, a man of giant brain, a delightful fellow, a good person, and a scintillating conversationalist. He was also something of a "TV visionary," if that's not too oxymoronic a phrase.

But, basically, he was a "big picture" person, a lofty thinker who created Utopian castles in the clouds, but only gummed up the works when he tried to get involved in the day-to-day operations of the office. And after a while we started to notice the office ran a heck of a lot more smoothly when he wasn't around.

Which was handy karma, because usually two, often three, and sometimes even four days a week The Man would be – as his twenty-three-year-old, utterly-useless-but-easy-on-the-eyeballs, naughty-librarian-type "office manager" aka secretary would curtly inform us, in tart tones of ersatz efficiency – "working from home that day."

He "worked from home" so much it became a running joke between Roger, the hyper-intelligent, twenty-six-year-old, goateed kid who actually ran things around there, and me.

busy, ladies and gentlemen: too busy to say hello, too busy to say goodbye. To tell you the truth, I've given up even trying to phone her during the day. I e-mail her now, with whatever thoughts are pinging around in my melon, or with late-breaking news flashes from the home front – e.g., that the dishwasher guy had come, and what he said. And she'll thumb-type me back her response, when – *if* – she has the time.

Me (muttering quietly to Roger): "Yeah, I was 'working from home' last night, too, and man do I have a headache today. Also, I think I may have injured my hip jumping off the speakers."

Roger (muttering to me): "Yeah, I was 'working from home' over the weekend, but it didn't go so well, either, because I knocked over my bong in the middle of a 'meeting.' Now I think I may have to rent a carpet steamer to get the smell out."

Don't get me wrong, ladies and gentlemen. I'm not pooh-poohing "working from home" in general. I work from home myself, and I believe great things can emanate from one's domicile. Many of mankind's greatest achievements, e.g. *Madame Bovary*, were created by people who were "working from home."

It's just that, in this particular gentleman's case, we weren't exactly buying it.

THE SANDS OF MY TIME

But all of this is neither here nor there. I'm just trying to give you a little background, a little "back-story" to the moment I, a producer on a TV chat-show, found myself staring at that curiously bifurcated e-mail from my boss:

Subject: "Dave, could you . . .
. . . come see me in my office, please?"

I knew full well what this e-mail portended, the fate that awaited me as soon as I stepped over the threshold of The

Man's spacious, book-lined, well-appointed corner office with a stellar view of the city's downtown core.

If expressed as a gesture, that gesture would be: [Dave slowly draws finger across throat, while making *kkkkkkkkk* sound with tongue pressed against upper palate].

I'm an old hand at getting canned, I'm afraid. I said in the Introduction that I am the King of the Faux Pas.

I am also, unfortunately, King Canned, the supreme ruler of the principality of anyone who's ever been pink-slipped, given the heave-ho, the shepherd's crook, the old bums' rush, been passed over, outsourced, outplaced, become otherly employed, or whatever handy euphemistic neologism you care to choose.

I've been fired from more jobs than you've had hot dinners, basically. With one exception, I've been fired from every job I've ever had – and I've had lots of jobs. I've even been fired from a *campus job* as a *dishwasher*.

Now, do you think you can top that?

The lone exception was *Newsweek*, where I quit a heinously dull job as a "Letters Correspondent" after a mind-numbing fourteen months. They were nice about it – even threw me a little party, complete with cheese-and-cracker trolley and little Dixie cups full of plonk.

But usually, my approach to any given job is to cling to it like a barnacle clings to the side of a rich man's yacht, until someone comes along and scrapes me off.*

---

* I have never had any personal experience with the quaint, historical concept known as "job security," in other words. Few people I know do. It's gone the way of the dodo, I'm afraid – perhaps to be followed, sometime later in the century, by the very concept of a "job," i.e., something you go to, every day, five days a week, and that gives you "benefits," its own self.

Which always (except at *Newsweek*) happens sooner or later. As soon as I show up on Day One of any new job, an invisible hand reaches out, overturns an invisible hourglass, and the sands of my time begin to run out.

"And now the sands of my time have run out at this job, too," I thought, sadly, staring at the e-mail summoning me to The Man's office. "Ah, well, it was fun while it lasted – sort of. Anyway, it paid the bills, for a time."

Now, I'm probably guilty, again, here, of making it all sound more casual and light-hearted than I actually felt.

In reality, I felt ill. My world was crumbling around my ears. Fired again? Pam was on year-long maternity leave with our third child (Adam), and at that moment, apart from the miserable pittance she received as maternity-leave benefits from the government, we were solely dependent on my income to be able to afford the goo we spooned into the one end of that baby and the diapers to catch what came out the other end; not to mention feeding, and clothing, our other two kids, and ourselves; and paying the mortgage to keep the rain and snow off the heads of the whole fam-damily.

Therefore it was with a sick, all-too-familiar churning in the pit of my stomach, a terrible sense of impending doom, and a single drop of flop-sweat trickling down my rib cage, I pointed my size-13s toward The Man's office and threaded my way past the desks of the still-employed, to receive news of my doom.

"Would you mind closing the door behind you?" The Man said, sure enough, as soon as I crossed the threshold.

I sat down in the little chair on the other side of his pool-table-sized desk, and proceeded to await what was coming next. He finished typing an e-mail. Then, finally, he looked up.

"The news isn't good, I'm afraid," The Man began, in his cultured, upper-crusty, mid-Atlantic accent.

Can't renew your contract, unfortunately, blah blah blah, nothing personal yadda yadda yadda budget cuts and la la la.

All of which turned out to be an overflowing diaper-full of stinking, steaming horse droppings, because, a few months later, The Man hired someone else to replace me.

KING CANNED VS. KING LEAR: WHO SHALL TRIUMPH?

What had I done wrong? It is probable that I shall never know. I worked my ass off for The Man and had thought I was doing a good job for him, as well!

But The Man was capricious, mercurial, and unpredictable. We called him King Lear because, since he was away from the office so much, he had to rely on spies for information,* and tended to trust his Regans and Gonerils over his Cordelias.

. . . I don't know how well you remember your Shakespeare. In case it's a little rusty, King Lear had three

---

* Particularly his hottie/naughty-librarian secretary, who in fact at age twenty-three wielded a terrible baton of power in that office because she had The Man's ear; therefore everyone attempted to curry favour with her, knowing she could get you fired with a frown, and a pout, in the direction of The Man, who was, like any man, shall we say *not insusceptible to feminine pulchritude*?

daughters: Cordelia, Regan, and Goneril. He decides to divide his kingdom among them and give the largest share to the one who loves him the most. ·

So both Regan and Goneril, Lear's two oldest daughters, immediately launch into flowery soliloquies on the topic of how much they love him, what a wonderful king and father he is, and so forth. Cordelia, his youngest, delivers a speech much more temperate and honest than her sisters'.

Which annoys the old man. "Where's my fulsome, flowery praise?" he wants to know. So he divides his kingdom between Regan and Goneril, and disinherits Cordelia. Then – well, a bunch of other stuff happens, but suffice to say it all ends in tears.

Like King Lear, The Man would often wind up firing his most loyal *consiglieri* and Cordelias, his best workers, and allowed the most devious, useless, incompetent, and treacherous among his minions to flourish and prosper.

Someone was always sidling or sidewinding into The Man's office and stabbing someone else in the back.

(You could tell when it was happening because he closed his door on these occasions.)

The Man listened to evil counsel and, a few weeks before firing me, had fired his biggest Cordelia of all.

Call her P. Maybe because she was a little in love with The Man, P worked harder than anyone. Whenever I worked late, or came back to the office because I forgot my briefcase or whatnot, there she'd be, sometimes all by herself, her lamp casting a funnel-shaped glow over her desk, all alone in the dark.

And she did a great job, by universal acclaim, and every-one loved her. . . .

But one morning, around eleven, two burly security guards materialized, one to the left, one to the right of her workstation. She was instructed to shut off her computer, then escorted out to the parking lot, wondering, no doubt (1) "What the *&^%$#@! did I do to deserve that?" and (2) " What the *&^%$#@! am I gonna do now?"

BUSINESS NEVER PERSONAL

What had she done to piss off The Man? What had I done?

Who knows? In a way, it matters more than anything else. And in another way, it doesn't matter at all.

People like to pretend it's all "business never personal." But that's pure fantasy. In an office, business and personal matters are all mixed together in a fragrant potpourri.

Firing someone – no matter which end of the transaction you're on – is one of the most personal, intimate interac-tions that can take place between two human beings.

When you fire a person, you're cutting off that person's air supply, pulling the hose out of the helmet of that person's spacesuit, and slitting the person's throat.

If the person you're firing has a family, you're taking away that person's ability to keep his or her kids in diapers and pabulum. You're "breaking his rice bowl"; and is there any-thing more personal than that?

You're sending that person scrambling, at the very least.

Between The Man and me, it was a particularly piquant transaction, because we'd been friends for more than a decade before he hired me.

(Before you say anything, let me tell you being his friend hadn't made it easier for me to get hired. If anything, he bent over backwards to put me through an extra-rigorous pre-hiring process.)

He knew he was cutting off my air supply. He knew Pam, with whom he was also friends, was on maternity leave; that I would have to start fucking hustling, working the phones, the second I left his office; that Pam would cry when she heard the news; and that he was sending my family spinning across a patch of ice, headed for a brick wall; or, to put it another way, we would have a tough few months.

But vis-à-vis the whys and the wherefores, The Man played his cards close to his vest.

We were both like Shakespearean actors playing roles, in fact, in his spacious, well-appointed corner office. We were both acting up a storm, during that uncomfortable transaction.

He was acting all like it had nothing to do with me, or him, that he was just a messenger, or emissary, of unseen Higher Forces, all beyond his control;* and I was acting like it was "cool," no problem, totally fine.

I even leaned back in my chair and attempted to affect a

---

* As John Malkovich keeps saying, chillingly, in *Dangerous Liaisons*: "It's beyond my control."

certain saucy insouciance about the whole thing, I'm ashamed to say.

As if this, my job, were just one of many far-reaching, international enterprises I had on the bubble, enterprises so pressing I, Richard Branson-like, was just about to have to tender my resignation in short order, anyway, and him firing me was almost a relief.

But what *should* I have done? It doesn't help to freak out, seek revenge, burst into tears, get angry, or anything else, really, either.

What can you do? I can tell you from being friends with several people who have been on the other end of this trans-action (i.e., have had to fire people), it's not really personal – or, at least, they don't really seem to be all that sorry for the person they're firing.

If anything, they feel angry. Because often the person being fired let them down, didn't live up to expectations, promised things he/she was unable to deliver, lied in the first place about his/her skill-set, or some combination of/something akin to the above.

Sometimes it really is just budget cuts – numbers, nothing personal. It's funny, though, isn't it, how the best of the best so often seem to survive these numbers-only layoffs? A notion I'm trying to drill into the noggins of my offspring: these days, it's no longer cool just to show up and half-assedly do your job (if it ever was). Do that, and you risk being looked upon as deadwood; and may wind up drift-wood, if you see what I'm saying.

You have to be talented in the first place. You have to kick ass, and keep on kicking ass, to "burn always with a hard, gem-like flame,"* if you have any hope of survival in the ultra-competitive world we live in today.

But once the decision has been made to let you go, there's not much you can do. Most of the time, all you can do is just accept the verdict, and move on.

(Though sometimes it's a better idea to fight back: something we'll discuss later in the chapter.)

I accepted The Man's verdict, and moved on. Work-wise, I'm actually pretty well diversified. I write for newspapers, TV, and magazines, and I'm hoping to write movies.

I'm a hustler, baby! I'm not even proud of it. I don't feel one way or another about it. These days, for most of us, anyway, you just have to be, and that's that.

But for now I'm going to start by assuming you don't want to lose the job you already have – that you'd like to hang on to it. Here at Damage Control, we understand.

So let's start out by talking about a few of the ways you can stay one step ahead of that axe in the first place.

HANG ON TO YOUR STASH, PANAMA RED

First, though, before we discuss how to comport yourself within the confines of the actual bricks-and-mortar office, let's talk about matters external.

* Walter Pater, 1839–1894.

Because we want you to adopt a "holistic" approach to your career. Or, to put it in less bullshitty, New Age-y terms: you should assume, whether it's true or not, that you're being watched, under scrutiny and surveillance, at all times. Not only when you're stewing and steaming in your cubicle or "workstation,"* but also outside the office, and, just, basically, every moment of your waking life.

As Oscar Wilde so eloquently put it: "I forgot that every little action of the common day makes or unmakes character, and that therefore what one has done in the secret chamber one has some day to cry aloud on the house-tops.†

Now, don't get me wrong. I believe everyone has the right to relax, and I like bourbon, fine wines, straight vodka, extra-spicy Bloody Caesars, and ice-cold beers on a hot summer's day, as much as (or maybe even a little more than)** the next guy.

But you don't want people to think you have a monkey on your back.

* In all my working life I have never had the honour of a cubicle of my own; I've always been assigned a "workstation." I've always been part of an "open concept" office.

† And in prison, which broke him and killed him. I love Oscar Wilde, he is my hero and easily No. 1 choice of historical figures I'd like to have dinner with, but a poster boy for poor damage control, I'm afraid. Of the many mistakes he made, the biggest, I think: trying to be funny at his trial.

** Writing is very thirst-inducing work, as I'm always patiently explaining to Pam. It's the mental equivalent of munching on extra-dry saltines all day.

On the other hand, nor do you want them to think you're a priggish, prissy little prude. Sometimes it's hard to know what to do. . . .

THE QUESTION

I work in a fairly staid organization. Recently my boss, who's forty and seems a little hipper than the rest, came over for a dinner party. We were having a really great night, and after dinner a few of us announced we were going to go out on the porch for a smoke. That's when my boss asked, "Don't you have anything stronger than tobacco? Too bad!"

We laughed, but when we got out on the porch my wife persuaded me to offer him a joint from my secret stash. She said it was my duty as a host, and though I didn't really think it was a great idea, I came back inside and asked, "Would you like some pot? Because I do actually have some." My boss looked puzzled, frowned, and said, "No, I'm good."

Turns out he was just joking! It was an awkward moment, and I'm mad at my wife for pushing me into it, but mostly I want to dispel the notion among my colleagues that I'm some kind of pothead. Is there any way back from this slip-up?

THE ANSWER

Well, since that cat's – *meeee-yowww!* – out of the Ziploc baggie, now, buddy, what I would do, in this case, when all is said and done, is: exactly nothing.

Any frantic attempts at spin-doctoring and damage control you do in this circumstance will only provoke further eye-rolling and eyebrow-raising. If you bring it up, it's likely that whatever they say, people will tend to think, "Whatever, *Panama Red.*"*

Or: "Methinks thou dost protest too much, *Cheech and Chong.*"

No, this case is a perfect example of an occasion where silence is golden† and the best way to deal with the subject is to drop it.

Having a stash is probably not something anyone, these days, including a boss-type figure, is likely to give you a hard time about. After all, offering someone pot isn't the heavy-duty electro-shocker it was in, say, 1957, when nobody smoked it except jazz musicians and bikers and people from "the wrong side of the tracks."

These days, most forty-year-olds, even if they've never smoked it, have experienced it swirling around their heads. Bill Clinton smoked it – though, in strict adherence to his policy of never quite telling the truth, he claimed he didn't inhale – and he's a former president of the United States! Even in George W. Bush's ultra-straight White House, the policy for hiring people apparently was "No marijuana after college." Because even eggheads, policy nerds, and

---

* What De Niro calls Ben Stiller in *Meet the Parents* when he finds out he smokes pot.

† Recall Rule No. 1 of Damage Control in Matters of Love and Courtship: Sometimes, silence is golden, because it is almost impossible to interpret, and you haven't gone on the record one way or another. True, too, in the workplace, where a little *omertà* goes a long way. Recall the admonition of Robert De Niro in *Goodfellas*: "Never rat on your friends and always keep your mouth shut." I love the gangsterish redundancy of that advice.

ultra-conservatives might be tempted to dabble at some point along the line.

Generally speaking, though, for most social situations you should not offer anything that might make anyone uncomfortable, unless it's something you know in advance everyone would enjoy.

Having said that – and this is "master class" stuff, so fasten your seat belts* – while doing a good job and being a good employee, maybe keep a quiet eye peeled for another opportunity to "party" with your boss. He sounds like he might secretly be up for it, and getting up to a certain amount of limited naughtiness with the person who signs your cheques can be a good thing. It can cement your relationship. It's a little something you share. Certainly it makes it harder for your boss to chew you out when you're both thinking, "Tee-hee, we were up to some shenanigans the other night."

But there are a few crucial rules of etiquette you must follow when illicit substances materialize in the vicinity of you and your employer. First: take all cues from your boss. If he/she passes, you must do likewise. If he/she accepts the proffered contraband, then and only then may you feel free to follow suit.

Secondly – and this is semi-crucial – what happens in the back rooms of clubs and second-floor bedrooms of parties should stay there.

Around the office, a strict code of *omertà* vis-à-vis out-of-office shenanigans must be observed at all times, upon penalty of being whacked.

* And if you tell people I advised you to do this I will, unfortunately, have to deny it.

In other words, keep your dang fool mouth shut. I remember once, at an office where I worked, a junior staffer was laughing and talking in a meeting about how loaded everyone was the night before, what a wild night it was, ha-ha-ha, including the boss – man, was he "wasted."

The boss just gave him a look. It was like the "long look" Robert De Niro* gives "Morrie," the too-talkative, hair-piece-wearing, soon-to-be-whacked gangster in *Goodfellas*.

It's a chilling scene. Morrie's been riding De Niro for an advance on the big score they just pulled off. Finally, De Niro says, okay, sure. But then, later, standing in a crowded bar, he looks across the room at Morrie, then looks away, looks over at him, then looks away. And we, the audience, know exactly what the look means: it means Morrie's bloody body will soon be wrapped in a blanket in the trunk of De Niro's El Dorado.

Well, I don't remember if the too-chatty kid in my office was whacked or not. Either way, though, we all knew, in that moment, he would never be a "made man."

So try to be a "wise guy" and keep mum, and this little faux pas could wind up working in your favour. Otherwise, pass on the joint without partaking (also without comment: to wrinkle your nose and make a pooh-poohing comment – which would be the height of hypocrisy, and annoying for a whole different set of reasons).

And the next time you have people over, probably your rep would be best served if you kept your stash in the drawer.

---

* Again: I guess I reference him a lot, sorry.

SAYONARA, YOUNG TURK

Okay, let's pack our shark-repellent and snake-venom serum, put on our thigh-high scum-boots, and wade into the murky, viperous waters of a typical office.

THE QUESTION

Six years into my career, I've just really started to make my mark in the advertising world. It's a competitive field, and this year a new wave of junior staff was hired, one of whom thought he was the shit, going around the office schmoozing, glad-handing the old-timers, charming the ladies. He had the wool pulled over everyone's eyes – he was green! He had no place commenting on business. He should've been humble enough to sit back and learn. Instead he tried to upstage a few of us veterans by criticizing our media plans during a number of company meetings. It was outrageous, yet some of the oldsters gave him credit where none was due.

They even put him in charge of a small account – a first for a three-month employee. I offered to screen his plan before a presentation to the clients, and I gave him some bum advice, intentionally. It was pretty obviously over the line to anyone in the business, but he walked into that meeting and laid it on the client without forewarning the big cheeses. We lost that piece of business immediately, and now this kid's going to lose his job. I feel bad about it but don't want to admit to playing a part in his downfall – it could negatively affect my upward mobility. Any way to make myself feel better without getting lumped in with this chump?

THE ANSWER

For starters I should probably say Damage Control does not condone or endorse such Machiavellian manoeuvres as deliberately misleading greenhorns into doing things that ultimately get them fired.

That is a sin, and you should probably say a few Hail Marys, confess to your spiritual adviser, or put a little extra in the collection plate. And promise me not to do it again.

It's a sin that can't be un-sinned, though, so the question becomes: where do we go from here?

First of all, I have to say: you *should* feel bad about it, but maybe not maximally so. After all, to tweak the old saying a little, you can lead a greenhorn to hot water, but you can't make him jump in. He did that all on his own.

And it sounds like the kid would've hoisted himself by his own petard, anyway, sooner or later. Showing you and everyone else up in front of the bosses? Fuhgedaboudit – if you hadn't whacked him, someone else probably would have.

If you want to feel better about pulling the hose out of this kid's space helmet, and probably putting him in a position where his girlfriend, rolling her eyes, has to reach for her wallet when the cheque comes and the ex-"hotshot" has to sit on his hands – well, you could tell yourself you're teaching him a valuable life lesson!

Like when I was a kid and my mother would take me to task for beating up on my younger brother and sister.

"Hey, Mom," I'd tell her. "I'm just trying to teach them a lesson about the cruelty and harshness of life! You should be thanking me, not getting mad at me!"

Mom never really bought this line of reasoning, though, for some reason.

But I thought then, and a part of me still thinks now: there is a kernel of truth in this statement. When you give an obnoxious/clueless upstart/greenhorn a little love tap, an immunizing inoculation of humility, you're doing that person a favour, right? Waking them up a bit? Toughening them up for what's to come?

It reminds me of a speech Michael Gambon, as cruel, tanned, ultra-villain Eddie Temple, lays on a pre-Bond Daniel Craig, who plays a wide-eyed young crook in the British gangster flick *Layer Cake*.

Gambon's just screwed Craig over royally: tricked him out of all the money *and* all the product (drugs), and then lays a speech on him explaining why it would be futile for Craig to seek revenge.

"Are you enjoying this?" a defeated-sounding Craig asks him, when he's finished.

"Take it as a compliment," Michael Gambon says. "You're a bright young man. This monkey business is in your blood, under your skin. You're not getting out, you're just getting in. I've every faith in you. One day, it will be you sitting here telling some young Turk the facts of life."

"And they are, Mr. Temple?" Daniel Craig says, from between gritted teeth.

"You're born, you take shit. Get out in the world, you take more shit. Climb a little higher, you take less shit. Until one day, you're up in the rarefied atmosphere where you've forgotten what shit even looks like.

"Welcome to the layer cake, son."

Pure poetry! Facts-of-life-wise, it sounds about right, to me, too – that is, if you're lucky. Most of us are destined to munch our way through the lower layers of that particular confection our whole lives.

So if your conscience is really pricking you about whacking this little prick, I suppose you could take the kid out, apologize to him for giving him such lousy advice (no need to blurt out that you did it deliberately), then maybe lay some sort of Michael Gambon-like speech on him, along the lines of:

"Listen, kid, I like you, and I think you have a bright future in this business. That's why I want to do you a favour and let you in on a little secret: how you messed up."

Then drop on him whatever knowledge and wisdom you've managed to accrue in your six years in the ad game, e.g., he should be more of a team player; it's all very well to want to be a star, but you have to learn the rules before you can play with the big boys; no matter how big a hotshot he thinks he is, he can benefit from the wisdom and experience of the "seasoned veterans"; and so forth.

You could explain all this to him. To be honest, though, all things considered, I wouldn't bother. His wounds are still pretty fresh; he probably won't be in the mood to swallow even the most friendly and well-intentioned advice.

Especially from you. I mean, look what happened last time.

No, if it were me, I'd just fuhgedaboudit, and move on.

And concentrate on watching my own back. I mean, it sounds like it doesn't take a heck of a lot to get the chop in your shop. Sounds like the waters are a little sharky. Also, now, stained with fresh blood. So maybe you best keep on swimming, there, *chum*. Swim or die.

If this kid's tough, and a true hotshot, he'll find a way back into the game (and then you better watch your back, buddy, because he could come gunning for you).

If not, well, maybe he wasn't cut out for it, after all. Maybe he was really meant for a different profession – so, once again, you did him a favour, pointing him in another direction! He should be thanking you!

If you do wind up taking the kid out, it might be a nice gesture if you picked up the tab, though.

After all, he might be a tad skint for a while.

"YOND CASSIUS HAS A LEAN AND HUNGRY LOOK": AVOIDING EARLY FLAME-OUT SYNDROME

Okay, that concludes the official portion of the advice, aimed at Mr./Ms. Machiavellian Backstabber.

But I'd like to do a bit of an extended remix here, aimed at kids fresh out of some program or another, new to the working world: like the kid who went from playing with the big dogs to swimming with the fishes in the previous question.

Because this sort of thing seems to happen a lot. Call it Early Flame-out Syndrome (E.F.S.). A Tom-Cruise-in-Top-Gun-type hotshot ("Maverick") comes swaggering out of some program or another, gets in the workplace, becomes the boss's fair-haired boy – for a while. But then something happens; and he/she swipes her security pass one day and it doesn't work, and all the security guard can tell him/her, staring puzzled at his computer monitor, is: "All it says here is you're supposed to see the outplacement counsellor."

And since ipso facto E.F.S. strikes at the beginning of a career, it can be quite devastating. I stick to my statement, above, that if a kid is made of stern stuff, he/she will bounce back and come back bigger/faster/smarter/better.

But obviously it's better if you can avoid all that drama in the first place; we do have a few thoughts we'd like to share about that.

Now, some of these anti-E.F.S. tips may seem a little counterintuitive, at first blush, but they're still right, we think. And I'm going to drag Shakespeare in again.

Okay? So: you've been warned.

Let me begin by saying I've spent quite a bit of time in the trenches of TV news. And I've seen a lot of fresh-out-of-journalism-school, would-be hotshots come and go. Especially when it comes to on-air types – well, they can put on a lot of airs, thinking, "Me, me, me, it's all about ➤ ME ◄ ! And I'm gonna be a STAR!"

But the ones who last longest, I've noticed, are the ones who always have a kind word for the grunts, the rank-and-file (e.g., the writers, who are the lowest grunts of all in TV news): a smile, a comment, a show of interest. Mmmm, how's your dog, Dave – Murphy, is it? You solve that flea problem yet?

The ones who don't last – well, their trajectory tends to go something like this:

After a short probationary period, the boss hauls the hotshot into his/her office, and says, "Kid, I don't even know what "it" is, but you got it! Everyone's loving you on camera! Keep it up like this, and you're gonna be a STAR!"

And it goes straight to the hotshot's melon, which starts to swell and become over-ripe. He/she starts twirling diva-liciously around the newsroom, chewing out camera-persons, criticizing editors,* pooh-poohing scripts, throwing hissy fits in the makeup room if the Pancake No. 11 isn't trowelled on just right.

That's when the murmuring begins. Then the mur-muring turns into muttering, the muttering into a low, rumbling grumbling: "*Grumble mutter* who does she think she is *rhubarb rhubarb* I'll tell you who she is: a bitch *mutter mutter* someone should say something *grumble grumble*," etc., etc.

Next thing you know the "Next Big Thing" is out on his/her keister on the street, except this time without a microphone, or a camera-person, or story to report.

It's a typical rookie/greenhorn mistake: thinking the only person they need to impress, when they get a new job, is the boss and sods to everyone else.

But nothing could be further from the truth, in my expe-rience. The offices I've worked in (see above) are more like an episode of *Survivor* (except without the bikinis and breathtakingly beautiful, lobster-filled tropical lagoons, sadly), and the boss is like the host, Jeff Probst: detached, materializing infrequently, only vaguely aware of the tribe's quotidian shenanigans, and ultimately willing to accept the tribe's verdict on who should stay and who should go.

If you want career longevity (and you do), you have to keep your new colleagues on your side. Okay, here we go again with the Shakespeare:

---

* And let me tell you, TV editors hate being criticized, even more than the rest of us. Editors are "touchy as a hunchback," as the Russian saying goes.

Caesar: "Yond Cassius has a lean and hungry look. He thinks too much. Such men are dangerous."

Marc Antony: "Fear him not, Caesar, he's not dangerous."

"Yeah, you're probably right," Caesar says (I'm paraphrasing). "I'm probably just being paranoid."

Of course, on the Ides of March, he finds out that he was right all along, and Marc Antony was wrong.

Not that it was much consolation . . . He never really had a chance to find Marc Antony and tell him "I told you so" after Cassius, Brutus, et al., shanked him. All he really had a chance to do was gurgle, "Et tu, Brute?"* and die.

Rather than trying to tear your new workplace a fresh one, be nice to your new colleagues. Lay back for a while, try to get the lay of the land.

Now don't get me wrong: I totally understand the impulse to be a "new broom," sweep aside the codgeriffic cobwebs of the old-timers, and usher in The Era of [Your Name Here].

But just take it easy in the early days, hot stuff. Go slow. Accumulate information before making your move.

It doesn't even hurt, in my view, if you appear a little thick (not dumb, but eager and interested to learn). The Chinese have a saying: "Masquerading as a swine to kill a tiger." It's based on an ancient hunting technique in which the hunter disguises himself in the hide and snout of a pig and mimics its grunting. The tiger thinks: "Mmmm, fresh pork," and prepares to pounce, until the last moment, when the hunter casts off his disguise and reveals himself to be that most dangerous of creatures: a hungry man with a pointy stick.

* At least, according to Shakespeare; historians dispute this and say he either said nothing or maybe "You too, child?" in Greek

Likewise, it might not hurt you, greenhorn, if you act a tad porcine for a while; lull your colleagues into a false sense of security before revealing the pointy stick of your ambition.

Until then, remember (1) fresh blood is usually the first spilt; and (old poker saying) (2) if you don't know who the sucker is at the table, it's probably you.

THE TERRIBLE, TRAGIC SADNESS OF THE OFFICE HOTTIE

Okay. Let's stay on the greenhorn motif a moment.

Let's say you, the newbie, have managed to hang on through your "probationary period." You've managed to impress everyone. You're a good, solid worker, a team player, a go-getter but not one that's trying to go-get everyone else's jobs (yet), thus upsetting the apple cart. Congratulations! Young Turk no more, you are now a valued young member of the team.

But . . . you're still young, with all that entails. Let's just say with all the hormones, pheromones, and hotties suggesting everyone go out for mojitos after work, some people find they have a hard time navigating the sexual minefield that is a modern-day office.

THE QUESTION
I'm very attractive and get a lot of attention from men. They're always flirting with me at work, but often it takes

me a while to notice because I'm not the flirty type at all.

At one job there was a colleague who was flirting with me constantly but never asked me out. I am told I can intimidate men, so I asked him out. We went out once and never again. It wound up being such an embarrassing situation I had to leave that job.

The same thing happened at my next job: I had to leave for a number of reasons, but partly because of a flirtation gone sour.

At my present job, there's a guy who likes me, though it took me almost a year to notice. When I did, I sent him a jokey e-mail asking to meet up. He never replied and now I am very embarrassed and do not want to face him. I do not, however, want to leave my job over this.

Why do men flirt so stupidly with no intention of following through? And why do I fall so stupidly every time, to the detriment of my work life?

THE ANSWER

Mmmm . . . hello, office hottie.

Come in. Make yourself comfortable. Welcome to Damage Control. Can I get you anything? Cappuccino? Bottled water? Hmmm . . . ooooh . . . I, uh, I like your top, it, uh, really, uh . . . well, it's nice!

[Advice guy shakes it off, snaps out of it, pulls self together; suddenly becomes brisk and businesslike.]

Anyway, where was I? Oh, yeah: you and your ilk have caused members of my gender a considerable amount of consternation, confusion, and suffering over the years. It's great finally to hear your side of the story.

First I would like to say: though I am not personally a sexy little *chiquita picante con salsa verde* driving all the men (and perhaps even some of the women) in my office crazy every time I bend over to pick up a pencil or tie my shoe, I, David Eddie, feel your pain.

Counterintuitive as it might seem, I've often thought it would be a drag to be trapped in the body of a too-pulchri-tudinous babe.

Surrounded by cheeseballs and adhesive horndogs at parties, all laughing way too hard at your jokes, even the unfunny ones: "Ah-ha-ha, Jennifer, that is too funny, you really hit the nail on the head with that one, you should do stand-up, ha-ha-ha," etc. Everyone pretending to hang on your every word, meanwhile trying to sneak peeks down your blouse and picturing you naked.

Annoying. And isolating, I would think. In William Butler Yeats's beautiful poem *A Prayer for My Daughter*, the poet is standing over his baby girl's crib thinking: "May she be granted beauty and yet not/Beauty to make a stranger's eye distraught . . . for such,/Being made beautiful overmuch,/Consider beauty a sufficient end,/Lose natural kindness and maybe . . . never find a friend."

I think I know what he means. It would be hard to make a real connection with anyone. My wife, Pam, was an early-blooming über-babe with fuel-injected turbo-curves, and she says high school was a nightmare because of the way the teenaged boys turned everything that came out of her mouth into a sexual double entendre:

"I like our new geography teacher."

"Oooh, I bet you do, Pam. I bet he'd like to map out your topography, hey? Bet he'd like to explore your Amazon rainforest, hmmm?"

Oy, change the topic, already, she wanted to say.* But they wouldn't. Besides being utterly boring, it wound up making her feel isolated and insecure.

And hotties have no one to complain to, the poor babies!

If they try to complain to a guy it goes like this: "Oh, Howard, you're my only true friend; whenever I try to talk to anyone else they just spend the whole time watching my lips move and trying to picture me naked – Howard? Are you listening to me?"

"Hmm? Sorry? What's that?"

If she complains to a female friend, her "sister" in arms just sits there thinking: "Oh, cry me a river. You've got all the guys drooling over you and now you're gonna whine about it?"

The good news, sister, is: while it lasts, you wield an unholy baton of power. Why are you wasting this awesome power on some ambivalent dude in your office? Why are you, especially with your track record, trying so hard to take things to the next level?

* She and I have an ongoing debate: which was harder, being a teenaged girl or teenaged boy. She says girl. I say: "Pam, no woman can ever know the terrible torments of the teenaged boy, driven to near-madness by lust." When someone asked Sophocles how it felt to be old, he said: "I am happy to be free of the fierce and savage master of lust." When I heard this, as a teenager, in a Philosophy class, I thought: Oh, man, I know exactly what he means. Fierce and savage master, indeed. I didn't want to be old, but I thought it might be nice to be, say, thirty, and not be driven to the brink of madness by this "fierce and savage master" (little did I know: turning thirty would not in fact change a fucking thing, nor would turning forty: I just seem to get hornier each passing year).

Personally, I'm not a big fan of the office romance. Don't get me wrong: I understand why it happens. These days, we all spend so much time at work. Naturally, sparks must fly, especially if one is, like you, a sexy little minx.

And I know a lot of these affairs work out. I have several friends who met at work, got married, had kids, and have lived (so far) happily married. My own father has been happily married to his former office manager for many years.

But it can go the other way, too. Most relationships do, after all. And if it does? Hello, nightmare. You have to encounter your colleague/ex everywhere: at the water cooler, in the lunchroom, shooting daggers across the conference-room table.

Even if everything goes smoothly, for my money it'd be a total pain. I don't know about you, but I like to keep my head down at work and concentrate on the task at hand. When deadlines loom and I'm up the creek, I can be gruff, curt, and blunt to say the least: exactly the opposite of the qualities necessary to sustain romance.

Anyway, this guy you're interested in is obviously ambivalent, to say the least, and who needs that? Maybe he's a little intimidated by you. Or maybe he's the one afraid, wisely, to "dip his pen in company ink." Maybe he's frightened of all the trouble it could lead to – and pardon me for saying so, madam, but you sound like Trouble with a capital T and that rhymes with P, which stands for Pink Slip.

No, I would say, rather than look upon your co-workers as a dating pool, you need to get out there and find your next boyfriend the old-fashioned way: at night. Take that booty you're bragging about and shake it around some clubs and parties. If you are all you say you are, it shouldn't be long before some guy sidles up with twinkling eyes and offers to buy you a drinkie-poo.

And that's what you want, really, in a guy, isn't it? Someone with the stones to approach you in awkward circumstances, out of the blue, in the field, despite your forbidding sexiness? Someone who knows what he wants?

Not some ambivalent salaryman who doesn't even know his own mind.

VICKI FEVER

Now, in the Introduction we said we like to look at problems from all angles. In a previous question, we looked at the problem from the POV of both the Machiavellian double-crosser and the greenhorn he sent to the abattoir.

We sympathize with both sides, but in the end perhaps can't help but feel like the greenhorn has the bigger problem.

Likewise, in this case of the office hottie, one can't help but feel the person at the other end of this transaction may, perhaps, be prodded with the sharper end of the stick.

We want to bend over backwards (or forwards, if you prefer, ladies) to show we are deeply concerned about, interested in, and sympathetic to the problems and challenges associated with those imbued with excessive hotness, and if you are a sexy woman who feels we haven't really paid enough attention to the issue, please contact either Pat or me via our publishers and we will be glad to arrange further elaboration in an in-depth session, perhaps over mojitos in a quiet corner of a local tiki lounge.

(Just kidding, Pam. Don't worry, no matter how many crazed advice-groupie hotties may throw themselves at me, I will always stand steadfast at your side.)

But Pat and I can't help but feel a certain twinge of fellow-feeling for the dude in the above scenario.

I mentioned the little hotsie-totsie twenty-three-year-old "naughty librarian"-type office manager who worked at the television station from which I was shitcanned as a producer. Did I mention she was also highly curvaceous, extremely flirtatious, and Polish, with a sexy Eastern European accent? And that she kept saying stuff like "Vhy are all ze good men taken?" (usually in the midst of a group of taken men) or "I only like older men" (usually when surrounded by older men).

Let's call her Vicky. She thought I was "zo *funny*" and laughed at all my jokes, even the lame ones; and she was the type who, when she laughed, laid her hand on your forearm and let it linger there just a microsecond too long (once, when we were all sitting around our desks, she laid her hand on my *thigh* and let it linger there a little too long).

She was also the type who became tipsy and emboldened after like half a beer. Once when we were all out for a drink after work, The Man asked her, "What are you thinking, Vicky?" She said, over the top of her half-empty draft: "You do not vant to know. I am thinking very bad thoughts."

Then shot me a smouldering look that almost set my boxers on fire!

———

She was the "office hottie." She had all the married and otherwise committed men, and I think even a few of the women, in a tizzy. At any given moment, at least three or four people in the office suffered the symptoms of what we called "Vicky fever."

Vicky fever was like a tropical fever – like malaria, dengue, or beri-beri, in that the symptoms might go away for a while, but they always came back.

In any case, I used to toy, as a young, jejeune, greenhorn advice columnist, with the notion that there might be some purchase to spending *too much time* with such a creature, becoming bored, and getting over "Vicky fever."

That perhaps one way to overcome a temptation is to *overexpose* oneself to that temptation.

But I now see that for what it is: terrible advice, and pure folly. Really, the only way to avoid temptation is to stay away. Give the office hottie as wide a berth as you can, boys.

What I did, anyway, after a while: turned down all Vicky's offers to go out for drinks after work, hook up with friends, hit clubs, and so on. She might pout; stick her full, bee-stung, Scarlett Johansson-like lips out in a little moue of discontent, knock my hip with her hip and say, "Ah, come on, Dave, vun little drink!"

But I stood firm.

Because here's how it happens, gentlemen. You think: "Okay, I'll go out for drinks with the sexy intern, but only with a bunch of people around." Then: "Okay, I'll go out for a tete-à-tete with her, but I won't go up for a nightcap in her apartment afterwards."* Then it's: "Okay, I'll go for a nightcap, but I won't have sex with her."

Next thing you know, you're sleeping in one of those hotels with a neon picture of Pegasus – or maybe it's Icarus – and a sign with a burnt-out, eternally sizzling letter: Ic-*zzt*-rus Hotel, Ic-*zzt!*-rus Hotel. . . .

If you must go out for some business-related drinks, stay sober (have only a "virgin mojito," if there's such a thing), and get the hell out of there at your earliest opportunity.

Where was I? Oh, yeah, damage control vis-à-vis one's career. The next question touches upon the heart of the matter, I believe.

AS IT TURNS OUT, "THE LAW" SUCKS

Yes, to me, this question is the crux. Work this one out, and everything else is "small beer."

THE QUESTION

After two years in the trenches, I just quit my job as a junior lawyer. I couldn't take it any more – from the long hours to the mindless articling to the culture of the firm – and just

---

* Once I did wind up in her apartment, just the two of us. It was some kind of "party" – maybe her birthday? – but for some reason no one else showed up. It was just me and her, drinking vodka and flipping through a photo album full of pictures of her in a bikini during seaside summers in Poland. A volatile situation. Finally, The Man showed up and I got the hell out of there.

blew a gasket last week. Let's just say that bridge is burnt. (Burnt!) This after spending ten years in school and two on the job. That's more than a third of my life, up in smoke, and now I don't know where to begin. My parents, who helped fund me during the university years and always pushed me to become a lawyer, like my dad, are furious. I can't go back to law, not just because I burned my contacts, but because after the long road getting here, I now know it's not the path for me. Is there a way to salvage some of what I've built and still make a good living or should I be looking at starting fresh, from scratch?

THE ANSWER

My college roommate, the esteemed Miami lawyer Charles Beeman, had a passion for the law since the age of twelve.

He went into law because it was in his bones and his blood, because he loved the law and understood the adversarial system down to his toes. That's who should go into law. And that's why anyone should go into anything: for one reason and one reason only – because you need to, because you have a yearning and a passion for the work.

As my mother (the nurse) always used to say to me, when I was a kid: "Whatever you choose to do, you should enjoy it, because you're going to spend so much of your life doing it."

Eight hours a day, or more: imagine spending that kind of chunk of time doing something you loathe.

Add on top of the fact that you'll be miserable the even more horrible notion that you'll probably suck at it and wind up getting fired. That's the reason I never find myself feeling envious when I hear about, say, a number-cruncher-type making millions.

For example, I have a number-crunching friend, an investment banker, who's made millions and even has his own nine-acre private island. His latest scheme is to put a tennis court on it, or possibly even a helipad.

But I, impecunious ink-stained wretch though I may be, feel no envy of this friend. Because I know that I would be terrible at this type of work, become dizzy and bored, get called on the carpet by my boss, and be forced to resign in shame, or find myself fired (once again).

I recall once playing squash with this friend in the basement of the building where he worked. Afterwards, we went up to his office, and I had to make a phone call. He took the opportunity to catch up on a little work, hauled out a spreadsheet, covered in tiny numbers, and started analyzing the tiny numbers.

As I observed him, I thought: "I could never do that." No matter what . . . I could never crunch these little numbers. I was calm and firm in this knowledge. I could try. But I'd get fired and it would all end in tears.

But it happens to so many who get lured into law. Too many people get into it because: (1) their parents want/expect it from them; (2) it pays well; (3) it seems solid.

But these are probably the three worst reasons to choose a profession, in my view.

Sure, law school may be something one could come to love. Anything with "school" in its description is bound to be at least a little bit fun.

But then the practice of the law cracks them. The 100-hour weeks, the mind-numbing circumlocutory otiosity of legal briefs – have you ever read a legal brief? They're like: "The party of the first part, See ALA, 201 F. Supp. 2d at 416 quod erat demonstratum, having tortified the olfactory mucosa of the nasal protuberance of the party of the second part, inducing sanguinary outflow thereupon, res ipse loquitor, VF 73-C of the penal code carpe diem in flagrante delicto see Robbins v. Supreme Court," etc. etc. when all they really mean to say is one guy punched another in the nose.

It's almost like everyone in the legal system is *deliberately trying to waste as much time as possible*. But why would that be? I mean, it's not like they're getting paid by the hour!

Oh, wait. Yes, they are. Six hundred dollars and up. Hmmmm . . . I guess if I made six hundred dollars an hour I'd want to stretch everything out to take as much time as possible, too.

But that's not what you want to be, not how you want to spend your brief twinkle on this planet, is it?

("They give birth astride a grave," as Samuel Beckett says. "The light gleams an instant, then it's night once more.")

People get into careers for all the wrong reasons.

Me, I'm a firm believer that you should find the thing that interests you, and the money will follow.

In fact, I would go so far as to say if my plane were to begin to shake uncontrollably and things began to look grim, I would grab a cocktail napkin and that's what I'd write to my boys: "Follow your interests, follow your passion, and the money will follow."

Of course, you should take whatever I say in this department with a grain of salt. I'm a writer, so I'm at the extreme end of the spectrum on this question.

Writing can pay off handsomely indeed, if you're one of the lucky few, e.g., J.K. Rowling, a former welfare recipient whose net worth currently stands at *one billion dollars*, making her, as far as I know, the planet's first billionaire author.

As for me – well, let's just say I'm still waiting to make my first billion from my writing.

But I love what I do. I can't wait to get up in the morning, have a cup of coffee, and tackle it. And I only wish the same for you, dear reader.

Don't worry about the years wasted! That's like the poker player who keeps pushing good money after bad into the pot, even though he's pretty sure he's going to lose, because he's already got so much in there.

The great tennis player Jimmy Connors once said: "Rather than viewing a brief relapse back to inactivity as a failure, treat it as a challenge and try to get back on track as soon as possible."

Same could be said of starting off down the wrong career path. Don't dwell on time lost. Treat it as a challenge and get on track as soon as possible. Think about the years ahead that won't be wasted, that'll be spent productively, creating a life's work you can point to and be proud of and say: "Behold, I did that."

Good luck to you.

DEALING WITH PESKY CO-WORKERS

Anyway, that's the big-picture goal: my "Utopian castle in the clouds."

In the meantime, I'm fully aware that one must do what one must do to put bread and meat on the table. And often that involves going into a *place of work*; where one encounters *people* (e.g., colleagues, bosses, etc.).

Which is a shame, because most people are naturally horrible in the first place; and they're at their worst when it's a matter of putting bread and meat on the table.

"Why you gotta be like that?" I find myself always wanting to ask the people I work with.

Jean-Paul Sartre had it right. In his play *No Exit*, three people die and go to Hell, which turns out, to their surprise, to be nothing more than a comfortably furnished room.

They keep waiting for their tormentor to show up, but no one comes. They start to chat, bicker, get on each other's nerves – until, finally, they have the horrible realization: no tormentor is ever going to arrive, it's not necessary because *having to deal with each other for eternity will be torment enough.*

That's when one of the characters utters the immortal line, beloved of misanthropes everywhere: "Hell is other people."

A sentiment I've shared, many a time, on the job – though of course I've also met people I like, some of whom have become lifelong friends.

THE QUESTION
My workplace seems to be populated with many nosy people who seem intent on forcing their own views on the rest of the world.

One of my colleagues is a fervently religious woman who is not content practising her faith on her own time, but instead interrogates her co-workers in their cubicles and preaches to them. On one occasion she followed me on my lunch break to a shoe store and chastised me for "shopping again."

I don't think she's a bad person, but for some reason she seems to feel it's okay to make her co-workers' personal habits and lives part of her personal crusade. And she's not the only one. I would say her behaviour is the norm rather than the exception. Any tips or advice for dealing with fascism in the workplace?

THE ANSWER

I've heard lots of toxic-office, psychotic-boss, and cantankerous-colleague stories. But following you out of the office on your lunch break, stalking you, then pouncing on you in a shoe store and chewing you out for shopping?

That's out there. If someone did that to me, I do believe they would soon find their hindquarters in intimate contact with the business end of a size 13 Adidas shell toe.

It's every working stiff's inalienable right to slither out of the office for a little "retail therapy" at lunch, for God's sake. Take that away from us and what have we left? If people stopped slipping out for clandestine shoe-shopping safaris on their lunch breaks, the entire footwear industry would grind to a halt and teeter on the brink of collapse.

And you say her type of behaviour is the "norm" at your office? Yikes.

My first impulse, as a professional advice-giver and distributor of carefully considered, thoughtful counsel, is to grab your lapels, pull your face within an inch of mine, and, with my eyes bugging out like someone in a zombie movie, say: "Run! Run like the wind! Submit your resignation immediately and hightail it as far from that toxic office as your feet will take you."

But it's too easy to tell people to quit their jobs. I'm going to have to go ahead and assume you've considered this option and decided against it, for whatever reason. Perhaps you enjoy the work itself. Perhaps it's the only place you can do the work you love. Or maybe it's just the warm, cozy feeling you get from having a roof over your head and groceries in the fridge.

In any case, why should one unhinged anti-shopping evangelist force you out before you're ready to go?

Now, my advice may seem a little counterintuitive to some. It may even seem a tad unscrupulous, underhanded, and Machiavellian. But demented shopping-denouncers call for high-handed cloak-and-dagger measures, so here goes: befriend her.

That's what I always do. The minute I get a new job, I seek out the most obnoxious, annoying, self-obsessed bore in the office and start chatting that person up.

Why? Because they're invariably the ones who know everything and everyone; who know what's about to happen in the company before it happens; whose connections run like an invisible network of veins and arteries throughout the building. That's how they keep their jobs, despite their odious personalities. And that's why you should not go over her head and complain.

I think your instinct is quite right, that if she feels she is allowed to get away with this sort of thing, it's probably because management smiles a warm and beneficent smile upon her zealotry and lack of boundaries.

So don't go upstairs. You could just be shooting yourself in the foot.

"Keep your friends close and your enemies closer." Never more true than in an office.

Generals, statesmen, and presidents have always understood the neutralizing effect of befriending your enemies and potential adversaries.

"Why, madam," Lincoln responded to a woman who chastised him for not calling Southerners enemies in a speech at the height of the Civil War, "do I not destroy my enemies when I make them my friends?"

Likewise, in 1971, after being the target of a failed kidnapping attempt, Henry Kissinger arranged a Saturday meeting with several of the alleged conspirators without informing the Secret Service or the Justice Department.

He totally charmed them. They gave him "Kidnap Kissinger" buttons and one of them remained his friend for years. In fact, colleagues often commented he was nicer to his enemies than his friends.

Because with friends all you have to do is maintain. With enemies you have to convert.

It takes a little work. Spend as much time with your cracked colleague as you can stomach. Learn about her hopes, dreams, aspirations, home life, where she wants to go for vacation.

Don't overdo it. It is possible to "over-befriend" one of these toxic characters; suddenly you're having lunch with her every day and she's trying to persuade you to go on surveillance missions with her.

Befriend her just to the point where she would feel guilty selling you out. Try to ensure the information flows mostly in one direction: from her to you. Usually I find these types of characters love nothing more than to talk about themselves and aren't really all that interested in anything you might have to say, anyway.

Which is good. Slowly accumulate information as you spray a sort of neutralizing foam of friendliness around her, a foam that slowly hardens into an immobilizing acrylic.

Information is power.

Meanwhile, as any career counsellor worth the stock his or her card is printed on will tell you, you should always, always be keeping your resumé in circulation, networking and plotting your next move.

There are good offices out there, where you can both do good work and have fun with your colleagues. I've seen them with my own two eyes. You just have to close your eyes, click your heels together, and believe.

WAXING TOXIC

Of course, it's easier to deal with toxic behaviour when it's a colleague, an "equal," someone on the same rung as you, power-wise.

When a boss starts to wax toxic, it's harder to know what to do. We said, previously, we will discuss times when it's appropriate to fight back. This is one of those times:

THE QUESTION

I recently went for a waxing, and on the morning of my appointment, my aesthetician called me and asked if she could change the time. No problem, I told her. She recently moved to a new salon downtown whose owner is, to put it kindly, a raging psychopathic witch who makes herself feel better by bullying and demeaning her staff. But once I got there, she told me the owner had yelled at her for ten minutes after the call, shrieking the whole time that she was incompetent, stupid, and inconsiderate to her client.

On my way out, the owner lit into my aesthetician again in front of me and several other clients, screaming at her and accusing her of undermining her and the business.

It only got uglier from there.

My aesthetician called me that evening to apologize and told me that she plans to leave at the end of the month.

I'd really love to have good triumph over evil, but what can I do?

THE ANSWER

First, despite any sanctimonious lip-flap you might've heard to the contrary, I firmly believe we live in a culture that not only condones but even celebrates bullies and bullying bosses.

"You're fired," Donald Trump smirks, his ludicrous comb-over practically twitching with *Schadenfreude* as he dispatches another would-be mogul on *The Apprentice*.

"The tribe has spoken," Jeff Probst intones, extinguishing the torch of hope for yet another *Survivor* contestant who has proved "weak" or "useless," and who must immediately leave the island without a word or backward glance.

Or what about *Hell's Kitchen*? Have you checked out this *bleep!*-ing show? As he puts his wannabe-chefs through their paces, Gordon Ramsay is not only a bully. He acts like a man teetering on the precipice of a full-blown psychotic "break."

He screams, throws plates, kicks garbage cans in his fury at the incompetence of his kitchen minions. And what a potty-mouth! He turns the air blue with his expletives. Every other word is bleeped.

"Ah, Sharon, these *bleep!*-ing scallops are *bleep!*-ing disgusting!" he'll scream – then spit the offending mollusks into the garbage, or dash the plate to the floor, or both. Or he might press the plate of food onto the front of an underling's chef jacket, so it leaves a huge, embarrassing stain the minion has to wear for the rest of the show.

Culturally speaking, I believe we've turned a corner with *Hell's Kitchen* – and not in a good way. What's next? Chef Ramsay pulls a gun out of his chef jacket: "Ah, Jennifah, this *bleep!*-ing risotto's undah-cooked!" *Blam! Blam!*

But you're probably wondering when I'm going to get to your *bleep!*-ing question.

I will say this: from a legal standpoint, your aesthetician friend is lucky to live in Canada. In the United States, it's pretty much: "Tough luck, get another job."

Here she has some legal recourse. In the past few years, the courts in this country have been sending a powerful message to employers that bullying bosses are not acceptable.

For example, in 2006, after an RCMP officer testified her hard-ass ex-military boss yelled and screamed at her ("Open your fucking eyes and look at the books!" he once bellowed at her) so much that the pregnant officer became ill, a B.C. court awarded her a settlement of nearly (and here I want you to imagine me bringing my pinkie up to the corner of my mouth here, and twisting it, Dr. Evil-style) one million dollars.

Now true, the largesse of the settlement was intended to compensate for the fact she was so scarred and damaged she could not continue to work in the foreseeable future. And that doesn't sound like the case with your aesthetician.

Still, according to Toronto employment lawyer Janice Rubin, she can sue for "constructive dismissal" – one of these misleading legal misnomers with which lawyers love to stuff their briefs (so their briefs will seem to be bulging with gravitas) that actually means: the atmosphere in the workplace became so intolerable you were driven to leave – it was as if you were fired.

And "constructive dismissal" cases carry damages, same as if you'd been fired. In the case of your friend, these damages may not amount to much. And your friend may not feel like hiring a lawyer at this moment. They're *bleep!*-ing expensive.

But a lawyer's a good thing for her to have in her corner in this circumstance. The only way to get a bully to back off is to sic an even bigger bully on him. Or, to put it another way, that's what lawyers are for.

Something like 60 per cent of people leave their jobs soon after being targeted by a bully.

Sadly, your friend appears to be one of that number, but she doesn't have to go gentle out that front door. She should stand up to the bully.

Even a letter from a lawyer, "educating the employer," as Ms. Rubin dryly puts it, "as to where the lines are drawn and how she crossed them," would, I predict, bring this sadistic salonista up short.

Bullies are usually cowards underneath, as we all know: she'll probably be quaking in her pumps, thinking, "What with the damages and the legal fees, I could wind up losing my business."

And if that were to come to pass (this would be sweet), your aesthetician could conceivably swoop in, with her savings or perhaps a consortium of investors, and snap it up herself.

I know that's a long shot, a far-fetched scenario.

But still, wouldn't that be an excellent *"Bleep* you!" to a bullying former boss?

NOT-SO-CONSTRUCTIVE DISMISSAL

Okay, so you did everything in your power to avoid problems and E.F.S.; you coated crazy colleagues in a neutralizing foam of friendliness; you fought back against toxic bosses; you kept your head down but your chin up, did a great job, played the game – but it still didn't work. Someone in the hierarchy decided the Old [Your Name Here] Magic just wasn't working for them, any more: therefore, you wouldn't be working for them, any more, either.

It's not the end of the world, sunshine. Keep fighting, keep moving the brand forward. Whatever doesn't kill you makes you stronger, remember that.

THE QUESTION

I was dismissed from a job I had for six years; I signed a non-disclosure form. To make a long story short, we settled out of court and now I'm looking for work. Most of the potential employers I've been in touch with request a reference from a past supervisor, and although I had bosses at my last job who would provide me with one, they are bound by this non-disclosure agreement and just can't do it. Needless to say, I am out of luck. How does one recover from being fired from a job and what do I tell my future employers without making them suspicious?

THE ANSWER

This is an excellent question, perfect Damage Control material, but a little outside the comfort zone of my skill set. So I took the liberty of enlisting the assistance of a certain Ralph Shedletsky, the chief operating officer of Knightsbridge Human Capital Solutions. Mr. Shedletsky is outstanding in the field of helping people deal with "being let go."*

Señor Shedletsky and I discussed your case, and agreed you left out a few crucial details from your question, e.g., why you were fired in the first place, why you had to sign this mysterious "non-disclosure" agreement, and how long you've been out of work. But working with what you've given us, he came up with some very helpful and, I thought, quite encouraging observations and suggestions.

He said, first of all, the world has changed and being terminated no longer carries the stigma it used to, so "stop acting like it does." (The one time in our discussion he sounded quite stern.) People are fired all the time for all kinds of reasons these days, mostly having nothing to do with performance. The shame we feel upon being fired is

---

* Curious euphemism, that, I've always thought: because so often it contains a kernel of truth. The person is often secretly chomping on the bit for release; also, because of the implication of ownership and constraint. It's what you'd say to a slave: "We're going to let you go. Now – *run!*"

purely vestigial, a holdover from a former era when it was a lot harder to lose your job.

That's deeply true, I thought. I recall another job I was fired from – another TV job. I was working as a lowly writer for a morning TV talk show called *The Gill Deacon Show*. The show wasn't bad, she was a crusading ultra-environmentalist and smarter, probably, than your average TV talk-show host.

But our ratings were in the toilet; no one was watching. On a good day, maybe 16,000 people watched, which just isn't enough eyeballs.

The network needed at least one more zero after the 16 – so one day, the executive producer called all thirty-five people who worked for *The Gill Deacon Show* and said, in effect: "Thanks for the hard work, but you're all out."

That time I knew without a doubt it wasn't personal: they were all enjoying my work and also That Dave Eddie Feeling™ people get when I'm around.

But still . . . I found myself squirming as I broke the news to my father and then, later, to my father-in-law.

My father, a former tenured professor, would have had to commit an act of "moral turpitude" to lose his job.

My father-in-law entered the banking profession at age twenty-two or thereabouts and stayed in the same company, moving steadily upward, until he retired at age fifty-five.

How could a man of that generation be expected to assimilate the two seemingly contradictory concepts that the dude married to his daughter was: (a) supposedly well-liked, hard-working, and talented; (b) out on his keister?

Mr. Shedletsky, an old pro at hearing tales of woe, listened to my soliloquy, then said simply and soothingly, "If he were to enter the profession of banking today, it would be a world he would simply not recognize."

Bankers are fired in droves now, Mr. Shedletsky said. Like all professions, theirs has become much more unstable.

No offence to bankers, but I found this to be quite reassuring, if not downright uplifting, information. If even bankers are sweating in their pinstripe suits and shaking in their Gucci loafers about losing their jobs, then truly all humanity is on its way to becoming one.

Anyway, the point is this: don't be afraid to admit in interviews that you were let go. Especially in this day and age.

If your old boss won't give you a recommendation, ask a co-worker. Usually, Mr. Shedletsky says, by the time they're asking for a recommendation the job is yours to lose – or, at least, they're "very interested." Often anyone familiar with your work will suffice.

Which is why you have to rock the interview in the first place. Or, as Pam puts it, "be good in the room." Be confident. Believe. That counts for a lot.

Above all, don't get discouraged. Mr. Shedletsky draws the analogy of personal relationships, of hunting for a girlfriend.

"If you were to pick out ten women at a bar randomly and tell them you've decided they were the one for you, you wouldn't have much luck, would you?"* "It's the same with looking for work. The equation has to work on both sides."

Good point, but if I, the layman, may offer one slightly dissenting thought here: in this analogy you are the drunken

---

* I thought, but didn't say, "You just pretty much described my twenties, and it worked for me once in a while." I let him continue.

bachelor and the company you hope to work for is the bombshellicious babe. Which, for most of us, for most of our lives, is probably an apt analogy for how it goes.

But I think it's important, too, as time goes on, to build your personal "brand." A lot of us lose ourselves in the protective shell, or maybe I should say the rut, of a job, and forget we were hired for a reason, as a commodity, and we need always to remind ourselves to continually hone our "transferable skills" and keep them sharp.

Then one day, or at least this is the hope, your work will speak for itself and you will no longer be beholden to any former boss for a recommendation. And that's the golden ideal, right? To be completely independent, just to say: "Hello, I'm [your name here]," and everyone would know exactly what was meant, and implied, by the simple statement of your name.

Like Brad Pitt. He doesn't have to circulate his resumé. All he has to say is: "Hi, I'm Brad Pitt." And people say: You're hired! How's $15,000,000 sound, for a few weeks' work? "I'll have to get back to you." Thank you, Mr. Pitt, for even considering our offer!

And at that point – call it The Pitt Point – you can tear up, or set fire to, or perhaps we should simply say delete, your resume. You made it, baby!

YOUR TAKEAWAY DOGGIE-BAG OF THOUGHTS

- **Getting canned happens to good people.** Don't let it faze you; it could be a stepping stone to an even brighter future. Be confident. Believe. That will count for a lot.

- **Don't talk about how hard you work; keep your head down, do your work. People will notice.** (Although we do admit it doesn't hurt to have a bit of an "aggrieved air" at the office, especially when the boss is around: people do seem impressed by an aggrieved air, and tend to think you're maybe busier than you are.)

- **Having said that, don't make the rookie mistake of trying to be "above it all."** When it comes to office politics the office Regans and Gonerils will bring you down faster than the statue of a deposed dictator in the town square.

- **It doesn't hurt to bring your skills to the attention of the Big Cheese: however, he/she is not the only one to impress.** Don't ignore the rank and file or they will TAKE YOU DOWN LIKE NIXON.

- **Keep your friends close and enemies closer.** Neutralize potential rivals with a slowly hardening foam of fake friendliness. Do not only not avoid, but actually *glom onto* the office bore. They, like the cockroach, have usually survived for a reason and will probably even protect you in times of trouble.

- **Put down that drink and slowly back away from the office hottie.** If you *are* the office hottie, why not try looking outside the office for romance? Basically, everyone, at work: keep all your bits inside your clothing, at the office, anyway. Otherwise it could have a deleterious impact upon your career longevity.

- **In professions, as with mates, it really helps if you choose right in the first place.** But if you really feel like you haven't, don't waste time kicking yourself. Cut bait and fish elsewhere, the sooner the better. You'll be happier in the long run.

DAMAGE CONTROL ON THE SOCIAL CIRCUIT

"The evening's a wonderful time, isn't it, Alex boy?"
— MR. DELTOID, *A Clockwork Orange*

"When we remember we are all mad, the mysteries
disappear and life stands explained."

— MARK TWAIN

CREATURE OF THE NIGHT

"I should like to know which is worse," says the Old Woman
in Voltaire's *Candide*, "to be raped a hundred times by
Negro pirates, to have a buttock cut off, to run the gauntlet
among the Bulgarians, to be whipped and flogged in an
auto da fe, to be dissected, to row in a galley . . . or to remain
here doing nothing?"

Throughout my twenties and a good chunk into my
thirties, that pretty much summed up how I felt, too. During
that era I would rather eat urinal mints washed down with
Buckley's cough syrup than sit home in my apartment,
alone like an owl, staring at the four walls and my oversized laminated poster of Michael Jordan stretching out
his arms.

So I went out, baby! I discovered the joys of socializing at age of fifteen, when I crashed my first party (held by some older kids: I wasn't invited). I started going out more and more. I would say that from the age of nineteen, when I left home (for university), to the age of thirty-one, when I finally met Pam, I would say that with a couple of dozen exceptions,* I went out *every single night of my life.*

I would have gone to the opening of an escalator,† a greenhouse, an outhouse. I turned down nothing but my collar.

The only thing I loved more than going out was the feeling, the rush, of *getting ready to go out.*

The thrill of anticipation. You alone in apartment. Pour Scotch on rocks. Put throbbing, pumping music on stereo. Try on one shirt – no good! Try on other shirt – no good! Try on another shirt – looking good!

Hips twitching to music, sipping Scotch, pointing to the man in the mirror and saying stuff like: "Two minutes for looking so good!" And: "Creature . . . of the night!" And: "This hick burgh's gonna *explode* under my pressure!"

---

* Each of which I felt keenly, with great pain. I remember one in particular: maybe I was twenty-seven, twenty-eight, it was a Friday night, and a friend phoned late. I picked up the phone and she asked: "What are *you* doing home?" I had no answer for her. I, who supposedly had numerous friends, had nothing to do and nowhere to go. No one had invited me anywhere. I was just sitting home, doing nothing. It was embarrassing.

† That's not even hyperbole. I did go to the opening of an escalator, once, in a high-end shopping mall. It was a pretty good party, actually. There were a lot of hoity-toity society types there, quite a few top-shelf babes, the canapés were delicious, and there was even free wine!

Then turn off lights in apartment, head down stairs –
don't forget to lock the front door! – and out into the night.

I loved that feeling, too: the feeling that I was *disappear-
ing into the night.* I was a creature of the night throughout
my teens, and twenties, and into my thirties.

Daytime was . . . well, I wouldn't go so far as to call it
merely a transitional interlude, during that era, a jumble of
hours simply to be endured until night rolled around again.
I had my ambitions (to pay rent by writing), and many
things I was hoping to accomplish in the daylight hours, as
well. But the emphasis, the point of my life, was definitely
all bound up in what took place after the sun set (I justified
all the drunken shenanigans and skirt-chasing as my writer's
"material").

And then right on into the wee hours: "All the *good stuff*
happens after midnight," as we used to say.

Socializing, as I now know, is primo Damage Control
country, a minefield of faux pas, zingers, everyone taking
your measure. . . .

Of course, I didn't pay much attention to that in those
days of yore. Going out was all about getting wasted and
getting laid! I was pretty much "au naturel" back then. A
social savage . . .

And I loved the shenanigans. Oh, Lordy, how I loved the
shenanigans.

Only anyone who has ever run with a "band of brothers"-type crew of nefarious villains and ne'er-do-wells in
their twenties can have any idea what I'm talking about.

Some of them (the shenanigans, that is) were dumb,

Lord knows. But I still giggle myself to sleep, sometimes, when I think about them.

Grown men climbing out of the windows of sexy women's apartments, tiptoeing down roofs, jumping onto the shrubbery, cursing in the night. Grown women popping their tops off at parties (which I loved, and sadly lament the passing of this phenomenon in my life), and dancing in their brassieres, while wriggling in time to the music on the dance floor, shouting out "Yow!" and "Yew!" as if they were being jabbed by invisible pitchforks (similar to the metaphorical ones, I suppose, we were all being jabbed by).

MELTING LIKE CHEESE INTO THE CROWD

One of my all-time favourite shenanigans, though, one that still causes me to snicker down the sleeve of my pyjamas, in the middle of the night, when I can't sleep, was a relatively minor incident; and I didn't even witness it personally.*

A friend of some friends of mine – call him "J" – was stumbling down the stairs at a football game, in a sudsy stupor, balancing a beer in one hand and a pizza slice on a paper plate in the other, when suddenly he tripped and accidentally pressed the pizza slice onto the back of some random (and fairly huge-seeming) guy's expensive-looking cashmere coat.

* This incident was originally recorded in the funniest unpublished novel I've ever read, entitled, I think, *Untitled*, written by a certain David Akerly.

For some reason the cashmere-coated guy didn't feel the slice being pressed to his back. (Perhaps he was enjoying a festive, sports-fan stupor of his own?)

And like a weird kind of anti-miracle, the slice just stuck there, cheesily clinging to the guy's back.

Now, obviously the noble way to go in this circumstance would have been to tap the huge guy in the cashmere coat on the shoulder and say: "Pardon me, old chap, but it is my unfortunate duty to inform you that I have, unwittingly and without meaning to, pressed my pizza slice into the back of your obviously fine, dry-clean-only garment. My deepest apologies and regrets. I am horribly, terribly sorry. Here is my card. Please send me your dry-cleaning bill as soon as you get it and I will make instantaneous reparations. Once again, I'm awfully, deeply, *personally* sorry about this terrible mishap and ask you only to attribute it to clumsiness and possibly a soupçon of intoxication on my part; but I assure you nothing could have been farther from my intentions than for this unfortunate incident to have taken place."

But "J" didn't go that way.

Instead, he stood, swaying, for what seemed like a long moment, staring with glassy-eyed beer-googles and an almost . . . childlike wonderment, and incredulity, at the miraculous way the cheesy, saucy, pepperoni-dotted triangle remained affixed to the guy's back; and then, with a guilty look, he melted, like cheese in a 600-degree oven, into the crowd.

Which is, allow us to reiterate, absolutely the wrong and the contraindicated thing to do in the situation described above.

But I confess, folks, when I think back on the incident, when I picture that pizza slice clinging with cheesy tenacity to the back of the unsuspecting dude's coat – well, I've been chuckling myself to sleep over that one for nearly twenty years.

DON'T TURN ON THE LIGHT!

And I, David Eddie, was not incapable of the odd shenanigan myself.

Once I was at a party or gathering at the home of a certain Mary Jo Eustace, noTORIous, now, as the ex-wife of reality-TV thingamajig* Dean McDermott.

Mr. McDermott dumped Ms. Eustace for Tori Spelling, of *Beverly Hills 90210*/daughter-of-Aaron-Spelling fame, just as Mr. McDermott and Ms. Eustace were adopting a second child – an era of her life about which Ms. Eustace has published a volume of her recollections, observations, and reflections, entitled *Divorce Sucks: What to Do When Irreconcilable Differences, Lawyer Fees, and Your Ex's Hollywood Wife Make You Miserable.*†

---

* Well, how am I supposed to refer to the bizarre, uniquely modern nexus of nonentity and celebrity this man occupies and embodies? "Reality TV . . . actor?" Hardly. "Reality TV . . . star?" No, that actually hurts. He is, as his IMDb profile says, "best known . . . for his marriage to Tori Spelling," and their various reality shows about same. So what is he? Who knows?

† These how-to books are getting so *specific*, these days, you ever notice?

But this was long before any of that happened, long before Mary Jo met Mr. McDermott, or Ms. Spelling, or wrote a book, or anything.

Back then, we were all just fresh-faced, innocent kids* in our mid-twenties. Life hadn't really started happening to us yet. Mary Jo still lived with her parents, in their elegant townhouse in a swish, fashionable part of downtown Toronto; she was dating a friend of mine, a certain Scott, also known as "the Maestro," for his chilled-out demeanour and masterful navigation of all thorny social situations (he should be writing this chapter, not me).

Anyway, we were sitting in the dark in her living room, by candlelight, for some reason that I don't remember. I suppose to create an elegant, romantic atmosphere.

A gesture that wound up kind of . . . backfiring, thanks to me. At one point I went out in the backyard to smoke a cigarette. And I must have stepped in . . . something.

Something warm; and brown; and fresh . . .

After I finished my cigarette, out back, I returned to the living room and the spot on the couch I'd occupied before. But then, after a while, in the candlelit semi-darkness, as we were all chatting and sipping wine, my nostril-hairs began to detect an unmistakable, one-of-a-kind, accept-no-imitations odour: doggie doo-doo.

"Good Lord, that's revolting," I remember thinking. "But what's that disgusting smell doing in the well-appointed living room of this fashionable townhouse?"

---

* Well, all except Mary Jo. She was a wised-up wiseacre even back then.

It took me a while, but eventually it came to me: "Oh, no. The . . . horror . . ."

And then I did a dumb thing. Poor damage control!* (Like I said, I was a "social savage," a bumpkin.) I tried, almost literally, to cover my tracks. While everyone else was innocently chatting, I sidled, as if casually, under cover of the candle-lit semi-darkness, over to the fire-place, and scraped the bottom of my shoes on the brick, hoping that, when it all came out, when the stinking, steaming reality of what happened "hit the fan," the horri-ble stench wafting around the room would not be attribut-able to me.

This was before I realized (a) my whole life was laid out for the amusement and entertainment of some divine and/or quite possibly infernal figure, or a rare collaboration between the two;† (b) people will always sniff out the truth, sooner or later – especially if it smells like dogshit.

Sure enough, after a while, one of the group sniffed and said, in the crepuscular, candlelit semi-darkness: "Can anyone else smell that?"

"I know, it's gross," someone else chimed in. "I've been smelling it for a while!"

"It smells like dogshit!" someone else said.

---

* Remember Rule No. 1: What's done is done and can't be undone/The sands of time, they can't un-run, etc.

† Jehovah and Beelzebub sitting on a celestial couch, munching pop-corn together, arms around each other's shoulders, having set aside ancient differences to enjoy my antics, laughing until the tears stream down their cheeks.

Mary Jo stood up, obviously to hit the lights. Just then I had a horrible realization: that a track of shit-prints probably led straight to me; then to the fireplace; then back to me; and that if the lights came on I would unmistakably be identified as the culprit, the guilty party, *el hombre culpable.**

All this occurred to me in the split second when Mary Jo was reaching for the light switch . . .

Which is why, without really thinking, I cried out, in a strangulated voice: "Wait! *Don't turn on the light!*"

But of course, in that exact moment Mary Jo snapped on the light, and there, like something from out of a cartoon, it was: a trail of shitty footsteps leading, first to me; then to the fireplace, where it became obvious to everyone I'd tried, in a vain effort to exculpate myself, to scrape the offending load off the bottom of my shoe; then back to where I had been sitting, in the dark, hoping no one else would notice the smell.

Busted! Oh, that one took a long time to live down, ladies and gentlemen.

"Don't turn on the light!" became a catchphrase people used whenever they felt guilty about anything and were afraid of being found out.

So one person might say to another: "Hey, someone saw you making out with Alison Stephens at a party on the weekend. Aren't you worried [your girlfriend] Priscilla might find out?"

"Don't turn on the light!" the other person would say.

---

* A "macaronic" linguistic mash-up. Please forgive.

And everyone would glance over at me – then burst out laughing.

For, like, *ten years*.

They never let me forget that one.

Oh, no. It was way too good, way too juicy. I wore that one, like a giant gold chain with a huge clock suspended from it, a pendant of shame and horror, around my neck, for a long, long time.

URBAN HERMIT

And, hey, it was all good, clean fun (well, maybe Ms. Eustace might not have seen it that way: she was probably on the blower to the carpet-steamer rental company first thing the next morning, frantically praying they'd be open on a Sunday); knockabout, roustabout stuff; the type of thing you expect and maybe even hope for in a certain era of your life.

But lately, I don't know, I guess I'm just not feeling as into that type of stuff as I used to be. Guess I'm getting old. These days, if a friend of mine were to press a pizza slice into some guy's cashmere coat, at a football game, then melt into the crowd, I'm not sure I'd even find it all that funny!

Sad but true. Something's happening to me. Once one of the most social of characters, lately I'm more like an urban hermit, a recluse.

For like, the last twenty years, every day, upon awakening, I, a man of repetition and routine, have always had the same thought: "What shall we have for dinner tonight?"

But lately, to my surprise and chagrin, a second thought has obtruded into my cranium upon awakening.

And that thought is: "Do I have to see anyone today?"

And if the answer is "No," then I can feel my spirits lift. If it's "yes," then they sink.

Maybe it's just all the work I've had to get done, lately. My plate's been piled as high as a sumo wrestler's at a luau.

And when you've got a lot to do, deadlines looming, and you go out – I don't know, maybe it's just me, but you feel twitchy and jonesy and off and not really able to contribute much to the festive spirit of the gathering. Always checking your watch and feeling antsy and uncomfortable – and with a bit of an edge.

And, of course, people sense your discomfort; so they try to make a little conversation with you.

They ask about your work.

Very natural. But that just makes it worse, only exacerbates the problem for the out-on-the-town workaholic! Like, for example, in the final stages of the preparation of this book, I kept my head down and pretty much worked night and day for a period of several months.

But, every once in a while – mostly because I was worried if we didn't go out once in a while, Pam would go stir-crazy and start going out to parties by herself and start dirty-dancing some random, Viggo-Mortenson-looking dude (him doing jiu-jitsu "air chops" on the dance floor, tattoos flashing) – Pam and I would get dressed up and go over to a friend's house.

And I'd be sitting there all twitchy and weird, thinking "Man, I should really be working on my book. I can't social-ize like this, I've got a deadline. No, no; take it easy, Dave. You're here to have fun. Don't be an idiot. Just relax, and enjoy." At which point someone would invariably ask: "So,

Dave, how's it going with your book deadline? Are you going to make it?"

And everyone would go all quiet, and turn to me: eyebrows bobbing up and down; smirking; shooting me querying, slightly pitying looks. All expectant. Could it be that Dave will fuck it up? If so, I need to get to a phone asap and disseminate this information to all and sundry, prontissimo. I need to "go wide" with this news.

Me wanting to grab them and knock their coconuts together, like Moe of The Three Stooges, and scream: "You fiends! I wrestled in a dark, sulphurous pit with my demons to take a break from those very labours so I could even come out at all tonight! I was hoping to seek refuge, to escape from having to think about my fucking deadline, and now that's all you want to talk about? You're assassins! All of you!"*

Of course, I didn't say that. They were just trying to be nice. But the fact that I even wanted to grab my dear, beloved friends and knock their coconuts together and scream out "You're assassins! All of you!" . . . well, obviously, that wouldn't be a good look for me. So mostly, these days, I just stay home and mind my own business, read and/or write and/or moodily sip a Scotch in front of the fire, and keep my mouth shut, when I feel oppressed by things I want to get done.

———

* This last bit is one of my favourite lines. It's what 1909 Tour De France winner Octavio Lapize supposedly screamed at race officials on getting to the top of a particularly punishing mountain-leg of the race: "You're assassins! All of you!"

Call me a curmudgeon, but the other inescapable observation I've had about going out, recently, is it just isn't as fun as it used to be.

I mean, I exempt my close friends. I can't remember who it was who said he wanted to "retire on the shady side of forty with a few choice friends," but that definitely sums up how I'm feeling these days.

I like small gatherings: dinner parties, sitting around a living room with four or five people.

When the numbers get a bit bigger – well, I've already filled you in on my Tourettic, blurtaceous, faux-pas-filled tendencies at larger gatherings.

But also I've begun to notice what zinger-meisters, underminers, interrupters, snobs, bores, and long-winded, self-important gasbags most *other* people also are. What a festival of irritation so many social gatherings have become, when you stand back and examine them with a cold eye.

Maybe it's just me, but sometimes it seems like even when people are complimenting you, out on the social circuit, they're working hard to dig the old knife in.

RETURN "INSULTIMENTS" WITH "APOLOBUKES"

THE QUESTION

I've always been heavy. Recently I lost quite a bit of weight, and have kept it off, through a simple regimen of walking and watching what I eat. The problem is some people are complimenting me too much. I know that might be hard to understand. But one friend in particular is over the top.

Every time I see her, she focuses on how fat I once was, how much "better" I look, to the point where I want to slap her. Last time I ran into her, I flipped out and told her that I thought she was way out of line and super-insulting. I know it was ungracious, but I had to say something. She hasn't talked to me since; and the last time I saw her walking in the park, she turned away from me, laughing about something with a gaggle of her skinny friends. Can I apologize to her without backing away from my convictions?

THE ANSWER

Ah, the "insultiment."

I'm familiar with it. Certain people love to candy-coat their obnoxious, unsolicited observations in a sugary shell of flattery.

Not too long ago I purchased a pair of giant, goggle-like glasses and was test-driving them around town, to see what sort of reaction they got. One of the "regulars" at my local, whom I know a little, zeroed in when he spotted them glinting in the half-light of the bar.

"I like your glasses," he said.

"Thanks."

"Yeah, they suit your face. And they kind of balance off all the weight you've gained lately."

From behind the enormous windshield-like lenses of my glasses, lenses that look like they need little wipers attached to them, I stared at him, speechless.

It was weird. I could not think of a single thing to say. I was so zinged I was tongue-tied, speechless; I could not think of a single snappy retort.

(Brilliant, witty, verbally dexterous writer, master of repartee and man-about-town that I am, I retorted with the following dazzling riposte: "Uh . . . thanks.")*

Now, I know many people kick themselves for not being able to come up with a snappy counter-zinger in these moments.

You just stand there, mute, and blinking, like an idiot. Only later does the perfect comeback occur: "Damn, I wish I'd said . . ."

The French call this phenomenon *l'esprit de l'escalier*, "the wit of the staircase." It refers to the moment the riposte to that insufferable guy's obnoxious crack at the party hits you – just as you're descending the stairs, leaving the party.†

Me, though, I think the reflex that paralyzes our larynxes in these moments is a good thing, a gift from above. See, 99 per cent of the stuff that might emanate from our pie-holes in these situations might satisfy our wounded vanity but would only escalate matters and lead to all kinds of further ugliness and damage, and that's no good.

In the case of my little friend and his insultiment about my glasses and weight, I just thanked him, as I said above, semi-moronically, then gave him a hearty clap on the back

---

* You know what I've decided recently actually makes a handy, all-purpose comeback for almost any kind of social situation? "Touché." No matter what insult or crack or zinger the other person lays upon you, all you have to do is say "touché," and you're out of there.

† A quintessentially Gallic, quintessentially *Parisian* expression, I feel, because it assumes not only that your friend lives in an apartment, but that it's a walk-up.

– okay, maybe it was a bit of a teeth-rattler, but hey, I'm only human – and said, "See you later."

I'm glad I didn't say anything else.

I'm also glad I didn't do anything else. He's a little elfin, troll-like, non-magical leprechaun of a man; I'm easily twice his size and double his weight. And for a split second felt a powerful impulse to lift him up and hang him on one of the bar's coat hooks, so no matter how much he wiggled his arms and legs he wouldn't be able to get down.

But I didn't – I suppressed this urge, thank God.

And you shouldn't say or do anything in these types of situations, either, ladies and gentlemen.

React with sublime mildness to all rudeness. Powerful, self-assured people, in my view, never freak out, never lose their tempers, never get involved in day-ruining exchanges with random insultiment-mongers or other assorted underminers or confounding confrontationalists.

When presented with obnoxious behaviour in all its myriad forms (and it seems to be on the rise lately, doesn't it, dear reader, in the gyms, at the bars, on the streets, at work? Or maybe it just seems that way), strong, grounded people just smile bemusedly with a slight forehead crinkle, as if to say to their interlocutors: "Ha, ha, you're quite a character, aren't you? Quite a 'loose cannon,' hey? Ha-ha-ha [checking your watch], well, I'm late for a meeting of sane, normal, non-passive-aggressive people, so, ha-ha-ha, good luck with all *that* . . ."

And edge away.

In your case, though, since you've already lost your temper, and you regret it – but also still have a point you'd like to make – why not return your friend's "insultiment" with an "apolobuke"?

(Apology + rebuke = apolobuke.)

Here's how it works. You spin a fluffy floss of syrupy-sweet apology around your real message. Something like: "Listen, I'm sorry I freaked out on you the other day. I know you were just trying to compliment me and I had no business going off on you like that. I guess I'm still sensitive about how heavy I used to be, and when you would go on and on about it, it would make me realize what a negative assess-ment everyone had of me back then. I mean, here I was assuming people were mostly judging me by my personal-ity and accomplishments. I always forget how much some people focus on the physical stuff. Anyway, again, sorry I was upset. I know you were just trying to be nice."

She should get the hint.

If not, well, you know there's no law that says you have to stop and talk to everyone you bump into.

When you see her coming, don't break stride. Just smile and wave and say: "Hey, Cindy, how're you doing?"

If her steps slow when she sees you, or she stops and turns, just say, in super-friendly fashion: "Hey, I'd love to chat, but I have to go."

And keep on briskly walking.

Remember: Briskly walking is how you got so svelte in the first place. In this case, by not breaking stride, the ben-efits you reap are twofold.

You are avoiding a passive-aggressive freak-show "frenemy" who's just going to undermine you and pop your balloon and make you feel rotten.

(Such people are like kryptonite; the secret of success is to avoid them and stick with positive people.)

And you're burning calories. Speaking of which, I gotta go. Gotta hit the gym. Guess that little punk's crack got to me after all.

THE "QUESTIONSULT/QUESTI-BURN" – A VARIANT

Recently I've come across an interesting variant on the "insultiment": the "questionsult" or "questi-burn."

The term comes courtesy of a friend of Pam's from around the neighbourhood, the mother of a kid who comes over and plays with our kids quite a bit.

Now, don't get me wrong. This is a person I like. She's cute and bubbly and smart and funny.

In any case, one evening she came by to pick up her kid and wound up staying over for dinner. I had some fresh sage our boys' part-time caregiver Shahnaz had brought from her garden, so I decided to make saltimbocca, chicken breasts stuffed with prosciutto, sage, and provolone.

So I, the family chef,* start cooking dinner, while the girls sit at the kitchen table, sipping white wine and chatting: a pleasant, peaceful urban scene.

Then little Miss Questiburn starts peppering me and Pam with questions, always in a very "interested/fascinated" tone of voice:

Interested/fascinated, staring at my ankles: "Dave, tell me: how do men decide, when they're wearing shorts, to

---

* I'm the cook. Pam can *maybe* fry a steak, bake a potato, and boil some green beans on the stove, in a pinch, or if I go away on a trip: for some perverse reason I'm proud of this fact.

wear their socks all pulled up tight like that – as opposed to scrunched down a little?"

Presented as a "fascinating question" on the differences between the genders.

I fumbled for an answer: "Uh, well, I guess I never really thought about it . . . one way or another . . . when I was, uh, getting dressed this morning . . ."

Meanwhile, Pam leaps up, comes over, and, seeming a little embarrassed (on my behalf), crouches down, and starts scrunching down my socks a little: "Yeah, you know, you shouldn't wear them pulled up so tight, with shorts, like that, Dave." Scrunch, scrunch.

A few moments later, patting Murphy, Little Miss Sock-Scrunchy turned to Pam and asked, bright-eyed, in interested/fascinated tones: "How often do you wash your dog?"

Pam: "Why? Does he stink?"

"Oh, no-ho-ho, not exactly!" Miss Questiburn said, brightly. "It's just sort of a funky, 'natural' smell!"

(Later, Pam told me, Miss Questiburn, peering into Pam's messy closet, asked brightly, in interested/fascinated tones: "How often do you do laundry?")

Then, later, when I'm pounding out the chicken cutlets for saltimbocca, Miss Questiburn asked, interested/fascinated: "So, is that how you always handle raw chicken?"

Me: "Uh, yeah, why?"

Miss Questiburn, brightly: "Well, it's probably for the best! Your children are probably developing all kinds of immunities that other children don't have!"

Although pressing the "bad dad" button usually makes me see red, I let that one slide. After all, she was a guest in my home and for some reason wasn't really bugging me.

Just kind of making me laugh. She has a . . . pixie-ish demeanour; that may have helped.

But then, a few seconds later, as I pounded the chicken, true, a little piece shot off the chopping board and landed on the floor.

"Ha-ha-ha!" Miss Questiburn laughed with a "tinkling of merry little bells" type of laugh. "Do you realize pieces of raw chicken are flying all over the room?"

And in a flash I could *see* her retelling this anecdote to her friends: "He was wearing shorts with his socks pulled up all tight and pieces of raw chicken were flying everywhere while he cooked! Men are so hopeless, aren't they?"

That's when I finally snapped. Me: "That's it! Everyone out of the kitchen!"

For the record, I always wash my hands and everything else in the vicinity both before and after handling raw chicken. I'm not exactly sure what Miss Questiburn was referring to, though it's possible too she may have had a point.

And, truth be told, her "questi-burns" were kind of funny, in a way; almost . . . charming, once you brushed aside the low-level irritation they provoked.

They were . . . charmnoying, let's say, while we're sitting around coining words.

And, hey, I got something out of it, too. (Rule No. 2: **Learn, baby, learn**.) Every time I wear shorts, now, I hear her interested/fascinated voice in my head, asking brightly: "I see you're wearing shorts today: is that how you're going to wear your socks with them – all pulled up, like that? I'm just interested!"

And I always remember to scrunch them down.

TRANSLATING THE DUDE CODE

Have you ever heard the saying "The opposite of a great truth is another great truth"?

If that's true,* and if we can safely say "insults are annoying," then we must consider the possibility the following two opposing statements are also true:

   1. "Insults can be fun, funny, and even . . . helpful."

   2. "Under certain circumstances, even the most enthusiastic, heartfelt compliments can be distressing."

Let's consider Statement 1 first.

THE QUESTION

My friend's girlfriend came home early when we were playing poker at his house and was horrified by the way we talk to him. It's true we ride him quite a bit, but it's all in good fun (well, mostly: some of it can be a little harsh, I admit). She stormed in, called us all "jerks," and broke up the poker game. A few days later we got an e-mail saying she did not appreciate our "puerile insults" and disrespect. Now he's been hard to get in touch with and we suspect she's told him he can't hang with us any more. We were just treating him the same as we did long before she arrived on the scene. Are we supposed to apologize to him? To her?

---

* And if it is, then the opposite of *that* statement ("the opposite of a great truth is another great truth") must also *ipso facto* be true. Whoah! I just blew my own mind!

THE ANSWER

Ladies: I know it's counterintuitive, but (some) men express their affection for one another via the insult.

This was well captured, I thought, in the movies *Knocked Up* and *Superbad*.

Judd Apatow and crew have a lock on this stuff. Lines like "Your face looks like Robin Williams's knuckles" (in reference to a character's beard in *Knocked Up*), or, from *Superbad*: "Fogell, shut the fuck up. And take off that vest. You look like Aladdin," ring pretty true to me.

And I'm McLovin it. For years the airwaves have been awash in treacly, *Sex and the City*, oh-no-that-top-looks-great-on-you-honey girly talk. Now, finally, the way men talk to each other when there are no women around is getting some onscreen representation.

Women, if I may continue boldly to generalize, tend to compliment one another in person and save the more critical material for, shall we say, discussion with a third party.

Men will just say stuff right to your face. I remember once a friend of mine, flipping through some vacation snaps, came across one of me in a bathing suit and merely said, "What's the matter, buddy? Lose your gym membership?"

Can you imagine? But I wasn't hurt. I know him to be not only one of my closest friends, but also a tireless supporter: one of my top lieutenants in the field.

Maybe it did sting a bit. But it helped, too. Hmm, I thought, maybe my physique could use a little de-pearification. I need to re-Adonisize myself immediately! Time to hit the gym!*

---

* Ladies, are you starting to sense a theme-let, here? Non-magical leprechauns commenting on my chunkiness; friends suggesting

And perhaps that's the point of "chop busting." To Taser each other forward to greater heights of self-improvement. I've certainly found that time spent in masculine society is an excellent antidote to ego preening, self-importance, and putting on airs.

But it can go too far, too. I know some men use "banter" as a cloak to take serious, wounding jabs at people – a Class A Dude-Code misdemeanour.

The Dude Code governs all male behaviour. It's a rule book not only unwritten but unspoken. (How else would you expect a male code to be?) It is simply understood.

And every man knows, deep down, when he has taken it too far, when chop busting for fun has edged over to the zings and poisonous arrows of genuinely insulting cracks.

So that's the bit of Damage Control you need to take care of first. Ask yourself: "Is our banter in fact friendly, only gently mocking? Does it come enwrapped in an implicit Twinkie of affection and support and love?"

If you cannot honestly answer that question with a "yes," then I think you need to take your friend out for a drink – maybe all of you at once, in a kind of anti-intervention – and say, "Look, upon reflection, we realize we've been riding you too hard and we're going to back off and take it easy on you from now on."

I know: it sounds like a horribly uncomfortable situation, and no doubt it will be, but the total elapsed time of this discussion, before someone coughs and changes the subject or waves the waitress over for more drinks, I would

gym-membership-renewals . . . Viewed from one angle, my whole life has been a battle: junk food and booze vs. brown rice and the gym. Which will triumph?

estimate to be in the neighbourhood of about seven seconds. And though he may not respond on the spot, you can bet your friend will think about it, and in the end appreciate it.

But if it is (mostly) just all in good fun, if you treat him with the same mixture of respect and disrespect as you do each other, I think you should approach the girlfriend.

I wouldn't apologize, except maybe to say you're sorry about how it "came off." But explain to her, as you did to me, that this is a standard feature of masculine interaction.

Maybe write it out as a note and include the note as part of a loot-bag peace offering that includes a bottle of Chardonnay and copies of *Knocked Up* and *Superbad* by way of audiovisual illustration.

Who could resist such a gift? Tell her that's the way men are, that they don't mean anything by it, it's just a way of keeping each other real, letting off steam, sanding down each other's rough edges.

Attempt to convey the difficult-to-swallow-but-consummate truth that it's only when you stop mocking and insulting her boyfriend that she should worry. Because that means his friends have decided either he's too fragile and "delicate" to take it or his faults (or girth) have mush-roomed to such proportions they now fall outside the purview of friendly banter, or both.

When they stop busting his chops, explain to her: that's the ultimate insult.

SPROI-OI-OI-O*ING!* ME LIKEY!

Now let's take a look at the second statement I mentioned above: "Under certain circumstances, even the most enthusiastic, heartfelt compliments can be upsetting and distressing."

Don't believe it? Check out the following scenario, in which a couple of guys paid a woman an inadvertent compliment.

But it didn't go down well. Not at all. And even though their transgression took place in a hot tub, when they got out they found themselves in even hotter water than ever . . .

THE QUESTION

My wife, Jill, and I have been friends for many years with my buddy Brad and his wife, Phyllis.

For many years we've enjoyed get-togethers at their cottage, during which we often go skinny-dipping in the lake or in the hot tub. It's always been casual, with no implications – until recently.

During a recent winter visit, the four of us were in the hot tub when Pam's sister Sarah came out to join us. She has a certain "look," and as Brad and I watched her approach we both became noticeably aroused.

My wife was not amused. She told me afterwards that Pam was partly embarrassed, and partly envious that I had reacted to her sister but never to her.

I just want to put the whole thing behind me. I'm still in the doghouse with my wife, and she has let it be known that there will be no more tubbing. How can I put things back the way they were?

THE ANSWER

Sir: Before I answer your question, I have one question to ask you:

May I join your social circle?

It'd be sort of like having your own around-the-clock pro-bono advice-dispensing columnist/author, bartender, and towel boy, all rolled into one: dishing out wisdom, mixing drinks, fetching people's bathrobes and wraps and flip-flops.

Things have been a tad tame in my world lately. We all have kids and houses and sit around talking about schools and money and "wall sconces," whatever the fuck they are.

Whereas you, sir! Sexy sisters vying for erotic supremacy; nude frolicking in a bucolic setting; unwonted displays of extramarital attraction causing ripples of drama in the hot tub.

It's like a movie on Showcase, or something.

Even the sex-perts I consulted for this question sounded a little envious of your lifestyle.

"I have to tell you," said Joan Marsman, a Toronto-based sex therapist, laughing, after I described the parameters of your problem to her, "apart from everything else, it sounds like a lot of fun."

She spends all day, she said, dealing with sexual dysfunction, penile malfunction, men who have to strain and struggle and pop all manner of pills in order to attain a satisfactory erection, so "it's kind of nice to hear about healthy, functioning men."

She did say that the presence of tumescence in this circumstance violates what you might call The Covenant of The Hot Tub, "the unspoken agreement that all this nudity is fun and not sexual," and the husbands definitely owe the wives some kind of apology.

I agree. What kind of apology, though, depends on where you stand on the question of whether men can "help it" or not.

There seems to be some disagreement on this score. Two of the three sex therapists I spoke to felt men could help it, one felt they couldn't.

Perhaps not surprisingly, the two who felt it is controllable were women; the one who felt it wasn't was a man.

"Of course we can't, David, as a man you know that," chided Dr. Alex Alterescu, a Toronto-based clinical sexologist. He also mentioned something about the superheated waters of the hot tub being a "vasodilator," thus making it even more difficult for the men to control their twenty-first digits.

Which sounded highly technical, and I was kind of buying it, until I spoke to Judith Golden, another Toronto sex therapist who scolded me from the other side of the fence:

"Think about it, Dave. You know perfectly well it's in your control."

To be honest, I'm not quite sure where I stand on this question. I guess I do feel that at the first sign of impending tumescence all you have to do is picture your grandmother crawling up your leg with a knife between her teeth, and the crisis will pass.

But I've never been in the erotically charged, superheated, vasodilatory situation described above. So let's leave the question open.

In any case, I do think you owe your wife an apology. Sometimes we have to apologize for our unintentional errors of taste, as well as the ones we fully intended to commit; and at the very least, you could say your actions, witting or unwitting, caused embarrassment all around.

Follow up by showing her you're attracted to her and she's the one for you. And maybe it's time everyone cooled off for a while, put on some bathing costumes: maybe some unflattering one-pieces for the women, and extra-baggy shorts for the men.

Also, give the sister a wide berth.

Then, maybe when things in the hot tub have cooled off a bit and become a little less steamy, you can go back to your old, *al fresco in flagrante delicto* ways, which all three therapists did say sound like a bubbling tub of good, clean fun.

When you do, send an e-mail to McClelland & Stewart, and I'll give you my contact information.

I'm a good folder, and I make a mean martini.

CONCENTRATE ON YOUR OWN OCULAR LUMBER, BLURT BOY

So as we said in the answer above, we have to apologize for our unintentional errors of taste, as well as the ones we fully intended to commit.

But do we have to apologize for everything we say that is of substance? Can we not speak our minds when we're out on the town? Is there not a place for truth, in social occasions?

THE QUESTION
My girlfriend's close friend, let's call her Tina, lost her mother in a car accident two years ago. She had a really

rough time accepting it, seeing as it followed on the heels of her father's passing the year before. In any case, since she lost her mother she's continually using her grief-stricken status to garner sympathy from anyone who'll listen. If she's losing an argument, she'll well up in tears and pull out the grief card. Criticize her taste, out comes the dead parents. My girlfriend and some of our friends have talked about it and agreed that it's a bit much to stomach, so when I called bullshit on her at a dinner party we hosted last week, I thought *someone* would have my back. No dice. The table went silent, and Tina started crying inconsolably. Two couples got up and left. My girlfriend lost her mind. And now I'm the black sheep just because I said what was on everyone else's mind. I can't take it back (and I won't). How can I get everyone else to own up to their honest feelings here? Just because I said something politically incorrect (but honest!), I shouldn't be an outcast, should I?

THE ANSWER
Two things that should never be delivered at a dinner party: (1) pizza; (2) home truths.

In fact, "truth" and "truth-telling," and being "blunt" and a "straight-shooter," and the like, are all highly over-rated as concepts, I feel.

In a way, this question and the earlier one about "insultiments" and "questionsults" aka "questi-burns" are related. Insultiments and questi-burns are "home truths" – e.g., "your dog stinks/your socks look dumb pulled up like that/the way you handle raw chicken is kinda freaking me out" – only expressed in *passive-aggressive* format.

You, sir, simply took the "passive" out of the equation.

I'm not sure it's any better. Let he or she who is without sin cast the first stone . . . and how would you like someone to deliver a bunch of "home truths" to you?

Once again, there's a *Seinfeld* that speaks to this issue.

George is sitting with his girlfriend, Patrice, at a diner. She's wearing chopsticks in her hair and talking about how although she's an accountant at the moment she'd like to eventually make enough to live on selling her papier mâché hats. George asks, "Papier mâché hats? What if it rains?"

She tells him they're art and are meant to be hung on the wall. When he asks if there's any money in it, she (mis)quotes Thomas Carlyle: "Whoso belongs only to his age references only its popinjays and mumbo jumbo."

He starts trying to break up with her, hands her his old "it's not you it's me" line: "I have a fear of commitment, I don't know how to love."

Oh, bullshit, she says: give me the truth. Finally, he explodes.

George: "The truth? You want the truth? It is your earrings. It is the chopsticks but it's so much more! You're pretentious! You call everyone by their full name! You call my doorman Sammy 'Samuel.' But you don't even say Samuel, you say Sam-you-EL! And 'pa-pee-ya machay'! What is 'papier mâché'?"

Thus the relationship ends. Later, as he's explaining what happened to his friend Elaine, she turns the tables on him.

Elaine: "How would you like it if someone told *you* the truth?"

George: "Like what? What could they say?"

Elaine: "There are plenty of things to say."

George: "Like what? I'm bald? What is it specifically? Is, is there an odour I'm not aware of?"

Elaine: " . . . You're very careful with money."

George: "I'm cheap? You think I'm cheap? How could you say that to me? I can't believe this. How could you say that to me?"

Elaine: "You asked me to."

George: "You should have lied."

He's right. What a terrible, dystopian society it would be if everyone sat around telling each other "home truths."

You wouldn't like it. I wouldn't like it. It would be fractious, disastrous, and catastrophic. There is a reason it's called "polite society," and that's because we don't just blurt out whatever pops into our head about other people.

The best line from that exchange is Elaine's: "There are plenty of things to say." Exactly. You may have something to say to Grief Girl, e.g., "Good grief, enough already!"

But just remember there are "plenty of things to say" about you, too.

Now, of course, if your friends had discussed this with you and didn't "get your back," there's kind of an issue there, no? I think you can take any one of them aside and say "Thanks for the support." Of course, if they say, "Dude, this is polite society, we didn't think you'd just blurt that out," they'd have a point, too. You've appointed yourself a "teller of truths," and you have to make peace with the fact that it can be a lonely vocation.

Now, some people who've known me for a long time might chime in here and say, "Hey, Dave, I seem to recall you were once known as 'Blurt Boy' and were infamous for your indiscretion, how can you dare to get on your high horse on this topic now?"

True, I was once known as Blurt Boy – but (a) I've changed since those days, I've learned to be discreet and double-check with my internal editor before things come flying out of my mouth; (b) when I blurt, I blurt out dumb stuff about *me*, things that might make me look bad, unwise, scandalous, etc.

It was never delivering home truths to other people. I was like the opposite of the guy in the biblical parable, the one Jesus abjures to "stop criticizing the mote in your brother's eye, why don't you pull out the friggin' beam in your own first?" (I'm paraphrasing.)

I was so busy trying to remove my own ocular lumber I could never worry about anyone else's.

That's how you should be, too. Worry about your own problems and flaws; let others worry about theirs.

In this case, I believe you do owe an apology. And it should be something humble, too. Because dressing down someone on a social occasion is right offside. I gotta don my striped shirt and blow my whistle on that one.

Approach the poor, grief-stricken girl you humiliated, and apologize from the bottom of your heart.

If you can't find the words, you don't know where to begin, allow me to make a suggestion as to an opener: "I know I'm not perfect . . ."*

And really believe it. Because, after all, who is?

---

* Recall Rule No. 3: CYH, Curb your hubris.

SKIP THE FUNERAL AND IT'S TIME FOR "CONDOLOGIES"

THE QUESTION

My sister's mother-in-law passed away last week. I was going to go to the funeral, but then a friend gave me once-in-a-lifetime tickets to a basketball playoff game. I couldn't resist. I mean, I didn't know the deceased that well – anyway, long story short, I skipped the funeral. I told my sister that, sadly, I had an unavoidable work commitment.

But then the friend I went with mentioned the game, and my sister hit the roof. Now both she and her husband have cut me off entirely and asked other family members to do the same, saying I disrespected the dead. How can I undo the damage I've done?

THE ANSWER

As you may recall from the Introduction, Damage Control's corporate motto is "What's done is done and can't be undone [skritch, scratch, the DJ drops a heavy beat, everyone at Damage Control Central starts to tap their toes, bob their heads, and twitch their hips in time to the rhythm]/the bell that's rung can't be unrung/uh! uh! the sands of time, they can't un-run . . ."

And so forth. (I had to take the needle off the record and turn off the stereo just there before a full-on party broke out, here at DC HQ.)*

But because you happen to touch on a topic I feel quite strongly about, I'm going to set aside company policy on

* Where we have a strict vinyl-only policy. No CDs, no downloads!

this occasion and say: you probably should have gone to that funeral.

There was a lovely piece called "Always Go to the Funeral" on NPR a few years ago, by a woman named Deirdre Sullivan.

She said her father taught her to "always go to the funeral."

She said his statement has always reminded her "to do things even when I really, really don't feel like it. . . . I'm talking about those things that represent only inconvenience to me, but the world to the other guy. You know, the painfully under-attended birthday party. The hospital visit. . . . In my life, the daily battle hasn't been good versus evil. It's hardly so epic. Most days, my real battle is doing good versus doing nothing."

Too true. All too true.

But she had me with "painfully under-attended birthday party."

Nothing is more embarrassing when you're alive than throwing a sparsely attended party.

But an under-attended funeral? If, after an embarrassing life and (probably) embarrassing death, hardly anyone shows up to my funeral? That scratching sound you hear from my grave will be me trying to dig my way even deeper into the earth.*

In all likelihood, if the deceased is a world-historical figure, the funeral will probably be the last party thrown in his/her honour. You have to go if only so that he/she can seem popular this one last time.

---

* Unless by some freak coincidence you happen to have stumbled near the undisclosed secret location of Damage Control's underground bunker: it could be the sound of the DJ working the "wheels of steel."

And to support the living, too, obviously – in this case your sister and her husband. It's a tough time for them – and a busy one, as well, in my experience. When someone dies, there's a lot to get together in short order: religious ceremony, choosing a venue for people to gather, burial or cremation, etc. A lot of decisions.

And you have to do it all in a daze. On top of your regular life. Your sister was not only grieving but tired, harried, and hassled. She might have needed not only your sympathy.

She might have needed you to roll up your sleeves and help.

So you can see why the mental image of you eating popcorn and watching a bunch of tall guys in shorts bouncing balls around a hardwood court while she was frantically dealing with everything might've been a tad . . . infuriating?

"Always go to the funeral." Even if you're not invited. A funeral is one of the few social occasions it's acceptable, even encouraged, to crash. (The concept being: the family's too stunned and grief-stricken to remember who all to invite and their contact information.)

It's up to you to figure out where it is and show up. It works out for you, too, trust me: free snacks, free drinks, good karma. And you've demonstrated you're a good friend, a solid supporter – a rock.

Anyway, enough said on the topic of "You should have gone."

Since you didn't, I would say your best bet now is to send your sister a note of both condolence and apology – a note expressing your sincerest "condologies" (memo to Hallmark, you should have this type of card, it'd be a big seller: "I'm very, very sorry for your loss – and also my behaviour – during your time of grief.") Be humble, don't try to justify. Say you're an idiot and really, really sorry.

Maybe now offer your services and help. After all, at least as far as the living are concerned, it's always better late than never.

Remember it's going to be you on that bier some day. If you die before your sister, who do you think is going to be front and centre on the organizing committee for all the . . . arrangements?

That's right: sis. So before the sands of your time run out – and none of us knows how much time we've got – you need to right this wrong. Smooth things over with your sister.

That way, if, God forbid, you're hit by a garbage truck or fall through a sidewalk grate, she won't pepper her comments with cracks about how you loved basketball during your life, so much so you were blinded to, etc., etc. And she'll be able to enthusiastically pour her energies into throwing you the last bash you surely deserve.

That way, you can still seem like a cool guy to everyone even after you've . . . cooled off a bit. That's showbiz, baby: You gotta go out on a high note. Leave them wanting more.

LITTLE WHITE LIE

THE QUESTION

I'm not a fan of babies, but when a senior colleague of mine invited me to his two-year-old's birthday party, scheduled for a Saturday afternoon, I unthinkingly said yes. But then some friends I hadn't seen in a while, including a girl I'm kind of into and a couple of people from out of town, invited me for some beers on a patio at the same time as the party.

So I told the guy in my office I couldn't make it because "I had to visit someone out of town," which was a total lie, but the prospect of going to my friend's house and standing around with a bunch of kids vs. hanging out on a patio with some cool people was just too much to take.

The problem came when a friend of the guy I'd blown off spotted me on the patio. This "spy" told the friend with the two-year-old that I'd blown him off. Now he's pissed at me. But Jesus, I had to, kids make me squirmy, and there's nothing interesting about them until they're at least able to walk and talk, right? Things have been really awkward ever since, and he's made it clear that he doesn't trust or believe much of what I have to say. This could fuck up my career, and all because I'm not into partying with Teletubby fans!

THE ANSWER

Okay, this question is quite similar to the one above about the funeral and "condologies." But I think it's a good opportunity to raise a crucial "learn, baby, learn" aspect of Damage Control on the social circuit.

It is quite simple: **The One and Only Iron-Clad Rule of Damage Control on the Social Circuit: No Matter How Much Fun the Thing You're Invited to Subsequently May Sound, You Must Always Honour the Prior Commitment.**

You got that, Slim? I know it can be tough. I know it can be hard. And I certainly share your chagrin at the thought of going to a party full of little short-stacks running around and spraying you with Silly String and pressing their open-faced peanut butter sandwich onto your trouser leg.

I'm a parent myself, but whenever I step into a house where a purported "party" is taking place, and little kids are running around, gobbling chips and drinking pop, or some dude with a little blob in a Bjorn is talking to another dude about which type of diaper he prefers, or whatever, my heart sinks. And I think: "Oh, so it's going to be one of *those* types of parties, is it?"

And basically, I just want to turn around and leave.

Now, it should be said, I *know* this is just me; that not many share this prejudice: "Oh, no, Dave, parties with kids are *fun*, what's your problem?" I can hear everyone clamour.

I don't know, maybe part of me just hasn't grown up. Maybe I'm a bit of a big baby myself. But whenever I go to a party, I like to think there's some danger in the air, that people will be exchanging ideas, engaging in witty banter, crossing swords, dropping bon mots, and popping canapés. That we are all sophisticated and soigné and urbane – illusions that all fly out the window when the unmistakable smell of a fresh-filled diaper wafts toward your nostrils.

But onward to your problem. You have to honour the prior commitment. I'm glad you brought this topic up, in fact; because even now, with people I know in their thirties and forties, many are still barking their shins on this problem, attempting to dipsy-doodle, pull off a Hail Mary, and winding up caught in their own web of lies.

And it's always the fun ones.

I have one friend. Everyone loves her, she's a lot of fun, everyone invites her to everything. She'll say "yes" to something – but then something more fun-sounding will come up! And she'll cancel the un-fun thing, with a bit of a fishy excuse (something that always tugs on the heartstrings a little, e.g., "My cat's not feeling well").

Then she'll go out and do the more-fun-sounding thing!

Which is all very fine and festive and kind of funny – as long as you're on the good end of this transaction. Like, a few times she blew off people she was committed to see on a certain night to come over to Casa di Pam and Dave for dinner.

And we felt very flattered. But when you're on the other end of the transaction, suddenly it's not so funny.

Her (over phone): "Dave, my cat's sick, I'm sorry I can't make it to your house tonight, I really should stay home and keep an eye on him."

Me: "Oh, gosh, no problem, boy, sounds terrible, hope he feels better!"

Then later I'll hear she was spotted out with some different people, laughing and sipping Chardonnay on some patio.

The message it sends to the person you're blowing off is "You're boring, I've found 'mettle more attractive.'"*

Which is a terrible message to send to a friend. And if you do it enough, people will start not inviting you out so much, any more, which is obviously the opposite of what you want.

So stick to the prior commitment. As soon as you say yes, write it down in your calendar, and say no to all subsequent invitations, no matter how fun-sounding. It'll save you a lot of trouble in the long run, trust me.

Because socializing is not only a matter of having fun, it is, like everything else, a test of character. And if you fail, as you quite rightly have intuited, it can hurt you both personally and professionally.

So: apologize to your senior colleague, lay upon him some version of the truth (e.g., you had a friend come in

* Shakespeare again: *Hamlet.*

from out of town, it was your only chance to see that person, and you became flustered).

And then: bite the bullet. Invite your colleague over to your house, *with* kid, and make a show of becoming friends with that person.

It could all turn out to be for the best, in the end.

WHEN THE BROMANCE IS FADING

Okay, let's take a look at a couple of questions that may have light-hearted aspects but address a serious issue for many of us: what to do when it seems like a friendship is starting to fade, and get blurry around the edges.

THE QUESTION

I met this dude in school and we've been friends for ten years. But the last time we spoke I had that feeling – a bit like the feeling you get when your significant other is about to break up with you. I'm thinking the bromance is over.

This is someone I used to look up to and admire. Now we are both married and have kids, but we have diverged somewhat. In the past, I would dump a friend for the slightest offence, but I stopped doing that because it seems petty. So now I think, well, I probably offended this friend without even knowing it. Should I just call it a day, or should I, after all this time, send him an e-mail asking WTF?

I don't talk to my wife about this because it has a tinge of gay to it. I mean, why would one dude be all knotted about another dude not calling him back, right?

THE ANSWER

If your "bromance" is starting to fade, maybe you should invite him out on a "man-date," and "bropose" to him, then the two of you can get "manried" and head off to a tropical "mancation" destination for a bromantic "manlimoon."

Ah, I'm just messing with ya, "bro."

Also, I guess I'm poking a bit of fun at the "brocabulary" of man-prefixed terms that have been in vogue lately.

But I think I've got it out of my system now.

First of all, cast off your fears of gayness, dude.

There's nothing wrong with loving your male friends. I have several male friends I'd be crushed to lose. If one of them said he was finally fed up with me and my antics, my heart would be bro-ken (okay, it's not out of my system). I'd have to walk around in the rain so no one could see I was crying, my manscara (okay, it's never going to stop) running down my cheeks.

Or I'd have to cut onions and if my wife asked what was the matter I'd say, "It's (sniff) just . . . the onions, Pam."

But if she pressed me I'd probably crack, break down, and sob onto her shoulder: "Oh, my God, I miss him, Pam. It hurts so . . . much."

Does that make me any less mantastic? Any less hetero-licious? I don't see why it should. Women – unless they're all lying to me – like a man with strong male friendships.

(And recall from our "courtship" chapter that meeting my "crew" was a crucial turning point in my seduction of Pam.)

In any case, I'm a big believer in keeping your friends at all costs. As Polonius says to Laertes in *Hamlet*: "Those friends thou hast, and their adoption tried/Grapple them to thy soul with hoops of steel." It's hard to find friends. So when I do, I hang on to them like grim death.

So they screw up sometimes: so do you. I thought it was a great sign of maturity that in your letter you wrote that you no longer cut off friends for slight offences. I've had to forgive most of my friends something, and most of them have had to forgive me something.

The worst was when one of my friends in grad school made out with my girlfriend in the bathroom at a party.

Meanwhile, I sidled up outside, wanting to use the facilities. "Man," I said, laughing, to a group of people standing nearby, after about fifteen minutes had elapsed, "whoever's in there sure is taking a long time." They shot me a funny look, I noticed, a look of pity mingled with consternation.

"What's with them?" I wondered. A couple of moments later my question was answered as my soon-to-be-ex-friend and my soon-to-be-ex-girlfriend stumbled out, clothes in disarray, hair messed up, lipstick smeared everywhere.

The humiliation and hurt were instantaneous and shattering, like a punch in the face from Mike Tyson. I thought I would never talk to him, or her, ever again in my life.

But life is long and in the end I got over it, and I'm glad I did. Today he's one of my greatest friends, a valued part of my world. And all that stuff that happened: it seems so long ago, now. It feels like it happened to other people.

So don't be afraid of making a "broverture" to your buddy. Not via e-mail: e-mail's too distanced and cool a medium for discussing friction and problems. Call him and offer to buy him a drink. If he says no, well, you have your answer.

But at least you gave it a shot.

So yes: go for it. Run, run like the wind, like a guy at the end of a bromantic comedy – or better yet borrow a motorcycle and zoom to his house, popping wheelies, the music swelling as you ride up on the sidewalk, weaving in and out of pedestrians and knocking over fruit stands – and materialize in his doorway with a UFC DVD in one hand and a six-pack in the other and, your face working with emotion, say to him: "Dude, it's killing me how we never hang any more."

Hang your heart out there. Show him how you feel. You've got nothing to lose, in my opinion, but your well-founded feelings of manxiety at the prospect of losing a good, old friend.

Okay, I'm really going to stop now.

EMBRACE A BRAVE NUDE WORLD

This type of fading-romance aspect of relationships happens between couples, too. If you have a good old couple-friend, it's painful to feel distance growing between the four of you.

It can happen for any number of reasons. Below is perhaps one of the more unusual ones. Remember Stéphane Deschênes, whom we mentioned in the Introduction as "outstanding nude in his field"? This is the question that brought him bounding, unfettered and as nature created him, into our world.

THE QUESTION
My wife and I have been very close friends with another couple for more than thirty years. We are all in our late fifties. We have shared and supported each other through the births of our children, the deaths of our parents, health

crises, and career changes. But over the past three years they started spending weekends away in a small trailer.

Being curious, and based on cumulative facts gleaned over time, we Googled some of their camping locations. It seemed our friends had become naturists . . . nudists. Then we saw their picture in a naturist magazine. Now, we are not prudes – skinny-dipping is not foreign to us. Our problem is that it seems our friends have decided to move on to a new chapter of their lives without including us. Do we tell them we know or do we simply ignore the whole thing and hope they will eventually take us into their confidence?

THE ANSWER

I said before I'm all about hanging on to old friends: "Those friends thou hast, and their adoption tried/Grapple them to thy soul with hoops of steel."

But on the other hand, there's such a thing as taking a hint. And it does appear, at first blush, your friends are kicking you to the hamper like yesterday's boxers.

Sometimes we need to peel off old friends, like a pair of too-tight jeans, in order to grow and evolve.

I discovered the truth of this when I went away to college.

My high school friends knew me as "crazy Dave." Class clown, streaker, stoner, shoplifter, bookworm, the long-haired hippie freak in ratty jeans, wire-rimmed glasses, and my dad's army jacket. I was also "no-date Dave" – in all of high school I had one date and the whole thing was a lecture on why I never got dates.

But to the downy-limbed beauties of Middlebury College in Vermont, I wanted to reinvent myself and be known as Dave the haunted, slightly troubled troubadour; Dave the romantic poet; Dave the playwright, dropping aphorisms and bons mots like President Johnson dropped bombs on Vietnam. Above all, Dave "the lover."

To my amazement and everlasting joy, they bought it! I'm not one to kiss and tell, but suffice to say for the next four years the new Dave was perhaps among the happiest young men on the eastern seaboard. I was a "brain on a plate" no more; I was part of the ebb and flow of nature, the rhythms of the sun, the ocean, and especially the moon . . .

But my high school friends would never have allowed this metamorphosis to occur. They would have mocked my scarf and pretensions. They wouldn't have allowed me to "fake it until I make it."

Maybe your friends are thinking along similar lines. Maybe they're worried that (warning: tortured metaphor approaching) unless they untether the belt of your friend-ship, they'll never be able to drop their old selves to the floor and step forward into the sunshine of a brave nude world.

To get a sense of whether this could possibly be the case, I spoke to Stéphane Deschênes, the "naturist" member of our Panel.

He said you shouldn't take your friends' secretiveness per-sonally. They're probably just nervous about your judgment.

Naturism is about many things, he says, including equal-ity: "When you're naked you can't express your feelings of social superiority over others through your clothing."

But when most people think of nudist clubs or societies (don't say "colonies," they don't like that any more: it sounds too much like a cult), they tend to think (or maybe this is mostly me) of alfresco sex; sudden, total-giveaway boners, popping up unbidden, as you talk to a pulchritudinous fellow-nudist, spoiling and derailing your soliloquy on the problems in the Middle East; and not knowing where to look when you're talking to someone.

(Personally, if I were a nudist and a hot woman, I'd get a tattoo on the upper part of my left breast, saying: "If you're reading this, you're probably not listening to me. Shall I repeat what I just said?")

There's still a stigma attached to it, and Mr. Deschênes said a lot of naturists find it hard (*cough, cough,* sorry) to tell old friends about their new clothing-optional lifestyles.

He says he didn't tell a lot of people at first. When friends found out after he appeared on a cable TV talk show extolling the virtues of doffing your duds, many asked him, "Why didn't you tell me?"

"Because it wasn't like I'd taken up golf and could ask them, 'Hey, why don't you play a few rounds with me?'" he says.

It's a ticklish thing and continues to be ticklish at times. He says to this day when people invite him to pool parties they sometimes nervously ask him if he plans to, you know – that is, if he wouldn't mind wearing a suit, please.

But he says that, especially if your friends have contributed to a naturist magazine, they're probably quite passionate about it. And he predicts that if you approach them, "you probably won't be able to get them to shut up about it."

In all likelihood, they'll feel a huge sense of relief, and be more than happy to welcome you into the fold, should you so desire.

So yes, I would say: doff your reticence, unzip your emotions, and whip out your newfound knowledge of the new direction your friends' lives are taking. Just say you saw them in the magazine and start talking about that. If you wind up nudists – well, I have to say it sounds like a fun way to spend your weekends. Send me a postcard.

Of course, there's a chance your friends' evasiveness might have nothing to do with naturism. And I can imagine a horrible, embarrassing scene where you're all standing around naked sipping Cuba Libres and they say, "No, it wasn't that we were embarrassed by our naturism. We were just bored with you guys."

But that doesn't sound like the case here. Mostly because of the timing. If you're as close to your old friends as you say, it's just too big a coincidence that they started being evasive about the time they became naturists.

If you approach them with open hearts and minds, I predict you will soon be a happy foursome once again, perhaps playing nude gin rummy in the sun.

If you do go that route, one last note, courtesy of Mr. Deschênes: naturists love being nude, they love playing basketball and frolicking in the buff, but they're practical about it, too. They understand the need for clothing as protection: "I like to tell people," he says, "'Wear an apron when you're arc-welding or frying bacon.'"

Now that, my friends, is what I call good advice. And don't forget lots of sunscreen.

YOUR TAKEAWAY DOGGIE BAG OF THOUGHTS

After socializing frantically throughout my teens, twenties, and thirties, I, David Eddie, have come to the conclusion that, with a few exceptions, I hate everyone, everyone's a bunch of crazy nutbars and zingermeisters and I'd rather just stay home and drink and watch TV and lie around with Pam and my family and do my work. Therefore I've decided to become an urban hermit and recluse, ready to embrace my ultimate destiny of embittered, angry old man!

But there's still hope for you, dear reader! Like Pat Lynch, you should get "out there" and have fun, as much as you can, while you still feel like it!

Just keep a few things in mind when you hit the social circuit.

- **Rise above everyone's zingers with serene aplomb.** At most, gently return their "insultiments" and "questiburns" with "apolobukes." (Another statement to file under D for "do as I say not as I do" because I mix it up with people all the time – but I always regret it, dear reader.)

- **Silence = golden.** Remember that nine times out of ten "*l'esprit de l'escalier*" is actually your friend. Why go on record saying something you'll regret?

- **If you run across a friend who's a persistent zinger-meister and underminer, keep briskly walking and don't break stride.** You're avoiding a passive-aggressive "frenemy" who could wreck your whole day – and burning calories, all at the same time! It's a win-win situation!

- **Exception: insults are the lingua franca of male friends.** Ladies, don't let it get under your skin if your man's male friends "bust his chops" a little. It's when they *stop* insulting him you should start to worry.

- Even compliments – especially those of the type that might pop up and break the bubbling surface of the hot tub – can be insults, too, sometimes. Sad but true, often in life we must apologize for our unintentional, as well as our intentional, errors of taste.

- Really, most forms of blurtaceous home-truth-telling are out of place on the social circuit and should be avoided. Remember: you're not perfect either, and the last thing you'd want is someone delivering a "home truth" to you in a social setting.

- Always go to the funeral.

- Lies can get you into as much trouble as the truth. Do not compound your lies with further lies. When you've been caught in a lie – *that* is when you start singing the truth like a canary.

- Friends are important. Whether it's a "bromance" that's fading, or a friend-couple that's drifting away, time to pour it on. I, David Eddie, may be turning into a recluse, misanthrope, and "urban hermit," but you should hang on to your friends as hard as you can.

DAMAGE CONTROL WHEN YOU'RE SPLASHING AROUND IN THE GENE POOL

SAY WHAT?

"They fuck you up, your mum and dad./They may not mean to, but they do./They fill you with the faults they had/And add some extra, just for you. . . .

"Man hands on misery to man./It deepens like a coastal shelf./Get out as early as you can,/And don't have any kids yourself."

So wrote the British poet Philip Larkin in his 1971 poem "This Be the Verse," one of his best-known and most oft-quoted works – and also one beloved by shrinks and family counsellors the world over.

Critics and profs have spilled a lot of ink trying to prove "This Be the Verse" is somehow "ironic" and what Larkin "really" meant to say was that we should forgive ourselves our foibles because we inherited so many of them from our parents, and la la la. I mean, ha-ha – he obviously didn't really mean people shouldn't have children, because that would spell the end of the human race!

But I have to say that, unlike, for example, W.C. Fields – who also maintained a staunch anti-kid stance in public ("Children shouldn't be seen or heard from – ever again") despite having children of his own – Larkin doesn't seem to have been kidding around.

Nor was he being "ironic," either, as far as I can make out. As a child himself, Larkin once said, he thought he hated everybody, "but when I grew up I realized it was just children I didn't like." Children, with their "shallow, violent eyes," were, in Larkin's view, "selfish, noisy, cruel little brutes."

And, no, he never had any himself.

Which is either too bad, or for the best, I can't quite figure out which. Obviously, with his attitude, Larkin might not have enjoyed being pummelled into a chunky salsa by the mortar and pestle of fatherhood.

Most of his life, Larkin was a librarian, of the distinctly non-naughty variety,* in the drab, dreary, English industrial town of Hull.

I've seen pictures of him, his home, and Hull; I sort of feel like I can visualize his life – especially in the mornings, for some reason. Yes, in a rare attack of Keatsian "negative

---

* Well, he was a *little* naughty – or maybe the word I'm looking for is creepy. Racist, misogynist, porn-obsessed ("one of those old-type natural fouled-up guys" as Larkin imagined a biographer putting it). But still a great poet, though.

capability"* I believe I can vividly visualize the morning routine of "England's unofficial Poet Laureate":†

Alarm goes off in Larkin's modest "bedsit." Larkin reaches out, turns it off. Sits up, in Marks and Spencer pyjamas, rubs eyes; and, face blank, feeling neither one way or another about it, thinks to self: "Another day has begun." Slips feet into slippers, shuffles into bathroom. Takes whiz, catches glimpse of self in mirror. Heaves heavy sigh:** what can you do?

In the kitchen, Larkin makes tea, toast. Prepares sack lunch: tuna fish, apple, cookie. Goes into bedroom: dresses. Ties tie. Knot not quite right. Ties tie again. Knot right. Dons jacket. Checks mirror again, heaves another heavy sigh: good as it's going to get.

Snatch or snippet of poetry pops into Larkin's melon. Larkin dutifully jots it in handy notebook, with handy pencil stub. Larkin pulls mac off coat rack, slips onto shoulders with a shrug. Umbrella, too, just in case. Affixes bike clip to trouser leg. Grabs bike, and pedals into thin mists and/or fine rain of another grim, grey day in Hull.

---

* Basically, the ability to put yourself in another person's boots and see the world through his/her eyes, like Keats did with "stout Cortez" and the Pacific.

† Larkin turned down the Laureateship in 1984, for some reason, the year before he died.

** Unlike his friend Kingsley Amis, the hotshot novelist and ladies' man, Larkin was far from dashing. He *looked* like a librarian: dourly peering at you with big, mournful eyes behind heavy horn-rims with inch-thick lenses, looking like at any moment he was about to bring his finger up to his lips and say "Shhhh!"

Kids might've leavened/livened/loosened things up a little! Larkin might've become a bit less of a stiff, a little less starchy, stuffy, and shirty.

Kids can make you laugh even before breakfast – and how many people can you say that about? My kids have made me laugh, in the morning, *before I've even had a cup of coffee*, and that's no mean feat.*

Sure, having kids might've fucked with Larkin's routine, now and then. Rough-housing through Larkin's kitchen, kids might've jostled the table and spilled his tea onto his toast, ruining both, and creating a mess.

Visiting him at the library on "Bring Your Children to Work Day," they might've started playing tag in the stacks and knocked a bunch of books off the shelves, playing havoc with both the Dewey Decimal System and Larkin's nerves. And if he attempted to reprimand them then and there, one of the other librarians might've had to bring her fingers to her lips, and say "Shhhhh!" to Larkin, thus causing ripples of scandal throughout the entire community of librarians – perhaps even harming his chances for job promotion.

Everything might've been thrown into chaos, disorder, and disarray.

But chaos and disorder can be a good thing, sometimes.

---

* I'm not a morning person. Before I've had my first cup of coffee, I would estimate I'm somewhere in the range of only 50 to 70 per cent human. I'm more like a mid-range primate, or high-functioning mollusk, at that point. Yet I have found myself chuckling at the antics of my offspring in these unholy, pre-human hours. Also, they want to snuggle, which is a great way to start any day.

Without the chaos and disorder kids bring, people can sometimes become too finicky, persnickety, precious, and tidy, I feel.

In fact, if you've ever had that worry – if you've ever frowned and wondered, "Am I getting too precious? Have I become so neat and tidy and organized that it's actually becoming sort of a *problem*?" – then Dr. Dave has a prescription for you:

Have a bunch of kids! They'll solve that problem for you, lickety-split! They'll turn that frown and, along with it, everything else in your life, upside down!

Say what you like about them ("Heaven and hell, all wrapped up in a diaper" – Martin Amis), kids are great at fomenting chaos. They're absolutely brilliant at breaking, permanently staining, and unravelling things; at snapping off the crucial little bit that renders the whole appliance, or expensive toy, or car door, utterly useless. They're also outstanding in the field of losing things, prodigies of misplacement and selective amnesia.

What they don't lose, they turn into junk.

Which may be a good thing, all in all. Maybe it makes you a little less materialistic? I know I've become less attached to material possessions since becoming a father. Favourite hat, favourite jacket, see it on Nick (my oldest, who's started wearing my stuff), and mentally I bid it "Adieu." Next it's gone. Who can get attached?

Kids are anarchy-artists, merchants of mess, carnie barkers forever ushering you onto a one-way, non-stop emotional rollercoaster of madcap madness!

Kids grind your nerves into a fine powder, then mix the powder with the residue of your hopes and dreams, and use the resulting paste to brush their teeth. Don't forget to rinse!

Kids take you apart like an expert mechanic takes apart a car. But unlike a mechanic, they don't then put you back together again. They leave all the parts on the shop floor and walk away. And then you're the one who has to do the rebuild.

And that's the (as) good (as it's gonna get) news. In the process of rebuilding, something fine happens, I believe: you leave out the inessential, the pretentious and purely decorative, and what's left is a stripped-down, nuts-and-bolts personality designed to get you from point A to point B with a minimum of fuss and a maximum of reliability, dependability, and practicality – like an ATV, Jeep, or dune buggy.

I wouldn't have it any other way. The love you feel for your kids, and them for you, pays it all off, with interest.

THE DELICATE ART OF PERSUASION

However, I will say this: in my twenties, I held fast to a distinctly Larkinesque viewpoint on the question of procreation.

Kids would kill my dreams of becoming a writer, I felt. To write, you need (1) peace and quiet; (2) low overheads; (3) time to yourself; (4) to be well-rested. All these criteria or preconditions to the writing life went out the window when you had kids.

I wanted, like Richard Ford, like Philip Roth, like David Foster Wallace, to make the principled choice not to have kids, in order to devote myself all the more entirely to my work.

Kids were for suckers, I felt, anyway, no matter what one's chosen vocation. Kids use you the way a "strangler fig" uses a tree, I felt: to climb into the world. Often the original "support tree" is killed, or at the very least zombified, petrified in the process: drained of sap and vital energy and left a hollow, lifeless husk.

Kids led to the wearing of Tilley hats and fanny packs, and the driving of minivans, and I wanted none of that! I was a punk, a rebel, an outsider, and, moreover, the artistic type.

No, having kids didn't sound like my kind of thing at all.

Which is why, a few months into dating Pam, when it was starting to become clear the two of us were up to something far more serious than "dating" – when, in fact, we had already begun to cohabit, I arranged my facial features into a mask of rueful regret and said something to the effect of:

"Sorry to drop this bomb on you, Pam, now that we're all in love and everything, but I feel it's only fair for me to inform you I made up my mind a long time ago that I really don't want kids, at any point. And I feel really strongly about it."

She returned my lachrymose and Larkinesque gaze with a gunslinger squint of her own: "Well, now, that's a shame, because I've *always* wanted kids, ever since I was a kid myself. And I feel really strongly about it, too."

Huh, I remember thinking, or words to that effect: *Interesting dilemma. She wants kids, I don't; yet we're in love and obviously soulmates and at this point our paths in life, once separate, are now inextricably intertwined. Wonder how this thorny conundrum will work itself out?*

Here's how:

Pam, one of the most strong-willed women I've ever met or even heard of, pondered this dilemma for two years; then, on her thirtieth birthday, dropped the following ultimatum upon my unsuspecting melon: "Agree now to fertilize my ovaries within the next three years or, much as I love you, I'll have to ask you to pack your bags."

She had it all worked out. She'd studied the . . . fertility charts? . . . or whatever and had decided the optimal age to get pregnant by – and therefore the age *she* wanted to be pregnant by – was thirty-three.

Therefore, if I held fast to my anti-kid stance, she needed the next two years to shag, tag, and bag a suitable replacement donor – oops, I mean suitor – so her diabolical plans for procreation and population increase (cue ominous organ music and bwa-ha-ha-type villainous laughter) could come to fruition.

What could I say? The intervening years had quashed all doubt that Pam was the one for me. I wanted her; I wanted her to be happy; and I wanted her to feel that, with me, she was getting The Whole Package.

So, like a windshield struck by a pebble, I cracked. Like a stale cookie, I crumbled. Like a disused mineshaft, I caved. That's how this "dilemma" resolved itself.

Or, to put it another way: I declared myself open to negotiation.

And the negotiations went like this: She always wanted two kids; I never wanted want any. So we agreed on: "One . . . and we'll see."

"One . . . and we'll see" quickly became two. Then, after two, Pam was all like: "I just don't feel . . . finished yet."

And that is how, ladies and gentlemen, I, a man who never wanted kids in the first place, wound up with three.

The delicate art of persuasion/negotiation.

I, CUCKOO

And I couldn't be happier about it. What joy! What a barrel of laughs! What love, such as I never knew was available to mere mortals, has been mine to enjoy and savour. Like the Grinch's, my heart has had to grow several sizes to accommodate it all.

Could I imagine life without the incomparable Adam, our third kid? I could not. I'm so happy, now, that Pam negotiated him into existence!*

Of course, it's a challenge, being a dad, these days. As one friend of mine, a father of three children, says when asked why he doesn't get a dog as well: "I couldn't stand to have another pair of eyes gazing at me, full of unmet needs."

---

* Though I couldn't imagine life with a fourth. A fourth would've sunk our fragile little skiff. You'd just hear a big BLOOP! and neither Pam nor I would ever be seen nor heard from again. Which is why, après Adam and a couple of subsequent pregnancy scares to add spice, I booked an appointment with Dr. Shakeyhands the Not-So-Christmas-y Nutcracker, and subjected my poor, wrinkled, beleaguered, much-maligned nutsack to the ultimate indignity, aka "the big snip"; a procedure about which the less said the better, boys, except (a) keep your eyes glued to the ceiling throughout – gentlemen: *do not look down*, and (b) next to marrying Pam, it was one of the smartest things I ever did. Never having to worry about birth control, ever again? Brill. And just to clear up any misconceptions, the vasectomee continues to produce sperm after the procedure, it just no longer shoots out the end of your Johnson. It's reabsorbed into your abdomen, which is why some of us vasectomees believe the procedure actually supersizes your mojo.

As succinct a summary of parenthood as I have had the honour of hearing: eyes gazing at you, full of unmet needs.

But it's a challenge to be anything, nowadays: mother, father, brother, grandmother, son, uncle, cousin, son-in-law.

All these branches of the tree have *special* unmet needs, and operate according to their own different set of rules.

On the bright side, family members are more likely to lend you money than mere friends are.

Your family's love is more patient, kind, and loyal than the love you tend to find elsewhere. It's not always true – people can, and do, become estranged for life from their own family members, and never reconcile – but it *tends* to be true, that no matter how much you abuse and attempt to ignore your family, they wait patiently in the wings for you to come around.

I, for example, was always the black sheep, the prodigal, of my family. Growing up, I felt completely unlike the other members of my immediate, nuclear brood. I looked like them, but otherwise was nothing like them (they were all number-crunchers, math/computer geeks – talking to them was like an ape trying to talk to an astronaut).

I was like a baby cuckoo. Cuckoos lay their eggs in the nest of other birds, so the other type of bird has to hatch and raise the baby cuckoo. At a certain point, one has to wonder if the young cuckoo bird says to him/herself: "Hmm, I'm nothing like these people." And takes off, seeking out other cuckoos.

So as soon as I was old enough, I sought out the companionship of my peers – of other cuckoos, i.e., people who were more like me. "My friends became my family," as I would say, somewhat belligerently.

But my cosanguinary confreres aka my family waited patiently in the wings, through the Sturm und Drang of adolescence, the sudsy soap opera of my twenties, enduring my many slights, insults, missed appointments, forgotten engagements, and so forth. Lending me money, shaking their heads in disbelief – but amazingly, never giving up.

Friends drift off, slink off, grow in a different direction, double-cross you, or disappear; bosses fire you; employees quit and find other jobs; but your family is always there for you.

The downside of all this "'there for you' crap," as they call it on *Seinfeld*, is that you're stuck with them, too. *They*'ll hit on *you* for cash, if you've managed to amass any; they'll get all up in your grill, and stay there.

Having children can be challenging, sure. But at least they're cute. The problem with uncles, cousins, in-laws, brothers, sisters, and so forth is their cuteness tends to be intermittent, at best.

They'll climb all the way up the Crazy Tree and start dropping coconuts down on your melon.

They stand on ceremony less than other people in your life. Family members don't bother to mince words. They'll just open their mouths and tell you what they think. It's extraordinary!

And talk about advice! Every relative I've ever seen or known does an unbelievable amount of pro bono work in this department.

Solicited or not, doesn't seem to matter much, where relatives are concerned. Take my mother for example. I might be motoring through the kitchen, where she's reading the paper, on my way to do something (I consider to be) important, and she'll stop me with a:

"David."

"Yes, Mom."

"There's something I want to tell you."

"Uh, Mom, uh . . ."

And she'll begin to download terabyte after terabyte of unsolicited advice on me.

"Uh, yeah, Mom, that's great, but . . ."

There's no stopping her, either, once she's launched into it. I could literally be dancing from foot to foot like someone whose bladder is about to burst, she just continues on until she's done.

And the really annoying thing is how often, when the smoke clears and the dust settles, she turns out to be right . . .

Basically, to put it all in a nutshell, I've got good news and bad news and they're both the same: you're stuck with your family, and they're stuck with you.

You can't "quit" your family in a huff. No matter how mental they may be, you have to figure out a way to deal with them; and they have to figure out a way to deal with you.

And although you can avoid family members, you can't avoid them forever. Sometimes, you can't even fail to invite them to things, or they go all sulky, snarky, and poopy-pants, as in the following circumstance:

THE MEANING OF FAMILY

THE QUESTION

I'm hosting a family holiday party this year, but I'm on a budget, so I'm trying to keep it small. To do that, I only invited my immediate family (no in-laws, no cousins, etc.) and asked them not to talk about it. Still, my sister told her father-in-law about it and he called me, enraged at being excluded, and lectured me on the meaning of family before hanging up in my ear. Should I bite the bullet and invite everyone now?

THE ANSWER

I'm curious to know what your sister's father-in-law said in his lecture on "the meaning of family."

Something like: "Listen to me, you *&^%$#@! young whippersnapper! We're all nuts! We're bananas! Fruitcakes! We're so freakin' out of our minds most people would slowly edge away from us at parties – but see, we don't get invited to normal parties any more! That is why we insist on being invited to all family functions regardless of whether the host or hostess wants us there or not, otherwise there will be no forum or venue for the dramatization of our particular brand of madness – or, as we prefer to think of it, our 'eccentricities.'

"And that, you little %&$#@! bitch, is the meaning of family!"

Click. Dial tone.

Now, that's a lecture on the meaning of family I for one would love to hear.

Dude's way out of line, basically. The only way to react to not being invited to a party is with grace and a shrug, emanating an aura that one doesn't need party invites.

Back when I was a social butterfly, I would feel the sharper-than-a-serpent's-tooth pain of not being invited to something I thought I might be invited to. When you're a social butterfly, there's no worse pain. Your wings go all limp, your antennae droop, and big hot tears fill your little butterfly eyes.

These days, I'm focused on work and family. But I still like to get invited to things! So when, say, my friend Liz says: "Hey, Dave, you going to that big bash we're all invited to Saturday?" and I'm like "What big bash?" I feel a ghost of the old pain.

But it's getting dimmer all the time. And I know that as long as I'm a decent, honest, interesting, engaged person, the invites will come.

All of which is moot, sounds like, when it comes to your sister's father-in-law. He's not going to wait around for people to find him interesting! He doesn't care what people think of him! He wants to be invited *on principle*, as part of his *droit de senor** as paterfamilias.

Well, if he wants to come so badly, let him.

The more the merrier, right? Hopefully, he'll be in good form. (If you're worried about money, ask him to bring a bottle and/or potluck foodstuff, perhaps.) If not, well, that sucks, but, ultimately, everyone's responsible for their own behaviour.

---

* Pardon this further macaronic mixture of languages, dear eagle-eyed reader. I'm trying to be funny, or at least just cute, I guess.

It doesn't really reflect on you. Well, yes, too many stiffs at a party and you start to wonder about the host's social cachet.

But one sulky stiff any party can handle.

So if your sister's father-in-law stomps in, sits in a corner muttering darkly about "the meaning of family" with eggnog in his moustache, that's on him.

His rep will be the one taking the hit, not yours.

MOM, YOU NEED HELP GETTING BY

On a more positive note, let's say, the flip side to "you can never get rid of your family" is "your family is always there for you." At least: ideally. When families fragment, and become fractious, it can be tough.

THE QUESTION

I need to put my mother into a home. She's lived on her own in the family's old house for close to a decade, since my father passed away. She's managed to remain independent. She refuses any help with shopping, with property upkeep, whatever, out of pride, I guess. I'm her youngest daughter, and the only one of her children who still lives close enough to visit, so I've been dealing with it first-hand and I help out with whatever I can. Over the last eighteen months her memory's begun to fail as rapidly as her body and last winter she took a couple of nasty falls that landed her in the hospital for days at a time. I'm afraid her pride's going to kill her if she stays on alone, so I started looking into care options.

My brother and sister, both of whom live across the country, think I'm jumping the gun. My brother actually accused me of trying to make Mom someone else's problem, and insinuated that I was trying to angle in on the house. Neither of them have any idea of her current condition, and seem content to hurl barbs from afar rather than come and see for themselves. I've made my mind up, and I've found a place where I think she'll be happy. How can I break it to her so that she agrees and helps me get my siblings onside? Can I compel her to go?

THE ANSWER
Legally, the bottom line is: if your mother is of sound mind, you cannot force her into a nursing home or assisted-living facility.

If she has another nasty fall, and a doctor decides she can no longer look after herself, he can get social services involved.

But these are all extreme situations. Let's hope it doesn't come to that.

Let's hope you can persuade her to go. Persuasion, as mentioned above, is a delicate art form – especially when it comes to relatives.

I can't tell you exactly how to persuade your mother to do the right thing. No one can tell another person how to persuade someone else to do something they don't want to do: because it all depends on your mother's personality, your personality, and the relationship the two of you have.

All I can offer you are a few general thoughts on the art of persuasion. These things, in cases like yours, especially, tend to (a) be a combination of strong and gentle persuasion; (b) be more in the nature of a war of attrition than a blitzkreig.

In other words, keep up the pressure on your mother. You do have "home court" advantage, for one thing. You can wear someone down easier if you see them all the time.

Another note: women who grew up in the pre-feminist era, I've noticed, are brilliant at it; they had no "power," technically, to enforce their viewpoint and the men could say "I have spoken" and so forth – yet the women would find a way to get their way.

We should look to them, before it becomes a lost art and no one knows how to do it any more, like Haida canoe-making.

Different women accomplished it in different ways, but here are a few introductory suggestions.

My grandmother was famous for asking people the same question, over and over again, until she got the answer she wanted. To my grandpa: "Do you think we need a new couch?" No. "Our couch is looking a little old and worn. What do you think: should we buy a new one?" No. "Look at this picture of a beautiful couch in the Sears, Roebuck catalogue: wouldn't that look nice in our living room?" Okay, okay, we'll get a new couch!

My mother, I've noticed, just states her opinion over and over again (solicited? unsolicited? Either way, doesn't matter much to her) until someone cracks.

Recently, for example, Pam had a crick in her neck – well, it was more than a crick: she couldn't turn her head from side to side, could only stare straight ahead, like a zombie; obviously a bit of a handicap for an on-air person.

She went to a doctor, and after an hour wait, the doctor prescribed Advil – thanks a lot, doc! Acupuncture didn't help much, either. Finally, I forced her to just get some rest, hoping her body would heal itself. Waited on her hand and foot for three days, and she was still no better.

"We should take her to the emergency room," my mother said. My opinion: what for, to sit there three hours and get some more Advil? Better she should rest.

"Hmmm, I think she should go to Emerg," my mother (who, true, is a former nurse) re-stated, a little later.

Then Mom went home. Then phoned our home phone, my cellphone, and Pam's Crackberry (if she were able to figure out how to text, I'm sure she would've left a text message, as well), leaving a message on each: "I think Pam should go to emergency. Let me take her."

Then, the next day, she asked Pam how she was feeling, then said to me: "I think she should go to emergency."

Fine, Mom, fine! Pam went to emergency, got some heavy drugs (including the best drug ever invented by man, Percocet), and, truly, began to be on the mend.

Anyway, the point is: war of attrition, see? Keep after your mother about it. Bug her, pester her, do not fear over-iteration or being too obnoxious. Remember, it's for her own good.

Maybe get her to try out a nursing home, or assisted-living facility, overnight: some people have some luck with that. The senior gets a taste of the reality of that type of life, one way or another: sometimes decides it may not be all that bad, after all.

If she still resists – well, I don't know how to put this, except to just put it out there: next time she falls, take her doctor aside, explain to him or her the situation, get him/her to strongly suggest to your mother she give it a try.

Sometimes stubborn old ladies who won't listen to their off-spring will listen to their doctors. Doctors (often convinced of their own godlike powers anyway) appear to have oracu-lar powers to stubborn old ladies.

But that's about all you can do, on your own. Vis-à-vis your siblings, encourage them to become more involved – to come out to wherever you are and lend a helping hand. To observe first-hand your mother's dire straits and urgent need and help you persuade her to do the right thing.

If they refuse, then tell them in no uncertain terms to become *less* involved – i.e., to fuck off – and drop the mate-rial preoccupations, because it's just messing everything up.

Vis-à-vis your mother, it's time for someone to take the lead, a strong lead, and that someone is: you. Tell your sib-lings that.

"I'm taking the lead, here, whether you like it or not. Your job," tell them, "is either to follow or get out of my way.

"Pick one."

WHEN PARENTS BECOME BABUSHKAS

Okay, let us return to the realm of the merely annoying – or, rather, allow me to say: to the strange nexus of love and irri-tation that comprises most run-of-the-mill family dealings:

THE QUESTION
My mother's driving me crazy with her criticism of my parenting.

She's always saying we spoil our children, going on and on about how she did it in her day, and so on.

I actually blew up at her on Mother's Day and I feel incredibly guilty. I love her to death, but it makes me crazy when she criticizes me about my kids. I think I'm doing a good job. How can I get her to back off without hurting her feelings?

THE ANSWER

Well, on the one hand, don't even get me started about how annoying unsolicited parenting advice can be. For years I was a stay-at-home dad.

Stay-at-home moms complain about all the unsolicited advice they get from random busybodies, sanctimonious babushkas, and Nosy Parkers on the street.

But imagine, ladies, when the babushkas got a load of me!

A huge, stubbled, perpetually puzzled- and worried-looking man trying to shut up a squalling, tomato-faced baby in a stroller, on the street, in the park, offering it treats, whipping a bottle of "express milk" out of the cargo pocket of his army pants and jamming it in the craw of his screaming kid, trying desperately to shut him up.

The babushka would freeze, her hump tingling with anticipation, the little hairs in her mole twitching with excitement. Her whole life – all 176 years of it – was a preparation for this moment. Throwing herself in the path of my stroller, she would point an ancient, crooked finger like a gnarly old oak twig at my then-infant son, Nicholas (who's now a brilliant, beautiful, eminently sensible, and exquisitely sensitive twelve-year-old, by the way, babushkas of the world), and croak out her edict: "Your baby cold! Needs another layer!"

Or – and this one would always kill me: "He needs his mommy!"

That line was like a knife in my heart, would make me want to drop to my knees, clutch the hem of the babushka's traditional mourning garment, and sob: "No, babushka, no. . . . Don't say . . . that. . . . I know the kids would probably be better off with her. . . . But see, times have changed since you were young, babushka. There are motorcars now, and computers, and women have joined the workforce. . . ." etc., etc.

But all I ever did was smile and say, "Thank you for your input. You've certainly given me something to think about." And roll Nick away with a frozen rictus of faux gratitude affixed to my kisser.

Why? Because, ladies, that became, in time, my policy.

At first, I would bristle and argue, but I came to realize there was no point, it was a fruitless waste of energy. People who love giving free, unsolicited advice (unsolicited is the lowest form of advice, people; and unsolicited advice to total strangers? That's off the rudeness radar altogether) are not going to change their ways just because you act haughty and say something frosty. All you do is create friction and bad blood.

And sometimes, horribly, the busybodies, babushkas, and unsolicited-advice-volunteers actually have a point. If you drop the bristling and listen, from time to time you can get good advice, even in this unsolicited, off-the-street format.

It can be tough to implement this "smile and say thanks" policy, I know – especially, I've found, in the face of parenting wisdom from people who don't actually have kids themselves.*

And FYI, having "nieces and nephews" does not confer expert parenting status on you, people.† Anyone can be an uncle. You come in, distribute a few presents, a toy or two, some loose change, maybe bust a couple of magic tricks, then leave on a high note, bidding adieu, pressing your bunched fingers to your lips.

Trust me, there are times we parents would also like to leave on a high note, bidding adieu, pressing our fingers to our lips. But we don't have that option.

That's not parenting. Parenting is *ipso facto* when you *can't leave*. That is the very definition of parenting.

---

* I'm guilty of it my own damn self, by the way; Pam, too. Before Pam and I had kids, we might sit around critiquing how her sister was parenting her kids. What we might have said I'll reserve for my final book of memoirs, *I Take It All Back and Sorry About Everything*, by Dave Eddie, but suffice to say we *both* roll our eyes at our jejune former selves for having the effrontery to think we had any idea what we were talking about. You can't know anything until you're in the DMZ of parenting for a while; until you get "salty," as they used to say of people who had been in the field for a while in 'Nam.

† I recall once an obviously gay flight attendant – not that there's anything wrong with it, my brother's gay: but my guess was he didn't have much direct parenting experience – dropped some ludicrous parenting advice to me on the plane. "Thank you, you've certainly given me something to think about," I said through clenched teeth. But he wouldn't drop it, kept coming back to it, until I finally asked him, "Do *you* have any kids, yourself?" "No," he retorted, "but I have nieces and nephews." As if that settled the matter.

Unlike various aunts and uncles, though, your mother does have a lot of direct parenting experience – from raising you.

And her experience was this: for something like the first thirty years of your life, you were wrong about pretty much everything. So it's automatic for her, it's second nature to correct and reprove you and attempt to steer you in the right direction.

Second, parenting has changed unbelievably since her day. And sometimes (like when I go to a restaurant where someone has brought their kids) I think parents of previous generations have a point when they say our kids are spoiled, undisciplined, and obnoxious, and we're too precious with them.

I think of my kids as reasonably well-behaved, but after a weekend in the care of my wife's parents, I'm amazed at the transformation. When we arrive back home, they file out of the kitchen, in single file, hair parted neatly on one side, seen but not heard, practically addressing Pam and me as "Madam" and "Sir."

Of course, it lasts only until the grandparents' car disappears down the street, but while it lasts, what a lovely, pomade-scented whiff of what it must have been like in the days of yore. And sometimes one can't help but wonder: what if they were like that all the time? Wouldn't that be *nice*?

Now I'm not qualified to say what way of bringing up kids is better or worse. All children are different and so are all parents.

Suffice it to say you could probably learn a lot from your mother if you stopped bristling and being defensive and kept an open mind.

But ultimately you're the one responsible for how your kids turn out. Therefore you have the final say in how to handle them.

There is such a thing as being polite yet firm, of saying something such as "Thanks, Mom, I appreciate it, but I prefer to do it this way."

Still, you owe her an apology. She gave birth to you in pain and suffering. She had horrible nights and frustrating days with you, as you now know. She compromised her dreams, ideals, figure, social life, rest, independence, and so much else to protect you and keep you warm, dry, and happy, as you also now know.

She's owed at least one day on which she is honoured with unstinting patience and tolerance. Since you ruined that with your outburst, why not make it up with a bunch of flowers, maybe a nice dinner, and a card that reads: "Mom, I appreciate everything you've done for me, including and especially bestowing upon me the gift of life."

Because hey: if she hadn't done that, you wouldn't be around to feel irritated, now, would you?

TURNS OUT THE OLD MAN WAS A HYPOCRITE

THE QUESTION
We buried my father last month. It's been rough on everyone, especially my mom, who, for the entire marriage, put my father up on a pedestal. He was the example for all the kids – moral, upstanding, self-sacrificing – and she never let us forget it. As it turns out, he wasn't any of those things.

At the funeral I noticed a couple of strangers and, presuming they were old work colleagues, struck up a conversation. They weren't colleagues – they were his kids, from another marriage. They both bore resemblances to Dad, his square chin, those broad shoulders, and they came holding lifelong grudges. He'd abandoned his other family when he met my mom, and never looked back. They'd tracked him down shortly before he died and found out about the funeral from my aunt, who was privy to the scenario for all these years. They assured me they'd be discreet, that they meant no harm to my mother, and they left after paying their respects.

I made the mistake of telling my younger brother, who for most of his life felt like he couldn't meet Dad's high expectations. He hated how pious Dad seemed, how righteously our mother viewed him. Now he wants to come clean with Mom and our sister, to destroy her image of our dad and to knock the old man down a few pegs, even though he's six feet underground. I should've kept it to myself, but it was an emotional time and I felt he had the right to know. Can I stop him from spilling the beans? Should I?

THE ANSWER
I'm going to set aside, or rather *put off*, dealing with the whole question of spreading your DNA seed indiscriminately, starting "franchise families" here and there, then abandoning them to their own fate, until the answer to the next question, because it comes up there.

For now, I'm just going to focus on having an imperfect father, and how, or whether or not, to shield your mother from information about his shady dealings.

I have to say, first of all, the truth has a way of bubbling to the surface of the family hot tub.

For instance, my parents split up when I was twenty-three. For whatever reason – youth, naïveté, solipsism – I never had a clue there were any third parties involved.*

And my mother's plan was to take whatever she knew to the grave with her. But it was a flawed plan, see, because she had quite a bit of anger. And then, when I became a stay-at-home dad for a while, she came over constantly, and I wormed it out of her, over about 1,000,000 cups of coffee.

Turns out Dad was a busy boy indeed, extramaritally. What a hair-raising tale it was, too, when it all came out. Yikes!

Did finding out about my father's extramarital exploits change my opinion of my old man? Absofreakinlutely. Dad was always the moralist and high-horse equestrian, complete with aggrieved air and fine-point lectures. It's a bit harder to swallow, once you think back on what he was up to, morally, the whole time he was moralizing freely in the direction of all around him.

Still, it's better I know the truth, I think. If I know my father was a bit of a dog and a bad boy, a man of weakness and temptation – well, for one thing, I get to know him a little better. My love for him takes on shading and nuance,

---

* I blush to tell you I matured slowly and was a "man-boy" at the time – or must have been. The fact that my father, post-divorce, was suddenly dating a woman who'd been his secretary for many years should've told me everything I needed to know, but I remained serenely, sublimely oblivious. Ah, the soaring, sweeping cluelessness of youth! Now all I have to do at a party is say, "Yeah, uh, my dad is, uh (cough cough) married to his former secretary," and they instantly fill in all blanks.

and I get closer to loving the real man and not some idealized portrait.*

Also, I learn, for myself – in this case, from his anti-
example. When I heard about his many infidelities and saw
the effect it had on my mother (devastating: slow torture), I
resolved with all the more steely resolve never to indulge
myself in this department – even though I have the blood
of a dog coursing warm though my veins. . . .

Why do I tell you all this? Well, it all applies to your case.

First of all, the truth will out, as I say. Especially, sounds
like, in this case. An angry, oppressed brother, itching to
tell: how long's he gonna keep that one bottled up for?

No, I would not discourage him from telling. Partly out
of self-interest. Since she's going to find out anyway, how do
you think your mother will feel if she discovers you tried to
keep this information from her?

Probably that your loyalty lies with your dead father and
not with her.

And the information will probably do her some good.
Better she should have a realistic assessment of the man she
spent all that time with than carry some false image of him
around with her.

For – and if I can impart only one thing to you, dear
reader, in this chapter, or indeed this entire book – it is that

---

* My father was, typical of his generation, a man of few words and rare
expression of emotion. I always thought: "If I'm supposed to be his ticket
to immortality, he's blown it, because I don't have a clue what makes
him tick." It's a big part of why I write. If any of my offspring or indeed
anyone at all wants to know what makes me tick, all they have to do is
pull a Dave Eddie™ book off the shelves, and boom: all is revealed; all
is known.

we must learn to love those around us not only despite but *because* of their faults, flaws, and errors of judgment, taste, and tact; or at least to have a sense of humour about it all.

So your father was a high-handed moralist who started another "franchise family" without telling anyone about it? That might not seem too funny right now, but it may, in time. Comedy equals tragedy plus time, right?

(Though in this case it might take another generation or two . . .)

And once it's all out in the open, I would think you'd want to get together with and maybe get to know the members of this other secret "franchise family." After all, you're related to them! They're your . . . half-brothers, and half-sisters, or something, right?

In any case, they're family, and the more family, the merrier, right? Who knows, maybe in a few years' time, you'll all be sitting around the campfire, roasting weenies and having a good old chuckle about what a rat-bastard scallywag your mutual father, in some ways, was.

Then, once you've got that out of your system, try to remember the good things about him, too. . . .

STICK WITH ANONYMOUS DONORS

But let's take another look at this question of depositing one's DNA indiscriminately, and the possible consequences it can have.

THE QUESTION

My lesbian sister and her life partner recently went through a major case of biological clock ticking. Both are in their forties and are successful artists and businesswomen.

They suddenly realized that "something" was missing: a child. So they decided that borrowed sperm would be needed. In their circle, the natural method has been used – sleeping with the donor, thus knowing exactly the provenance and quality of the genetic material.

Now to me. I was asked to be the donor. My genetic material would ensure that the offspring would look like my sister (we look like twins but are not), or so it was explained. I would have to relinquish all parental rights, and the child would never be told of my role in the situation. I said no and have now essentially lost my sister.

Should I really try to mend this fence? I feel that I did nothing wrong.

THE ANSWER

I don't think you've done anything wrong, either.

Your sister, though: oy. What – and I mean this in the most positive, supportive way – is she thinking?

Thirty seconds' reflection would reveal this for what it is: a really, really bad idea. Oddly enough, a similar dilemma is unfurling in the midst of my own milieu. A gay friend of mine is "mulling," as the tabloid headline writers say, the idea of donating sperm to a lesbian friend who wants kids.

Now, he hasn't asked my opinion. But if he were to ask, and I happened to be in a mood to drop some pro bono Eddiefication™ on his derrière, I would say: "For God's sake, man, don't do it! You're going to bring a child into the world but pretend for its entire life that you're not its father?"

These things tend to end in tears. I remember we used to have a mayor, here in Toronto; a man, far from flawless, named Mel Lastman.

Physically, he was, and is, quite distinctive. A man of prognathous jawline and Brillo-pad-like hair, before he became mayor he was famous for his ads for "Bad Boy" furniture, his company: "Who's better than Bad Boy? Noooooo-body!"

Well, turns out Mr. Lastman was (allegedly) a "bad boy" not only in the arena of low-priced furniture. He had two (alleged) secret love children, Kim and Todd Louie.

As time went on, and Kim and Todd Louie hit their thirties, they got tired of everyone saying, "Damn, you guys look a hell of a lot like Mel Lastman! Have you ever considered the possibility he's your father?"

They stroked their exactly-like-Lastman's chins, scratched their Lastman-replica thinning hair-Brillos, and thought, "Hm, it's true Mom used to work for him at Bad Boy."

She told them what happened, then they sued Mr. Lastman for millions in retroactive child support.

He admitted to a fourteen-year extramarital affair with the mother, Grace Louie, but neither confirmed nor denied fathering the two mini-Mels. The judge tossed the Louies' lawsuit, comparing Mr. Lastman's legal status with that of a sperm donor.

So Mr. Lastman beat the rap. But is that the kind of father you want to be?

Because it'll play out in a similar fashion for you. I mean, children are only so gullible for so long. As this kid grows older, he's going to look at your sister, and he's going to think: "Hmmm. True, I look a lot like my 'other mother.' Which is nice. But if I've got this whole birds-and-bees thing straight, there's really no way she could actually have inseminated my birth mom."

Then he's going to take a long look at you. And he's going to think, "Hmmm. I also look a lot like my uncle."

And a light bulb's going to go on above his looks-exactly-like-yours head. Then he's going to want to play catch with you. And go to baseball games.

Now, becoming a father is one of the best and most profound things that can happen to a man, in my opinion. It's one of the greatest joys life has to offer. But it involves much more than the donation of 500 million sperm.

It's tying skates. It's drying tears. This morning (as I write this) I rolled up my sleeve and reached with my bare hand into a toilet bowl full of floating turds to extract a toy motorcycle my youngest son had dropped in there while going "No. 2."

Why? Because I love him, and I want him to be happy.

I know I'm not exactly doing the world's best sales job on fatherhood here, but you're going to want that too. You're going to want to be involved. And your child's going to want it. He or she is going to want to spend time with you, believe me. To hold your hand. To give you a hug. To say, "I love you, Dad," and have you say it back.

You're going to turn your back on that? You'd have to have a heart of stone. So if you secretly want to be a father, and you can make some sort of arrangement with your sister where you can be involved, have some visitation rights and so on – some sort of "Uncle Dad" thing – go for it.

Otherwise, you're doing the right thing by saying no, no question.

Sit your sister down and explain all this to her. Tell her that unless you are going to be involved in the child-rearing, then it's in the best interests of all parties – you, her, the unborn child – for her to get an anonymous donor. A donor, preferably, whose identity the child cannot discover by hook or by crook, charm or bribery.

Because the kid will try, I bet, even under those circumstances. I know I would. I'd want to find my dad, even if he didn't want to be found. Deoxyribonucleic acid (a.k.a. DNA) can act like a powerful drug. It can really mess with your head.

If she still stays angry, that's her problem. Yours too, it's true. But trust me, having your sister mad at you is a minuscule problem compared with the one you'd create – a problem that would keep growing and growing and growing – by saying yes.

UNPEEL KLING KONG, THE ADHESIVE TWIN

That's one end of the spectrum of familial problems: people who are, or are trying to be, completely detached, disinterested, and uninvolved.

There's plenty of friction at the other end of the spectrum, though, when family goes all Velcro on you.

THE QUESTION
I am currently dating a twenty-five-year-old fraternal twin. He seems to be adjusting to an independent life, but his brother is very clingy, controlling, and aggressive. He hits

my boyfriend and criticizes every move he makes. Over the course of our relationship, my boyfriend has vented to me about his brotherly issues.

But the damage stems from several occasions where I have stood up for my boyfriend. I wasn't verbally abusive in any way – I just backed up my guy's conclusions. But since that time, his brother has been treating me like Public Enemy No. 1. Now he makes all sorts of accusations about me to our mutual friends and claims I am "stealing" his brother. I really don't know what to do, and I have stopped trying to defend myself. I am worried he may hold some sort of resentment toward me. What should I do?

THE ANSWER

I know twins can have a profound connection to one another. You often hear anecdotally about cases of "twin telepathy," where one twin can supposedly read the other's thoughts, and of "twin empathy," where if one has a heart attack the other feels a terrible pain in the chest, and so on.

There was even one experiment where they put eight-year-old twins in separate rooms, and the needles on the polygraph hooked up to one purportedly jumped when the other plunged his arm into icy cold water or was surprised when a toy snake popped out of a box.

But it's not clear how legitimate this experiment was, or whether the phenomenon of twin empathy has been proved to the satisfaction of the scientific community (and I have to admit to my own bias: extreme skepticism when it comes to this sort of thing).

It is well-documented, though, that twins often finish each other's sentences and seem unusually in tune with one another. Sometimes, growing up, they even develop their own language, which no one else can understand, called "idioglossia."

So the bond can be really strong. And obviously your boyfriend's twin brother is feeling the pain and anxiety of separation – and perhaps a little envy, hmmm?

It's hard enough for us regular jocks when anyone around us scores something we want. "Why him/her?" you think. "Why not me?" Imagine how hard it must be for a twin to watch his other half succeed.

I know I'd hate it if my twin was out on the town, scoring all the babes, popping champagne bottles, accepting awards, laughing and twirling on the dance floor, while I sat home with a bag of Cheetos watching *Stuck on You* for the millionth time, dabbing tears from my eyes.

So try to be sensitive to the twin's pain and what he may be going through.

But at the same time, you and your boyfriend need to set some boundaries with Kling Kong, the adhesive twin. I mean: he hits your boyfriend? Did I read that correctly? At the age of twenty-five? How does he even have the opportunity?

Really, I feel there's only so much you can do in this circumstance. Your boyfriend is the one who needs to step up. Where is he in all this? "Venting" to you like a little 'fraidy-mouse half-man? You're defending him; why isn't he defending you?

He needs to practise Clause 23-B of the Damage Control Code of Ethics: "If someone starts trashing someone in your crew, you come back at the trash-talker with maximum hostility and aggressiveness."

This part of the Code is not a guy thing or a girl thing.

It's gender-neutral, and in fact the best example I've ever seen of the application of this maxim was by a woman.

At a party to celebrate her recent nuptials, a friend of mine "peaked early," shall we say, beverage-wise, found herself a tad over-refreshed in the early going, and by 9 p.m. had to crawl up the stairs and curl up under her duvet.

Afterward, observing this, some random guy (at the party, which continued unabated and no whit dimmed), standing next to her best friend, the maid of honour, said something to the effect of "How lame is that, getting so trashed at your own wedding party that you pass out at nine o'clock?"

The maid of honour's reaction was instantaneous and unequivocal. "What do you know about it, Fat Neck? Don't even talk about her! She's great and she can do whatever she wants! Who are you anyway?"

It was cool. Though she was a good foot shorter than him, she was on him like a pit bull on a Shih Tzu. His mouth snapped shut and stayed shut.

Now that, I thought at the time, is a good lieutenant. She should be given an immediate field promotion for outstanding loyalty and aggression under fire.

I think something similar is called for here. Your boyfriend needs to sit his brother down, offer him a stick of Doublemint gum, and say: "Listen, we're not kids any more. Grow up, stop acting like we're conjoined, stop saying nasty things about my girlfriend, and get on with your own life."

And the next time your boyfriend's former uterus mate punches him, I think your boyfriend should reach out, grab his brother's nipples through the fabric of his shirt, and twist one clockwise, the other counterclockwise, until this toxic Tweedledum screams out in pain. Then he should lean forward and say (maybe in their private idioglossia, if they have one, for added intimacy, intimidation, and effectiveness): "If you ever hit me again I'm going to break a chair over your fucking head."

Normally I don't advocate violence, but cretinous brothers call for Cro-Magnon measures. Of course, feelings may get hurt. Feathers may be ruffled. Your boyfriend may find it difficult after all these years to stand up to his domineering doppelganger. And if there's any truth to twin empathy, your boyfriend's own nipples may wind up being sore for a couple of days.

But sounds to me like it'll do them both a world of good to grow up, and apart, a little. Now's the time to do it.

And hey, sometimes tough decisions, ruffled feathers, and sore nipples are the price you have to pay for being in a romantic relationship.

Ladies, am I right?

WHEN KIDS START TO JUDGE

By the time this book comes out, my oldest son, Nick, will be a teenager (thirteen). He's not there, yet, thank God: he's still a "tweenager," or, as he prefers to be called, "a pre-teen."

Almost since infancy, he's always been a "boy of principle," a real philosopher who lives his life according to his ever-evolving belief-systems, and I have a feeling when it comes for him to judge me, he's going to judge me *hard*.

Fair enough. Pure karmic backlash, and I deserve it. As a teen, I judged my old man, hard, and also gave him a wild ride.

He was too "bourgeois" for my taste. I remember I, the teenage David Eddie, walking behind my parents, scruffy-jeaned, face hidden behind my Wall of Hair™, seething with anti-materialistic ardour and full of desire to *"épater le bourgeoisie"* as my parents innocently strolled along the avenue and pointed out one house after another and exclaimed:

"Ooh, look at that one, that's a nice house, isn't it?"

"What the *&^%$#@!" I'd think, walking behind them. "It's just a *thing*, man. Who cares?" Why didn't they care more about art/poetry/friends/love and "expanding their consciousness," as I was, through the frequent use of numerous mind-altering substances and various assorted intoxicants?

But so much of life comes full circle, doesn't it? I laugh whenever I catch Pam and me, walking down the street, oooh-ing and aah-ing and pointing out the features of various houses and gardens, the kids trailing behind us, bored stiff.

And if, in a few years, when Nick starts to seethe and stew as he observes me from behind his own Wall of Hair – well, so be it. I'll deserve it.

Still, I've spent the last few years trying to nip it in the bud.

THE QUESTION

My husband and I are agnostics, or at least we're non-practising. Recently our ten-year-old daughter has become a devout Christian. She reads the Bible and prays, and now she's been agitating for us to take her to church on Sundays. And the other day she calmly informed us that we were probably going to hell.

I got really upset at that and gave her a time-out, which I now regret. I mean, I shouldn't be punishing her for what she believes or telling her how to think. But I'm worried she's going to become intolerant of others' views. It just feels weird to have someone with such a different belief system in the midst of our family – one who also believes we're going to hell. And, to be honest, going to church is about the last thing I feel like doing on Sunday mornings. Any advice?

THE ANSWER

You're at the nexus of two ticklish topics – religion and parenting – so I'll try to tread carefully.

First let me say I know how it feels. I too have a highly religious child in the midst of our mostly secular family.

To clarify: I believe in God, but don't go to church. My wife is an agnostic and believes it's "lights out" when we die. (And I've noticed, over the years, a curious phenomenon: she almost always turns out to be right about everything. I just pray she's wrong on this one.)

Last year, Nick went with his best friend, who's part of a devout Christian family, to Bible camp and came back indoctrinated to the eye-teeth. Now he wears a cross,* reads the Bible, and prays every night. (I suppose he thinks his mother and I are both going to hell, but I've never asked him.)

Personally, I'm glad he's a spiritual kid and that he's found something to believe in. But I also believe intolerance and extremism are the things to be worried about, and should be dealt with early, and firmly.

* As do I.

A few summers ago we went to Prince Edward Island, and Nick, who loves animals, was horrified by all the lobster boils and clambakes.* One morning he was glaring at me, so I asked him if there was a problem.

"I prayed to the Lord last night that something bad would happen to you and Uncle John because of the way you *torture* lobsters and clams," he said – then burst into tears.

"Hey, hey, *hey*, kid!" I said. "That's not Christianity! That's not the Christian spirit!"

So we had a serious chat about respecting other people's beliefs, not judging people, not wishing ill on family members, especially in the name of religion, and so on. I'm happy to say that that's all it took, for now: a serious chat. Because when all is said and done he's a reasonable kid.

And that's job one, isn't it – the raising of reasonable children? Children are naturally extremists: you have to teach them to be reasonable.

Internationally renowned parenting expert Barbara Coloroso agrees. She believes nipping things like intolerance and extremism in the bud can have huge consequences. In her book *Extraordinary Evil*, she basically blames the various holocausts of the twentieth century on bad parenting.

I told her about your case and she said you should sit your child down and ask her to ask herself if she is using religion as a "vessel or a weapon. . . .

"Ask her if she's using religion to honour the intrinsic spirituality of human beings," she said, "or to create intolerance toward differences."

* Hey, I love animals too, especially seafood. I am, along with barbecue guru Ted Reader, a member of PETA: People for the Eating of Tasty Animals.

Ms. Coloroso says children are highly susceptible to indoctrination, to "swallowing whole" what somebody tells them. Obviously there's not much you can do about who gets to them first (and it's often occurred to me that if Nick went to Jewish camp he'd be walking around with a tallis and a yarmulke now). But you can help them to become "religious literates," i.e., teach them about other religions and belief systems, so at least they can make an informed choice.

Now, Ms. Coloroso is opposed to punishment of all kinds and believes everything can be talked out; a position with which I am not necessarily in wholehearted agreement. But I would say if you give time-outs in other areas, you shouldn't feel guilty giving time-outs in this area, too. After all, you're not punishing your daughter for *what* she believes, but rather *how* she expresses that belief.

As for going to church, well, I hear you. I want to like church. I wish I liked church. But on the blue-moon occasions I go, I always emerge blinking in the sunshine and thinking "Damn, that was just as deadly dull as I remember it from being a kid."

Still, why not go to church with your daughter? What do you have to lose, except a little time? (And if she's right about there being a God and a heaven, then you stand to gain it all back, and then some, on the back end.) There are such things as fun churches. When I lived in New York I used to go to services at a Baptist church in Harlem: people sang, swayed, clapped their hands. The sermons were funny, and the congregation would heckle the priest. My kind of church – the opposite of the dour, funereal Lutheran tradition I was brought up in.

Maybe there's something a little more lively like that in your neighbourhood.

Even the worst service leaves you with something to think about, a chance to step back and reflect on your pursuits and the passage of time. Maybe go for some Eggs Bennie after, to reward yourself. It'll be nice daughter-mom time, and you'll come to understand her beliefs better.

And you want to show her agnostics can be flexible too, right?

I'll make you a deal: if you do go, write me, and perhaps, inspired by you, I'll start going to church with my son.

Then he and I can pray together that I will be cured of my sins and shellfish ways.

YOUR TAKEAWAY DOGGIE BAG OF THOUGHTS

- **You're stuck with your family so you might as well figure out how to deal with them.**

- **Even if your family's acting mental, invite them to stuff.** If they comport themselves with less than ultimate propriety, it's on them, not you.

- **It is extremely difficult to compel a family member to do something, even if it's in his/her best interests. Use the gentle art of persuasion, instead.** Solicit the help of a trained professional/expert to weigh in and help your cause, for example.

- **Respond to unsolicited parenting advice with supreme mildness.** Smile and say, "Thank you for your input." To yourself, say, "Forgive them, Lord, they know not what they do." It may be annoying, but you can actually learn from unsolicited parenting advice, as well as the other (solicited) kind.

- **When it comes to dark secrets and family skeletons – what the hell: better to know the truth.** Then, you can love your family in "warts and all fashion"; what you love will be the real person, not some idealized portrait.

  Even if all is not necessarily sweetness and sunshine – well, you can learn from the example of your older relatives; but it is also possible to extract numerous valuable lessons from their *anti-example*.

- **Do not spread your DNA lightly or indiscriminately.** You bring a creature into the world with your genes, you're responsible for it, end of story.

- **Set boundaries with overly clingy family members.** Same goes for in-laws or even family members of someone you're just dating.

- **The goal of parenthood is the raising of reasonable children.** Children are naturally extremists who see things in black and white. Help them temper their idealism with reason and to shade in the grey areas of the world they're growing into.

DAMAGE CONTROL MASTER CLASS

WELCOME TO THE NEXT LEVEL

Okay, so you survived the obstacle course of courtship. You kept an open heart, avoided making bitter, angry generalizations about the opposite sex; you weren't too intense; but you did go strong to the hoop. You made it past The Fortnight Test, established yourself as a definite "possible," and possibly even a "definite." A keeper.

Maybe you even took it up a notch, got married, entered into a cohabitational arrangement, tattooed the name of your beloved on your bicep, or all or some combination of the above. You took off in a plane called Commitment; survived occasional turbulence, possibly some heavy weather, and loss of cabin pressure, perhaps even the crash of the entire craft. You walked away scarred and charred, possibly; but after brushing off the shrapnel and flaming chunks of fuselage lived to soar above the clouds once more.

At work, you dodged the blow-darts, snakepits, and booby traps; you made allies of enemies by coating them in a neutralizing, slow-hardening foam of friendliness; you curried the boss's sweet-and-sour favours both inside and outside the office.

But you didn't show off too much. You were mindful, also, of the esteem of your co-workers and took care not to create too many Cassiuses. Thus you avoided Early Flameout Syndrome, or, if not, handled yourself with aplomb during the outplacement process; worked to get yourself back in the game; and lived to praise your boss's tie, or brooch, or cooking, or cowboy boots, another day.

Out on the social circuit, you gritted your teeth, suffered the zings and arrows of everyone else's outrageous "insultiments" and "questi-burns"; you apologized humbly, profusely, and without reservations for your own faux pas, uncouth utterances, and outright obnoxiousness, and left everyone wanting more, as you fluttered butterfly-like out of every social gathering, pressing your bunched fingers to your lips and bidding the crowd "*Adieu, adieu, je ne regrette rien,*" leaving everyone thinking "Now there goes one hell of a guy/gal."

Vis-à-vis your family, you tolerated their madness and minimized the drama; you invited them to stuff themselves, tried to ignore their crazy opinions, along with the mustard stains on their blouses (that look a little like a silhouette of Abraham Lincoln) and crumbs in their beards. You strove to raise your own children to become the most reasonable human beings possible, while simultaneously remembering to keep yourself on an even keel and remain a colourful, interesting, non-Tilley-hat-or-fanny-pack-wearing member of society.

Well, congratulations! You've managed to hang on, and not lose any ground, in all these departments! Kudos and hearty, teeth-rattling backslaps all around! Here, have a glass of bubbly! We make it ourselves, in some old industrial tubs in a disused shaft in one of the bunker's subterranean cata-combs, made from grapes we grow on the southern slopes right above our mountain retreat.

And hey, while you're at it, have a cigar, direct from the bunker's humidor, you deserve it! Kick back, relax, take a load off. Because these days, life is so complicated, treach-erous, and tortuous, just avoiding losing ground is an accomplishment in itself. We're proud of you for coming this far, for reaching this plateau, in your "journey."

But we're hoping that reaching a plateau, flipping open a lawn chair, and deciding to hang out there and get a nice tan is not your style.

We want you everlastingly to strive onward and upwards, no matter how well you feel you're doing, to keep punch-ing your way forward into the future.

It's not healthy, we feel, to stand, or sit, or lie still; at least not for a prolonged period of time. Stasis = death, people! You're like a shark: swim or die.

A friend of ours, Andrew Livingston, once bumped into Robin Leach, the *Lifestyles of the Rich and Famous* guy, in Europe.

"Hey, man, I'm sorry to ask you this, you probably get asked it all the time," Livingston said. "But I got to know: is there one particular quality you've ever noticed that is common to all rich and famous people?"

"That's a good question, and actually, I haven't been asked it," Robin Leach said (according to Livingston, anyway). Then, after a moment of reflection, scratching his chin: "No, all in all, I can't say there is."

Then he thought a moment longer and said, "I'll tell you this, though. When someone thinks they've made it? When they feel they've finally arrived? They're usually on their way down."

In other words, even a hotshot like Johnny Depp probably doesn't think, "Ah, I've made it, I'm Johnny Depp, I can relax, now." He's probably always striving, pushing, angling for the next thing.

It's the complacent dopes who say, "Ah, I've made it – I've arrived!" and as a consequence let their guards down, who are in the biggest danger of a royal comeuppance/flameout.

CYH – remember?* Thus does it all come full circle.

Now, perhaps, for one reason or another, you have let your guard down. You've lapsed, or been lulled, into a false sense of complacency – or worse, the reverse: given up hope of any future progress or improvement. Decided: "Ah, what the heck, I'm never going to make it, it's not 'all gonna happen' for me. Uncle. I give."

Perhaps you've sunk, like a horse and buggy, into a pool of quicksand, into a brief rut. Perhaps you feel, as I did, from time to time, during my stay-at-home dad years, that you've

* "Curb Your Hubris," just in case you forgot.

wound up in the doldrums, that one or more aspects of your life – whether personal, career, social, familial – has drifted into the "horse latitudes."*

Don't let it throw you! Don't let your rut become a trench, and, ultimately, your grave! Recall the wise words of Jimmy Connors, the greatest tennis player who ever lived, mentioned earlier: "Don't look upon a period of inactivity as a failure. Rather, treat it as a challenge and try to get back on track as soon as you can."

I never gave a fucking shit about tennis, incidentally, growing up; or, indeed, any televised sport at all. But Jimmy Connors was something else altogether. I was pinned to the TV, as a child, when he came on.

Because he never, ever, ever gave up. Shots other people would just throw up their hands at and say "Impossible!" – he would go after! It was a mesmerizing spectacle, because you were kind of cringing for him and pulling for him at the same time.

His opponent would have him completely fooled, and heading in the wrong direction, with a cleverly placed drop shot or surprise cross-court volley – in any case, a clear winner.

"Ah, tough luck, Jimmy," you'd think. "Better luck next time."

But then, with a curious admixture of shock, horror, and faint hope, you would see – he's going after it! You could

---

* A part of the high seas where no winds blow. So named because after a while, when a sailing vessel of the days of yore had been stranded without wind for long enough in the "horse latitudes," the crew would start throwing horses (because they drank too much of the onboard supply of fresh water).

scarcely believe your eyes! The television announcers expressed their open incredulity, sadness, and pity bordering on disgust, at the ludicrous display unfolding before their horrified eyes.

"Ah, no," you'd think, egged on by the commentators' pooh-poohing comments. "Jimmy . . . no . . . oh, Jimmy, don't . . . you're just embarrassing yourself . . . This is just sad . . . Oh, my God, I can't watch . . ."

But then – he'd get it! Crazily, marvellously, he'd dive or pirouette, or leap, or (at least, as I seem to recall, on one occasion) slide toward the ball – and return the shot!

Then it would be his opponent who was flummoxed, cross-purposed, and short-circuited: the one standing there stunned as Jimmy's return dribbled over the net, to win the point.

That's why Jimmy Connors is, in our humble estimation, "the greatest tennis player of all time." You can have your Federers, your Borgs, your Agassis, and Arthur Ashes. They probably have, or had, more talent in their throbbing elbows than Jimmy had in his whole frame.

But that's the point. Connors famously had no forehand, a sucky serve, and even his trademark double-handed backhand probably wouldn't be much to write home about, in the modern game, anyway, and probably wasn't even then.

But he had heart – the "heart of a lion," the heart of a champion, and that's what *made* him a champion. He might lose. But it was never because he gave up. To win, you'd have to beat him, and he didn't make it easy.

And that's how he won eight Grand Slams, despite whatever handicaps he may have had in the talent department.

That's how we want you to be. As Jimmy Connors was to

tennis, so should you be to life. If you never give up and try to salvage every lost cause where others in your Chuck Taylors might give up, you'd be surprised what you can pull out of the fire.

And it's precisely when everyone thinks you're finished; fucked; sunk; flamed out, Icarus-style; that you are, perversely, in a strong position. What've you got to lose? And if you can somehow pull it out of the flames at that point, you can fly higher than ever.

Let's take a look at a couple of high-profile examples of how this phenomenon could possibly work and see what juice we could possibly extract from them.

HUNGOVER, HOOCH-LOVING HONCHO FACE-PLANTS! STAGGERS OUT OF PUBLIC LIFE FOREVER!

Something that happened to Ralph Klein, the popular former premier of Alberta, is the best example of this phenomenon we know.

Mr. Klein rose to power on his folksy, "man of the people" image – an image that was belied somewhat by the events of one night during the Christmas season, 2001.

On his way home from a Christmas party packed with many of his fellow plutocrats, oligarchs, and government-fat-chewing bigwigs, a somewhat over-refreshed Mr. Klein instructed the driver of his limousine to pull over near a homeless shelter.

He may have *intended* his visit to be folksy and man-of-the-people-ish.

But it didn't really work out that way. Slurring his words, Mr. Klein started chewing out the poor, trembling, homeless men and women, huddled over their plastic trays of dried-out turkey and from-a-box instant mashed potatoes, berating them for not having jobs, and so forth.

(Many of them did in fact have jobs and were part of Edmonton's "working homeless": the capital of the oil-rich province of Alberta had at that point a 1 per cent vacancy rate and it was tough to find a place even if you had a job.)

He then became embroiled in a loud altercation with several of them, before his driver managed to grab him and hustle him out of there. As he left he continued shouting imprecations at the homeless people, and also contemptuously flung a fistful of money on the floor.

Obviously, when news of these events got out, the press made a meal of it.

And at first, perhaps thinking the scandal would blow over quickly, the premier's office did some fairly standard-issue, b.s.-filled damage control, of the lie-deny-spin variety.

The premier's chief of staff, Peter Elzinga, denied the premier had been drunk at all (!). He claimed the premier had stopped into the shelter "out of the goodness of his heart" and had merely, in twinkly, avuncular fashion, out of purely altruistic motives, distributed about seventy dollars to the poor unfortunates he encountered there.

Then Mr. Klein himself publicly apologized for the "commotion" he caused at the shelter and also denied being drunk. His interest had been piqued, he said, by recent reports of the rise in homelessness in Alberta and his visit to the shelter was purely educational/philanthropic in nature.

"The purpose of my visit," Mr. Klein smoothly orated, "was to chat with residents and find out what their situations are like. During my time in politics, I have periodically made such unscheduled visits because they give me the opportunity to chat privately and honestly with people from different walks of life."

Which is . . . I mean, it's just so . . . Sorry, excuse us, one second [Dave and Pat whip out hankies, dab away tears].

Sorry about that. It's . . . not that we're so moved by Mr. Klein's mendacious speechifying. We were . . . We've just been chopping some onions, that's all. Sorry. We've got it together now.

The problem with this damage-control approach was fourfold: (a) it was obvious b.s.; (b) no one bought it; (c) it underestimated the intelligence of the listener; (d) there were too many witnesses to gainsay it and provide their own version of events.

Like Mark Shea. He'd recently moved to Alberta from Nova Scotia but, despite getting a job at a gas station, was having a hard time finding an apartment. So he was temporarily bunking at the shelter until he found something suitable.

After finishing his work shift, he arrived at the shelter, he told the *Edmonton Journal*, and "lo and behold, there he [Mr. Klein] was in the middle of six or seven guys, yelling at them at the top of his lungs" to get a job, stop being such shiftless moochers and bums, and so forth.

"I don't drink or do drugs and he's telling me to get a job when I already have one. If I wouldn't have gotten arrested, I would have slugged him."

Despite efforts to manage the situation, the anti-Klein editorials started to pile up. The murmuring for his resignation became a muttering; the muttering became a clamouring. He was hemorraging points in the popularity polls.

All of a sudden he was in a bubbling tub of political hot water, and the temperature kept going up.

He knew he had to do something. Something different from what he'd done. But what?

The move he chose was a bold one indeed. He called a press conference to tell everyone that, basically . . . he was a drunk.

Blinking back tears, Mr. Klein admitted to a thirty-year drinking problem and even admitted it probably affected his ability to work, at times.

"When you wake up with a hangover it affects your job performance. It's happened more often than I'd like."

He also admitted that sometimes he needed a bit of the old "hair of the dog" to get himself going in the mornings, to shake off the shakes and brush off the alcoholic whim-whams.

"When you get up and you're feeling rotten and you wonder, 'You know, gee, I feel this badly, do I really want to get on and do the work of the day?'" he asked the reporters present, who were no doubt scribbling furiously in their notebooks, double-checking to make sure their tape recorders and cameras were really on to witness this historic, confessional comeuppance.

He said he had thought about resigning, but had resolved to carry on and beat the "awful beast," as he described his drinking problem. "I think I have the ability to carry on with the job. I think I have the ability to fight this devil and win.

"I have resolved to make sure drinking does not affect me personally or professionally in the future," he said. He planned, he said, to "take it one day at a time."

He didn't even promise to quit drinking!

I can only imagine the thought-balloon that must have arisen above the collective melons of the reporters present at that press conference.

"Oh, man," they must've thought. "I can't believe I'm witnessing this Icarus-style flameout first-hand. Man, it's just like they told us in journalism school: we're on the 'front lines of history,' for sure! Wonder what headline they're going to give my write-up back at the newsroom? PREMIER TIPPLES, TOPPLES. Or maybe: HUNGOVER HONCHO FACEPLANTS, STAGGERS OUT OF OFFICE FOREVER."

But a funny thing happened. The citizenry of Alberta removed their collective Stetsons, stared across the dusty prairies at the eternally, coitally churning oil derricks, and said to themselves:

"You know what? I don't give an oilrigger's outhouse crap. H-E-double-hockey-sticks, I don't mind the odd nip myself, after a long, hot day! Hanging around these god-damn dusty prairies can make a fellow thirsty, doggone it! And I suppose it's affected my job performance from time to time. Anyways, I always liked this feller's style, and I appreciate his honesty. I forgive him. Jesus on a popsicle stick, I reckon I like him even better than before."

Mr. Klein's approval ratings went through the roof! And he continued putting up big numbers until he voluntarily decided to retire a few years ago.

Now, we don't want you to extract any too-literal lessons from this scenario.

Obviously, we're not suggesting that the next time you screw something up, you call a press conference to inform the world you are a drunk wrestling with the demon alcohol; that it sometimes affects your job performance; but you plan on dealing with it "one day at a time."

But some useful juice can be extracted from Mr. Klein's case, we feel.

First of all, it's a testimonial to the power of apology and of people's capacity for forgiveness.

Recall, if you will, for example, for starters, that both the premier's spokesperson, then the premier himself, initially attempted to enshroud the circumstances of that as-it-turns-out-not-all-that-fateful December night in a dry-ice fog of lies and deception: "Oooh, me not drunk! Me sober! Me pay *philanthropico-educational* visit to stinking, steaming, mooching bums!"

It was only when it didn't seem like the public really bought it that he switched tacks.

But you think the people who forgave him just simply *forgot* that he lied?

No, they remembered.

But *they forgave him that, too.* The citizens of Alberta said to themselves, I believe, "Dagnabbit, I might've lied in that feller's boots, at first, my own dang self."

When he finally came clean, in his *mea culpa* press conference, it was, in a way, that much easier to forgive him. He was only "human," after all.

So let's make that **Master Class Rule No. 1: People's capacity to forgive tends to run deeper than you might think, as long as you are humble, hubris-free, and human.**

Corollary: People can forgive you just about everything, as long as you don't insult their intelligence.

See below:

THE QUESTION

I've always hated the office holiday party, so this year, I had an excuse at the ready when the invite came. A couple of days after I declined, when my boss asked about my upcoming "charity night" (my excuse), I drew a blank and he called me on it. He considers attendance at the event a show of company loyalty, and now he's pegged me as a "lying weasel." What can I do?

THE ANSWER

A wise man once said to me, when he found out I was the Damage Control guy: "You know, I've always felt people can forgive just about *anything* – they can even forgive when you lie to them. . . ."

"Right!" I said, interrupting him rudely (I'm an "advice nerd" and can't help myself, sometimes). "Because deep down they know they might have done something similar in your boots."

"Yes," he said coolly, ignoring my interruption. "The one thing they can't forgive, though, is when you insult their intelligence."

The wise man was righteously on the money. You can lie to people. You can screw them over. You can cheat them. You can cheat *on* them. You can insult them, insult their husbands, political beliefs, haberdashery – and still find forgiveness in the end. But insult their intelligence and they'll come after you with pitchforks and blowtorches; they'll get medieval on your derrière.

So you lied to your boss. With this we can deal. But don't you dare insult his intelligence by clinging to your cheesy lie or it could all end in tears.

Ruefully admit to your mistake. Maybe throw in a little self-promo action and say you're more worker bee than social butterfly, you prefer spreadsheets and pie charts to cocktails and canapés (careful, though: again, if you think you'll insult his intelligence, don't go there).

Then suck it up and show up. Woody Allen said 80 per cent of life is showing up, and the office Christmas parties definitely qualify.

You don't have to stay long (especially if you're a parent, all you have to do is tap your watch with a concerned look and say, sadly: "The . . . sitter . . . gotta go": works every time).

Work the room, then leave on a high note, leave everyone wanting more. That's showbiz, baby!

Yes, people hate it when you insult their intelligence. When you insult their intelligence, that's when they come after you with the buckets of hot tar and bags of feathers.

But let's return for a moment to the Ralph Klein example.

Because I want to take note of one other interesting little aspect of it:

Note how, in a feat of almost prestidigitation-like misdirection, Mr. Klein's apology completely changed the subject under debate.

Suddenly, the debate no longer centred on that which really bugged *me* about the scenario, anyway, which was: supposed man-of-the-people plutocrat, *driven to a homeless shelter by his chauffeur*, chews out trembling homeless people in a decidedly non-man-of-the-people style.

No, it was: *Mr. Klein bravely admits to battle with bottle.*

It became all about his honesty, his character, and the whole "chewing out the homeless" aspect of the story was left in the dust.

So let's make that **Master Class Rule No. 2: Use your apology to frame the terms of debate.**

Say one of your underlings at work screwed up, but it was your responsibility to keep tabs on that person's actions. You must go into your boss's office to apologize. But the way you apologize to him/her will frame the terms of debate in the future.

Is the debate whether you're a good manager? The competence of the underling? Hiring practices in the future? You decide. It's all in the subtle way you word your apology. We're not going to tell you how to do that; it has to do with the specifics of the personalities involved; the details of the situation; your conscience; the security of your position; and a hundred other variables.

But suffice to say, short of out-and-out backstabbing, it's probably best if you frame the debate in a way that ensures your continued success.

HOW CAN I GET OUT OF HERE WITHOUT GOING ANYWHERE NEAR THAT GARAGE?

Mr. Klein's example also brings up the knotty question of *transparency*.

Transparency is an error-rectification strategy to be used judiciously. Sometimes it's your best friend; sometimes your worst enemy.

For an example of the former, we were charmed, recently, to read the story of a certain David Cowan.

In the year 2000, Mr. Cowan was having dinner at a friend's house in Silicon Valley, when the friend told him two "really smart Stanford students" were renting her garage and in it they were building an Internet search engine.

Mr. Cowan was a partner with Bessemer Venture Partners, one of the oldest and most distinguished venture-capital firms in America. As such, his job was to seek out and invest in fledgling companies.

But his interest was not piqued by the two geeks in his hostess's garage.

"How can I get out of here without going anywhere *near* that garage?" he recalls saying to himself upon that occasion.

Gentle reader: have you guessed, already, where this story's going? Did you get there ahead of me?

The geeks in the garage were none other than Sergey Brin and Larry Page, and the little-search-engine-that-could they were building in the hostess's garage would later come to be called . . ."Google."

Perhaps you've heard of it?

Mr. Cowan's incuriosity cost his company not only millions but *billions*.

He also on another occasion turned down a pitch from a fledgling online trading company, thinking: "Stamps? Coins? Comic books? You've *got* to be kidding."

That online trading company would later be known as eBay. Perhaps you've heard of it, too?

And how do we know these facts? Because Bessemer posts them on their website, in their rueful, self-deprecating "anti-portfolio" of missed opportunities and fortunes never made and now forever lost.

In this case, "transparency" is both a charming and highly effective corporate strategy, because it makes you think: (a) "What a trustworthy company," and (b) "They must be *really powerful* to be able to confess to these types of oversights."

Which is great, if you are a large, powerful, investment-capital firm.

Less so, we feel, if you're a fledgling intern or new at a company.

God, I remember my first "real" job, as a journalist. I was a reporter for *The East Hampton Star*, on Long Island.

I was fresh out of journalism school, twenty-six years old.

And I remember bouncing along on the Jitney,* on the way to my first day on the job, saying to myself: "Not only will I forthrightly and virtuously confess to my own mistakes, but I will also, in certain circumstances, 'fall on the grenade' for one of my newfound colleagues, and admit to *their* mistakes as well."

(In other words, I would claim I had made the mistake someone else had in fact made.)

What a rube! What a greenhorn! What a bumpkin! Now, some twenty years down the road, I mock, pooh-pooh, and urinate down upon my former self, as if from a great height.

When my newfound colleagues discovered this was my policy, they dumped their mistakes on me wholesale (and they, a bunch of "coasters" if there ever were any, whose jobs were mostly an afterthought to their beach-based lifestyles, and all of whom had trust funds anyway and were only really pretending to work, made *tons* of mistakes).

* The name of the bus that takes you from Manhattan out to the Hamptons.

At the end of that summer, my contract was, as they say, "not renewed."

From this episode we can extract **Master Class Rule No. 3: Most people just are not worthy of your "noble" gestures; make sure your own ass is covered before attempting to cover anyone else's.**

And also: **Master Class Rule No. 4: "Transparency" can be a powerful damage-control weapon; but, like any other powerful weapon or drug, it must be used judiciously.**

Time, I'm sorry to say, has convinced me there's a lot of truth in Robert Greene's ultra-Machiavellian book *The 48 Keys to Power* (the book all the rappers read in order to turn themselves into music "moguls" and label owners and CEOs), where he says:

"Most people are open books. They say what they feel, blurt out their opinions at every opportunity, and constantly reveal their plans and intentions. They do this for several reasons. First it is easy and natural to always want to talk about one's feelings and plans for the future. It takes effort to control your tongue and monitor what you reveal. Second, many believe that by being honest and open they are winning people's hearts and showing their good nature. They are greatly deluded. . . . By being unabashedly open you make yourself so predictable and familiar that it is impossible to respect or fear you, and power will not accrue to a person who cannot inspire such emotions."

Therefore: "If you yearn for power, quickly lay honesty aside, and train yourself in the art of concealing your intentions."

Recall the words from Sun Tzu with which we began this book: "All warfare is based on deception." A few people,

I've found, are worth your trust and confidence. But with everyone else, it's probably better to play your cards a little bit closer to your vest.

FINGER FOOD: WHEN TO GO ON THE ATTACK

Sometimes, not only are people not on your side; they are openly hostile to your interests.

In this case, you are making a mistake if you let them pursue their nefarious agendas. You are also making a mistake if you passively lie back and *fail to attack*.

Remember Yeats's line: "The best lack all conviction/ While the worst are full of passionate intensity." Thus (in Yeats's view, and I do think he hit the nail on the head) is evil allowed to flourish in the world.

Don't lack all conviction and let your enemies walk all over you with their passionate intensity.

Yes, most of the time we are students of Lao Tzu's gentle, bend-like-a-reed-in-the-wind approach to damage control specifically and to human interaction in general.

But when times get tough and your troubles surround you, sometimes you have to turn to the other Tzu, Sun Tzu (no relation), who advocated not only defeating but annihilating your enemies.

(Apparently this is Lance Armstrong's approach to bike racing, as well: not only to defeat, but to crush, annihilate, and *humiliate* his competitors. That's what we read, once, in a Tour de France book, anyway. How it's possible in a bike race, we're not 100 per cent sure; but that's what they say.)

We want you to be considered a nice person and a "good egg," yes; and that's really the best long-term strategy of them all.

But sometimes, in the short term, someone pushes you, and you have to push back.

Take Wendy's, the fast-food restaurant chain.

In 2005, the scandalous story hit the news that someone had found a severed human finger in a container of Wendy's chili, in San Jose, California.*

Wendy's did an investigation, found no severed fingers among its employees, and assured the public that standards were rigorously maintained, and there was no problem with health or security.

But of course media outlets "went long" with the story, endlessly re-running the juicy, "sexy" footage of a severed finger, and business at many Wendy's went into free fall, especially in northern California, where business was off as much as 50 per cent.

So Wendy's, in cooperation with San Jose police, began to focus on their accuser, a thirty-nine-year-old woman named Anna Ayala. It came to light she'd launched a number of similar, and possibly fraudulent, lawsuits in the past, including a sexual-harassment lawsuit against an ex-supervisor and a lawsuit against several car companies, claiming a wheel had fallen off her car. It also came to light

---

* I am indebted for this anecdote, as well as several of the facts to follow, including the Kobe Bryant apology, below, to another book called, by sheer coincidence, *Damage Control*, by Eric Dezenhall and John Weber.

Ms. Ayala had won a settlement after her daughter became ill after eating in a Mexican restaurant.

San Jose police searched her home. Suddenly, in the media, footage of Ayala's home being raided replaced shots of the severed finger.

Then it was discovered that the finger Ayala "found" in her chili had in fact belonged to someone her husband worked with, who'd had it severed in an industrial accident – and had given it to her husband in lieu of fifty bucks he owed him.

Ayala and her husband pleaded guilty, and in this cloud of scandalous, slightly disgusting, and ludicrous details, the whole debacle was laid to rest.

Moral of the story: **Master Class Rule No. 5: Sometimes, rather than being cowed by the person attacking you, it pays you to attack back.**

True in marriage, the social whirl, family matters, and certainly the workplace (less so in courtship, though perhaps it could apply to rivals for the object of your affection).

Both Pam and I have had this experience, in the workplace. Suddenly, someone – and it's particularly frightening when it's a boss, but often it's a colleague, too – will target you, attempt to isolate you from the herd, and run you to ground.

Why? Who knows? Some people are just like that. Often, the best tactic is to turn the spotlight on that person, attempt to isolate your attacker, and run him/her to the ground.

THE POWER OF APOLOGY

Mostly, though, when you're in the wrong, the best idea is simply, humbly, and with some kind of grace, apologize.

Apology is a powerful thing. And a necessary one, I've found – at least if you hope, for starters, to be happily married, or married at all.

I think I may in fact speak for many long-term married men when I say: the apology is a central weapon in your quiver, no less than the secret elixir by which one may continue to be married.

I apologize to Pam on a daily, if not hourly, basis. She also, should circumstances dictate, apologizes to me from time to time, which I appreciate.

As every married person knows, there are several different types or degrees of apology.

The lowest level* is: "I'm sorry *you* feel hurt by what I did/said." This type of apology has a certain meaninglessness. What it's saying, in effect, is: "I feel I did no wrong."

But it's also saying: "Despite my feelings of innocence in the matter, I want to make peace with you. Making peace with you is *as* important to me as being in the right."

Let's call this The Mealy-Mouthed Make-peace Apology.

Mealy-mouthed though it may be, it is actually a highly useful form of transitional apology, and tends to be appreciated by the recipient, as long as he/she understands that it's delivered, as it were, from between clenched teeth; but that it's motivated by love, and a desire for reconciliation

---

* Well, the absolutely lowest level of apology is the "apolobuke," mentioned earlier; but we'll leave that one out of the present discussion.

and peace. And in truth this type of apology does tend to go a long way toward smoothing things over.

At least, let's say: this type of apology is better than no apology at all.

In the public sphere, this type of apology was exemplified by basketball superstar Kobe Bryant. In 2004, a rape case against him had already been dismissed when his accuser refused to testify, when he issued to her (through the media, of course: it was a *mediated* apology) the following statement:

"Although I truly believe this encounter between us was consensual, I recognize now that she did not and does not view the incident the same way I did. After months of reviewing discovery, listening to her attorney, and even her testimony in person, I now understand how she feels she did not consent to this encounter."

Notice all the verbal dipsy-doodling, double-dribbling, and alley-ooping Mr. Bryant has to perform in order to maintain a fine balance between "I didn't do it" and "I'm sorry."

Now, some may find this type of verbal hairsplitting unconscionable, but recall that much was riding on this statement (a $136-million contract with the Lakers, numerous lucrative endorsement deals); when you're talking about legal snafus, an apology that contains an admission of guilt can be a very dangerous thing to do; it could land you in jail.

It may be painful and humiliating, but a well-timed, well-executed (even possibly genuine) apology can also be career-, reputation-, and face-saving.

At the other end of the apology spectrum from the **Mealy-Mouthed Makepeace Apology** is the **Full-On Mea Culpa**, and its variant, the **Tearful Mea Culpa**.

Remember the two televangelists, Jimmy Swaggart and Jim Bakker?

. . . and if you said "Jim Who?" in response to the latter name, we say, "Exactly."

Mr. Bakker was once, along with his wife Tammy Faye Bakker (who used to bawl over her love of the Lord, streaks of mascara running down her cheeks – remember *now*?) head of the powerful televangelical empire, PTL, short for "Praise the Lord" – also not all that affectionately known as Pass the Loot, for the way they raked it in from their "flock" (I love how openly televangelical types refer to their followers as sheep).

Mr. Bakker "sinned" first, when it was revealed he was having an affair with his secretary, Jessica Hahn, who went on to get breast augmentation surgery, pose nude for *Playboy*, and become a regular on Howard Stern's radio show.

Mr. Swaggart also had his own televangelical empire, STARCOM (Swaggart Television and Radio Communications), and shared Mr. Bakker's taste for the dalliances of the flesh. But in a way, Mr. Swaggart's "sin" was worse. First, he pooh-poohed Mr. Bakker from a great height and called him a "cancer on the church" for committing the sin of adultery.

Then *he*, Jimmy Swaggart, was caught having sex with a prostitute in a Florida motel room. She referred to Mr. Swaggart as one of her "regulars." And she was apparently one of many.

Ms. Hahn, before all her *Playboy* appearances and breast augmentation, was merely a meek, mild-mannered church secretary who tempted Mr. Bakker from the shiny path of righteousness.

In a way, that makes Mr. Bakker's transgression seem like the lesser sin.

Mr. Swaggart, on the other hand, was guilty not only of the sin of hypocrisy for denouncing Bakker, but also of the extra-sinful practice of paying for it with a Jezebel of "the world's oldest profession."

Or, if you prefer, a "sex worker."

But in the end, their damage-control approaches made all the difference.

Mr. Bakker prevaricated, attempted to obfuscate, and pointed the finger in every direction but toward himself. No one really bought it and as a consequence, he disappeared forever.

Meanwhile, Mr. Swaggart went on TV, cried, apologized ("I do not plan in any way to whitewash my sin or call it a mistake. . . . I have sinned against you and I beg your forgiveness"), and lived to preach another day.

His empire is almost better off than ever. The Jimmy Swaggart Telecast (on cable, true) still rakes it in by the millions.

Such is the power of apology.

Oh, and one last note, before we wrap up the discussion of the power of apology.

The highest form of apology, but also in a way the lowest, is the type described in the question below – the type Pam sometimes tries to extract from me. The kind that not only expresses genuine regret, but also promises that the crime will never be repeated. Equivocation is the Achilles heel of many an apology. If you've finally made up your mind to apologize, say it like you mean it, with an **Apology Without Equivocation, Followed by a Promise Never to Repeat the Offending Action Again.*** As should the person in the case below:

THE QUESTION

My twenty-four-year-old daughter was in a relationship for about three months. It started off well and he was very attentive. Gradually, his phone calls and e-mails started to dwindle. Days would go by and he wouldn't get in touch with her. My husband and I really liked him.

He had a good job and seemed really mature for his age (twenty-five). Two weeks ago, he stopped calling and answering her text messages.

I couldn't take seeing her like this and I e-mailed him to call me, then had a discussion with him about how he was treating her. He was extremely polite and said he would try to sort things out. My daughter was furious with me when she found out I had talked to him.

---

* Pam, always on the lookout for fresh frontiers in this department, recently introduced an innovative variant: the Gratitude-Filled Apology. We were at a cottage, she had awoken me from a nap in the living room by having what I felt was an entirely spurious conversation with Nick in the room. I arose grumpily, was a little snippy and shirty with her about her being "inconsiderate" – check it out, gentlemen: she wanted me not to apologize to her for my snarkiness but also to *thank* her for keeping the kids quiet while I napped (up to the point when she didn't). I met her about halfway on that one.

That evening, he text-messaged her to say it was over. She blames me and said I was the cause of the breakup because I scared him away.

My daughter is not talking to me and says she will never tell me anything again. We had a great relationship before this and I am dismayed and sad now that it's over for her. Help!

THE ANSWER

Before launching into my advice proper, I would like to take a moment to send up a little prayer: O Lord, thank You for sending me, in Your infinite wisdom, only male offspring.

But I remember being a young man, in my teens and twenties. And all I can say is: thank God my kids are going to be the perpetrators of all the scurrilous, scandalous skull-duggery about to come and not the ones upon whom it is perpetrated.

All of which is my way of saying, mommy dearest: I feel your pain, the pain of being the mother of a dating daughter in her twenties, right in my breadbasket.

I also understand your puzzlement: but this young man "seemed really mature."

The operative word here, madam, is "seemed."

Oh, sure. In our twenties, we all seemed mature when talking to our girlfriends' mothers: "Oh, yes, Mrs. Cosgrove, I agree that the parliamentary system has certain flaws. However, could it also not be said that in the context of modern Western democracy. . . ."

But then as soon as we got out the door we went back to our Jägermeister-shooting, multiple-girlfriend-juggling, up-with-exes-hooking, off-the-speakers-at-concerts-jumping regular selves.

Looking back, (a) I'm glad to be alive and not paraplegic and/or enrolled in a permanent detoxification program or psychiatric facility; (b) I can see it must have been very difficult for our girlfriends' mothers to bite their lips and refrain from picking up the phone and ripping us all a new one.

But that's exactly what you must do, *mamacita*: (1) bite lip; (2) remove proboscis from daughter's affairs; (3) attempt to re-establish trust.

Your first step is to issue to your daughter the type of apology my wife will occasionally try to wring from me, the most abject and humiliating kind known to humanity, the type where you have to say: "Not only am I sorry for what I have done, but I promise never to do it again."

(If you find this galling, try what I sometimes do: later, repeat the same speech in the mirror, only pulling faces and using an ultra-sarcastic, sing-song type of voice.)

Between us parents, I think we can agree that if this guy could be so easily put off your daughter, he probably wasn't worthy.

(Even if we overlook the fact he broke up with her via text message, probably the most callous and cowardly way to do it.)

But your daughter needs to make her own mistakes, madam, to learn to handle the cretinous, crunked-up cads (for those who don't know, crazy + drunk = crunk), booty-calling bounders, and narcissistic numbnuts she's bound to rub up against in her twenties on her own..

In order for your daughter to trust you, she has to believe that, when it comes to her dating life, you will remain a bystander, a spectator. You can listen and advise, but never interfere.

And above all, pray to whatever deity or entity you believe in that your daughter makes it through the next few years relatively unscathed, and when the dust and the boys around her have settled down a bit, she meets a suitable suitor, a young man who not only pretends to be, but is, in fact, mature enough to appreciate and deserve her and make a proper commitment.

SOMETIMES, IF THE SCREW-UP IS DEFINITIVE ENOUGH, IT DOESN'T REALLY MATTER WHAT YOU DO, JUST TRY TO MAKE A GRACEFUL EXIT

Now, before signing off, it would be unfair if we did not, in the interest of being "honest" and "transparent" our own selves, admit there are some times it doesn't matter how brilliant your "damage control" is.

You're going down.

Take Eliot Spitzer (*por favor*).

If you recall, he's the former governor of New York who, at a hastily called press conference declared that, effective immediately, he would cease and desist all gubernatorial pursuits, when it was revealed by an FBI sting operation that he was routinely cheating on his wife with a $1,000-an-hour "sex worker" in a $500-a-night hotel.

Now, I feel I should continue to be fully "transparent" and full of full disclosure here and confess that I'm only mentioning Mr. Spitzer because the head of Damage

Control's Marketing and Brand Expansion team told me I "absolutely had to."

His name's Brad. And he was really adamant about it.

But to tell you the truth Eliot Spitzer's name doesn't even come up all that often around the old bunker. He isn't a very positive example. He's just another one of those people who's kind of beyond our reach.

Of course, we all stopped whatever we were doing and crowded into the bunker's Media Room to check out the press conference in which he resigned, on March 10, 2008, his wife stony-faced at his side.

(Oh, man, was she stony-faced. If you looked up "stony-faced" in the encyclopedia, you'd see pictures of the faces on Easter Island, and her.)

But when the press conference was over we all dispersed, without comment. No one even bothered to pipe up with any suggestions about what could be done for Mr. Spitzer; a couple of days later, at our Monday morning meeting, the subject didn't even come up.

Because everyone at Damage Control HQ, down to the lowliest junior staffer and student intern, knew: there was nothing we could do for the poor man. He was finished; he was fucked.

He had no friends left, only enemies. He'd been caught doing the very thing he'd pooh-poohed and denounced other people about his whole adult life. He did about the only thing he could do: hastily called a press conference, resigned immediately, no questions please, then melted into the crowd, into the mists of obscurity, to "spend more time with his family" (and won't that be delightful?) not to mention lawyers, marriage therapists, and other career-flameout and downward-mobility specialists.

And if we here at Damage Control were to be fully "transparent," we'd have to admit we didn't get too exercised about the flame-out and downfall of this particular Icarus. We never liked the guy all that much anyway.

THE SECOND ACT CAN BE THE SWEETEST ACT OF ALL

But cases like Mr. Spitzer's are rare, we feel! That's the positive note we'd like to end on!

There is almost always something, in almost every circumstance, you can do to set things right! Remember: God/the devil is in the details; take action; take *charge*; learn, baby learn; spin, baby, spin; be humble, human, and humorous; in short do all the things we've been encouraging you to do since the very beginning of the book; and everything will work out fine.

F. Scott Fitzgerald said, "There are no second acts in American lives." But he couldn't have been more wrong about that, we feel.

America itself is based on a second act. It's the second act of a bunch of settlers who were tired of a first act of religious oppression and excessive taxation and crossed an ocean under great duress to hack a second one out of the bush.

Take Martha Stewart (please). When she got caught with her fingers in the cookie jar, Ms. Stewart had a pretty big empire, a pretty solid fan base, an army of busybodies and floral-arrangement-obsessed women ready to fall on their knitting needles to save her ass.

But my sense, also, is that, in the process of building a massive, multi-billion-dollar empire by churning out tips on how to turn, say, chocolate-dipped pine cones into the perfect centrepiece for an outdoor dinner party, she lost touch with much of her fan base, the everyday women and (I suppose) men who relied on her for the latest advice on caramelizing your Christmas decorations, or whatever.

You could sense the mood in the way she was being written about, talked about, even the way she was being satirized on TV. She was no longer a "woman of the people."

Which is why it's just possible that getting caught for insider trading, put in a high-publicity trial, sentenced for fraud, and doing time in jail were the best thing that ever happened to her.

When she was indicted, her wartime *consiglieri*, Charles Koppelman, advised her (and let's go ahead and make this **Master Class Lesson No. 6: "Take control of what you can control"**).

In this case, what she could control was her business. After her indictment, Ms. Stewart stepped down as CEO of her company.

Then, rather than trying to mount a lengthy appeals process, Ms. Stewart took her "pinch" like a man; used her time inside to coordinate a comeback; and emerged from prison with a veritable fistful of deals: for an *Apprentice*-style program on NBC, several how-to DVDs, her own TV show, a Sirius satellite radio show, and even a deal with a home construction company to build 650 homes, versions of her own residences, in "Martha-branded residential communities," whatever the hell that means.

"F. Scott Fitzgerald?" she might well have said, upon emerging from prison: "Bite me."

So: to reiterate: these are the rules of Master Class Damage Control:

MASTER CLASS RULES

Master Class Rule No. 1: People's capacity to forgive tends to run deeper than you might think, as long as you are humble, hubris-free, and human.

Corollary: People can forgive you just about everything, as long as you don't insult their intelligence.

Master Class Rule No. 2: Use your apology to frame the terms of debate.

Master Class Rule No. 3: Most people just are not worthy of your "noble" gestures; make sure your own ass is covered before attempting to cover anyone else's.

Master Class Rule No. 4: "Transparency" can be a powerful damage-control weapon, but, like any other powerful weapon, it must be used judiciously.

Master Class Rule No. 5: Sometimes, rather than being cowed by the person attacking you, it pays to attack back.

Master Class Lesson No. 6: Take control of what you can control.

So don't let anything that happens discourage you, dear reader. If disaster strikes, maybe it's just the beginning of a second act.

Whatever happens, take it on the chin, dust yourself off, pick yourself up, and get back into the game. Never give up, never say uncle, never knuckle under.

Whatever you've done wrong, you have to do something about it. You screwed up? Deal with it. Take care of it. This game is yours to lose, baby. We love you, everyone here loves you, and we have every confidence that no matter how badly you mess up, you're going to pull out of it, come up smiling, everyone clapping you on the back, sticking cigars in your mouth and lighting them, thinking more highly of you than ever.

You'd better. We've got our eye on you. You're on the monitors of the Surveillance Room 24-7. And we only want the best for you. We want you to be happy, healthy, and productive. To enjoy everything life has to offer, despite the fact you may screw up, fall short, and stick your foot in your mouth from time to time.

We're pulling for you.

Every last one of us.

ACKNOWLEDGEMENTS

I would like gratefully to acknowledge the contributions of Morgan Grady-Smith, recently promoted to Team David Eddie Lieutenant First Class; and of course Pat Lynch; for helping make this book, such as it is, what it is, *miglior fabbro*-style. Also Doug Pepper, as always, for believing in me; and to my agent, Elizabeth Sheinkman, who delivered a fresh human being into this world around the time I delivered the manuscript (can't believe you beat me to the punch, but then I'm a slow writer). Congratulations, Elizabeth. You're gonna be – and I'm sure already are – a great mom.

The rest of Team Dave Eddie: you know who you are. Keep standing by me, I need you.